# Praise, Claim God's Promises, & Pray Your Way to Victory

## 366 Days of Praying for Others

### Crystal Whitten, Ph.D.

# Praise, Claim God's Promises, and Pray Your Way to Victory

# 366 Days of Praying for Others

Copyright © 2020 by Crystal Whitten

Cover by Christopher Campbell, at Unsplash.com

ISBN: 978-1-7352988-0-1

Library of Congress Control Number: 1735298808

All rights reserved. No portion of this book may be reproduced, stored in a retrieval system, or transmitted in any form or by any means, including electronic, mechanical, photocopy, camera, recording, scanning, or others, except for brief quotations in reviews or articles, without the prior written permission of the author.

DISCLAIMER

The author would like to thank all those who have given permission to include quotations in this book. Every effort has been made to acknowledge copyright holders. The author apologizes for any error or omission that may remain, and for those concerned, please contact the author so full acknowledgment is made in future printings.

All Scripture taken from the King James Version of the Bible unless otherwise noted:

AMP: Amplified® Bible – Copyright © 1954, 1958, 1962, 1964, 1965, 1987 by The Lockman Foundation. Used by permission. (Lockman.org)

AMPC: Amplified® Bible, Classic Edition – Copyright © 1954, 1958, 1962, 1964, 1965, 1987 by The Lockman Foundation. Used by permission. (Lockman.org)

ASV: American Standard Version – Copyright © 1901 by Thomas Nelson & Sons. DARBY: Darby Translation – Copyright © 1867, 1872, 1884.

ERV: Easy-to-read Version – "The HOLY BIBLE: EASY-TO-READ VERSION © 2001 by World Bible Translation Center, Inc. and used by permission."

ESV: English Standard Version – The Holy Bible, English Standard Version® (ESV®), copyright © 2001 by Crossway, a publishing ministry of Good News Publishers. Used by permission. All rights reserved. Terms are intentionally loose.

GNT: Good News Translation – Scripture taken from the Good News Translation in Today's English Version- Second Edition Copyright © 1992 by American Bible Society. Used by Permission. Not more than 500 verses may be used.

ICB: International Children's Bible – Scripture taken from the International Children's Bible®. Copyright © 1986, 1988, 1999 by Thomas Nelson. Used by permission. All rights reserved. 500 or fewer verses is gratis use.

LEB: Lexham English Bible – The Lexham English Bible. Copyright 2012 Logos Bible Software. Lexham is a registered trademark of Logos Bible Software.

MEV: Modern English Version – Copyright © 2014 by Military Bible Association. Used by permission. All rights reserved.

MSG: The Message – THE MESSAGE, copyright © 1993, 2002, 2018 by Eugene H. Peterson. Used by permission of NavPress. All rights reserved. Represented by Tyndale House Publishers, a Division of Tyndale House Ministries.

NASB: New American Standard Bible® – Copyright © 1960, 1962, 1963, 1968, 1971, 1972, 1973, 1975, 1977, 1995 by The Lockman Foundation. Used by permission. (Lockman.org)

NET: New English Translation – NET Bible® copyright © 1996–2006 by Biblical Studies Press, L.L.C. All rights reserved. (Netbible.com)

NIRV: New International Readers Version – The Holy Bible, NEW INTERNATIONAL READERS VERSION®, NIrV® Copyright © 1996, 1998 Biblica. All rights reserved throughout the world. Used by permission of Biblica.

NIV: New International Version – THE HOLY BIBLE, NEW INTERNATIONAL VERSION®, NIV® Copyright © 1973, 1978, 1984, 2011 by Biblica, Inc.® Used by permission. All rights reserved worldwide

NKJV: New King James Version – Scripture taken from the New King James Version®. Copyright © 1982 by Thomas Nelson. Used by permission. All rights reserved.

NLT: New Living Translation – Holy Bible, New Living Translation copyright © 1996, 2004, 2007 by Tyndale House Foundation. Used by permission of Tyndale House Publishers Inc., Carol Stream, IL 60188. All rights reserved. New Living, NLT, and the New Living Translation logo are registered trademarks of Tyndale House Publishers.

NRSV: New Revised Standard Version® – Copyright © 1989 by Thomas Nelson Publishers. NTE: New Testament for Everyone – Copyright © Nicholas Thomas Wright 2011.

RGT: Revised Geneva Translation – © 2019 by Five Talents Audio.

RSV: Revised Standard Version Bible – Copyright © 1946, 1952 and 1971 the Division of Christian Education of the National Council of the Churches of Christ in the United States of America. Used by permission. All rights reserved. Up to 500 verses.

TLB: Living Bible – The Living Bible copyright © 1971. Used by permission of Tyndale House Publishers, a Division of Tyndale House Ministries, Carol Stream, Illinois 60188. All rights reserved.

TLV: Tree of Life Translation of the Bible – Copyright © 2015 by The Messianic Jewish Family Bible Society.

TPT: The Passion Translation® – Copyright © 2017, 2018 by Passion & Fire Ministries, Inc. Used by permission. All rights reserved. (ThePassionTranslation.com/)

VOICE: The Voice™ – Copyright © 2012 by Ecclesia Bible Society. Used by permission. All rights reserved. Fair Use Guidelines: (all must apply) gratis use when 500 or fewer verses used.

WEB: World English Bible – 1901, public domain.

WYC: Wycliffe Bible – Copyright © 2001 by Terence P. Noble. YLT: Young's Literal Translation – 1862, 1889, public domain.

# Dedication

This book is dedicated to two powerful prayer warriors: my mother, Evelyn Culpepper Whitten (1934– 2009) and my grandmother, Hallie Tessie Spraggins Whitten (Mimi; 1912– 2012). It is also dedicated to my recent and not so recent prayer partners, Grace Iacono and Bozena Wentland, and to my first prayer partner, Julianne Aranda.

Woods

Oh, give me a woods to walk in walk in
Where the cedar and pine are talking.

While the rest of the trees are asleep
And the yellow jasmine creeps.

To the top of the pine and the top of the gum,
As if to say, "Oh come! Oh come!"

Oh, give me a woods to walk in
Where the purple violets peek
Beneath our happy feet.

Where the laughing brooks bid you stay
And the wild ferns nod, oh yea!

Where the birds sing while you sit by the spring
And talk to the One who created these things.

And listen to Him as He talks to you of perennial spring
In the earth made new.

Where the evergreen trees bend low in the breeze,
And nothing will harm you.

Where the flowers bloom and the birds sing.
Oh, give me a woods to walk in.

Hallie Tressie Spraggins Whitten, 1967

# Epigraph

## Prayer moves mountains!

"Prayer is the answer to every problem in life. It puts us in tune with divine wisdom which knows how to adjust everything perfectly. So often we do not pray in certain situations, because from our standpoint the outlook is hopeless. But, nothing is impossible with God. Nothing is so entangled that it cannot be remedied; no human relationship is too strained for God to bring about reconciliation and understanding; no habit so deep rooted that it cannot be overcome; no one is so weak that he cannot be strong; no one is so ill that he cannot be healed. No mind is so dull that it cannot be made brilliant. Whatever we need if we trust God He will supply it. If anything is causing worry or anxiety, let us stop rehearsing the difficulty and trust God for healing, love and power."

—*The Daily Word,* 18 June, 1952

## We believe God hears and answers our prayers

"Children and youth may come to Jesus with their burdens and perplexities, and know that He will respect their appeals to Him, and give them the very things they need. Be earnest; be resolute. Present the promise of God, and then believe without a doubt. Do not wait to feel special emotions before you think the Lord answers. Do not mark out some particular way that the Lord must work for you before you believe you receive the things you ask of Him; but trust His word, and leave the whole matter in the hands of the Lord, with full faith that your prayer will be honored, and the answer will come at the very time and in the very way your heavenly Father sees is for your good; and then live out your prayers. Walk humbly and keep moving forward."

—E. G. White in *Messages to Young People,* 123

# Contents

Foreword ............................................................................................................. i
Preface ............................................................................................................. iii
Introduction .................................................................................................... xvii
Chapter 1: For Whom Should We Pray? ............................................................ 1
Chapter 2: When Should We Pray? ................................................................... 3
Chapter 3: Where Should We Pray? .................................................................. 5
Chapter 4: Types of Prayers .............................................................................. 7
Chapter 5: Prayer Formulas ............................................................................. 19
Chapter 6: Prayer Activity ................................................................................ 23
Chapter 7: Praises for Victory .......................................................................... 27
Chapter 8: My Blessings .................................................................................. 31
Chapter 9: Demonstrating Gratitude ................................................................ 33
Chapter 10: Bible Promises ............................................................................. 39
Chapter 11: Prayer Connects Strangers .......................................................... 51
Chapter 12: Answers to Prayer Build Faith ..................................................... 55
Chapter 13: Last Words Before Signing Off .................................................... 59
Chapter 14: The Ten Commandments ............................................................ 61
Chapter 15: My Current Prayer List ................................................................. 63
January: Pray for those who have made your life more difficult .................... 65
February: Pray for your family and loved ones ............................................... 79
March: Pray for the poor, oppressed and downtrodden ................................. 93
April: Pray for friends and loved ones with financial issues ......................... 109
May: Pray for non-politician public figures .................................................... 125
June: Pray for your prayer partners and spiritual leaders ............................ 143
July: Pray for couples and families in distress .............................................. 161
August: Pray for world leaders ....................................................................... 179
September: Pray for missionaries .................................................................. 197
October: Pray for the sick and for those who need healing ......................... 217
November: Pray for elected political leaders ................................................ 237
December: Pray for orphans, prisoners, singles, widowers and widows .... 257

# Foreward

Dear Reader,

Prayer is an amazing connection with the Power Source of life. In this book, the author has artfully combined her inquisitive nature, research skills, and heart-warming social skills, connecting all with that Power above who created man and spent His life saving humankind. The selected biblical references are poignant and direct our thinking to that source of Power and daily strength. They encourage us to reach out to others in mind and heart.

It is with joy we recommend absorbing the value of prayer for yourself, and also for others. Crystal Whitten is a generous and hospitable friend and scholar who loves people and socialization with them. She encourages us to get together with God and people. See how a connection with the God of heaven works wonders in your life, and then how your prayer for others works miracles in their lives and circles back with joy to you.

Keep a record here!

Leona G. Gulley, Ed.D.
Professor Emerita in Psychology, Southern Adventist University, Collegedale, TN

Norman R. Gulley, Ph.D.
Professor Emeritus in Systematic Theology, Southern Adventist University, Collegedale, TN

# Preface

*The prayer of a righteous person is powerful and effective (James). For where two or three gather in my name, there am I with them (Matthew). Even before they call, I will answer; and while they are still speaking, I will hear (Isaiah). The LORD is near to all who call on him, to all who call on him in truth (David). Is anyone among you in trouble? Let them pray. Is anyone happy? Let them sing songs of praise (James). Pray in the Spirit on all occasions with all kinds of prayers and requests. With this in mind, be alert and always keep on praying for all the Lord's people. Pray continually. Have no anxiety about anything, but in everything by prayer and supplication with thanksgiving let your requests be made known to God. I urge, then, first of all, that petitions, prayers, intercession and thanksgiving be made for all people—for kings and all those in authority, that we may live peaceful and quiet lives in all godliness and holiness (Paul).*

*Love your enemies and pray for those who persecute you, that you may be children of your Father in heaven. He causes his sun to rise on the evil and the good, and sends rain on the righteous and the unrighteous. When you pray, do not keep on babbling like pagans, for they think they will be heard because of their many words (Matthew). Do not conform to the pattern of this world, but be transformed by the renewing of your mind. Then you will be able to test and approve what God's will is - his good, pleasing and perfect will (Paul). If we confess our sins, he is faithful and just and will forgive us our sins and purify us from all unrighteousness (John). Then you will call on me and come and pray to me, and I will listen to you (Jeremiah). Therefore, confess your sins to each other and pray for each other so that you may be healed (James). May the grace of the Lord Jesus be with God's holy people (John).*

Most of us don't realize we are on an epic journey. We go to bed and wake up with endless to do lists, dread, anger, guilt, fear, anxiety, and a host of other toxic thoughts. Some of us wake up exhausted and require nervous system stimulants to function and get out of the house. We fail to wake up refreshed, energetic, with total equanimity and love for our fellow humans. Instead of living an analog life full of nuances and beauty, we choose a digital existence ruled by an endless series of "on" and "off" switches. Our lives are choked by distress and negative emotions. Tasks such as driving to work or getting along with our co-workers are existential in both the physical and spiritual realms. The alternative to basic subsistence is a life brimming with optimism, love, and heightened gratitude. We wake up and contemplate God's goodness. As we walk through the neighborhood or along a remote trail, we marvel at nature's love notes written just for us. We appreciate the intense beauty and loveliness of walking through life with the creator.

Recently, a speaker, when referring to Enoch walking with God, described how one day as God and Enoch were walking and talking together, they just kept on walking all the way into heaven. First Kings 8:58 describes what it means to walk with God. "That he may incline our hearts unto him, to walk in all his ways, and to keep his commandments, and his statutes, and his judgments which he commanded our fathers." Many are under the false belief that walking with God is burdensome or boring. This demonstrates the convincing nature of Satan's lies.

When we walk with the Lord, one day, as Enoch, we will be with Him forever. Makes me wonder what God and Enoch discussed. Were their conversations hurried, rote, full of begging and desperation, or were they humorous and full of praise and philosophical articulations? We want God to save our marriage, save our children, help us find us a high-paying job, make our boss go away, prevent a friend from taking his life, enlarge our paycheck, help us find a boyfriend or girlfriend, or help us find a better boyfriend or girlfriend. Instead of trusting in God's sovereignty, we present our requests to God as desperate pleas for His intervention (i.e., we expect a heavenly magic act as opposed to a Bible-based outcome). Instead of taking time to know Him, we focus on our desperate needs, oftentimes at the expense of developing a lovely relationship, and almost always at the expense of lifting up others in prayer.

The regular discipline of combined praise, contemplating Scripture promises, and prayer not only unites us with others, but also links us in mind and purpose with the Creator. Our prayers are now a part of the language of heaven and the duty of our angels. Our angels convey our prayers to the Father above, bringing each of us hope and relief. During times of danger we can claim God's promises, such as Psalm 34:7: "The angel of the Lord encampeth round about them that fear him and delivereth them." In faith we can claim this promise and others and be 100 percent certain God has heard our prayer. Every single promise in the Bible comes with the power of heaven. Only our unbelief and doubt limit access to these promises. Sometimes we experience a direct and even robust answer to prayer, and some answers are even miraculous. But most importantly, prayer changes us into His likeness and into His vessel. For some, prayer may be the only tool in their toolbox to help others.

But wait, let's slow down and be more purposeful about our lives. Let's learn to think about the reason we exist. Let's learn to use our God-given intelligence and reason from cause to effect. Let's make meaningful plans for the future which require forethought and delayed gratification. Let's live a reasonable life that upholds a biblical standard and lifts up society. Praise and prayer are keys to living an uncompromised life that exhibits the fruits of the Spirit.

Praise, promises, and prayer nurture within us the most important blessing God bestows on His people: the vision of love. Love for the person who abused us or our family, love for our flawed politicians, love for our faulty church leaders, love for those who are different from us. Love is the answer. It is easy to love those who love us, but what about the rest, the "jerks," "dummies," and the "low lifes" we all deal with every day? Why is it so hard to love those who have wronged us? Are we fake Christians if we fail to love others? Jesus hung out with societal rejects. He saw how the scars of sin mar our lives, choices, intentions, and our families and friends. However, when Jesus interacted with us, He saw a perfect and beautiful person, someone he was planning to die for. He saw Lucifer's deception manifesting in a degraded human race. If we could see each other as Christ saw us, our lives would truly change. The call of Christianity is to love even the most unlovable people in the world.

In a lesson study at church several years ago, we discussed the hypothetical situation of a Christian substituting their life so a non-Christian could live. We discussed the extreme hypothetical example of standing between a bank robber and the responding SWAT unit and being willing to take a bullet and die in place of the robber. Christians should have complete assurance of salvation, while someone robbing a bank may not have such assurance. If it came down to the innocent Christian bystander or the bank robber, wouldn't it be better to substitute the Christian's life? This would give the robber a greater window of opportunity to choose eternal life. This conversation troubled me for years. This hypothetical situation, while improbable, does present a moral and spiritual dilemma. Would this sacrifice make a difference for someone who might otherwise be lost?

Some psychologists might argue that self-actualized people (positively contributing to society and using all their talents and gifts) or people living life at level 6 of Kohlberg's Six Stages of Moral Development (regularly living Christlike ethics and principles), might be willing to sacrifice their life for a complete stranger, even one committing an illegal or violent act. Most people see this as unnecessarily giving up a productive, valuable life. But what does the Bible say about our lives? John 15:13 describes a level of spiritual development rarely seen in humanity: "Greater love hath no man than this, that a man lay down his life for his friends." In Romans 5:7, Paul tells us, "For scarcely for a righteous man will one die: yet peradventure for a good man some would even dare to die. But God commendeth his love toward us, in that, while we were yet sinners, Christ died for us."

Not every person has a circle of praying family members and friends. These people need our prayers. As part of a prayer ministry, seek out those who need prayer. There is no lack of people needing prayer. Every day in the United States, an average of 631 teenage girls get pregnant; 533 teens give birth; 2,363 women choose an abortion (2017 data); and thousands of children suffer abuse, develop drug addictions, become addicted to pornography, struggle with their sexual orientation,

*There is no lack of people needing prayer.*

drop out of school, run away from home, etc. Every day, almost 7,000 couples finalize their divorce, and their children (when present) experience the pain of their parents' divorce. Every day thousands of elderly fail to make a single social contact, thousands fall ill and suffer, and almost 7,500 people die every day. Of those who die every day, about 125 people commit suicide.

Ironically, thousands of Christians are at war with each other, judge each other, and call each other racists and bigots. We learn to take pride in our version of Christianity, while criticizing those who also study scriptures and believe differently. Every year, thousands of Christians break their promises, sell defective items to each other, have affairs with their neighbor's spouse, etc. Thousands of Christians fail to love, fail to forgive, fail to purge their anger, fail to see the miracle of everyday life, and fail to be thankful that God woke them up for another day of life.

*The Lord rebuke you!*
*Jude 1:9*

Many Christians, even pastors, seem eager to call each other out and embarrass, publicly criticize, and shame others. This is one reason the Bible says that Jesus must increase and we must decrease. (See John 3:30.) We also read in Jude 1:9 (NIV): "But even the archangel Michael, when he was disputing with the devil about the body of Moses, did not himself dare to condemn him for slander but said, 'The Lord rebuke you!'" When we slander others, we hurt ourselves. We stand in place of God as judge and jury. I heard a preacher make a comment that went something like this: "We might be fishers of men, and from time to time we might catch a fish, but once the fish is caught, let God do the cleaning."

Everyone needs prayers, love, and friendship. It is Jesus who wins the hearts of those redeemed from the earth. We hide behind the greater glory of Jesus Christ. As we lift up Him, all men are drawn to Him. Anything short of this goal damages us. When we stand behind Christ's glory, we are deaf and blind to insults, reproach, scorn, sleights, neglects, etc. When we live life apart from God, we continually guard ourselves against mortification and insults. Living for one's self not only clouds our emotions but stunts our intellect and leads to deep unhappiness and sorrow. Jesus is the only way; praise and prayer help us to know him better.

My heart ached for an acquaintance whose husband had left her for someone he met while online. His family, as well as a number of close friends, had serious concerns. Yet, some of his friends stuck by his side and refused to take a stand against his moral shortcomings. They offered up advice such as, "Things don't always work out." Or my favorite: "You deserve to be happy." Instead of an "iron-sharpening-iron" conversation with him, they were giving him their support and "I'm there for you" assurances. He needed more than feel-good platitudes condoning adultery. He needed a reality check, one delivered in love and compassion for his soul. One that was biblically focused on honoring the commitments he and his wife made before God and aimed at restoring their marriage. The good news is, hundreds of people prayed for this couple and the situation turned around. Prayer really is the answer.

The fruits of the Spirit distinguish from those who are Christian in name only (CINOs). It is important to avoid a life which exists within an echo chamber. I have seen inbred, dysfunctional churches do irrational things because the pastor used sophisticated psychological ploys to pit the church and its members against the rest of the world. This allowed the pastor to put on an Oscar-worthy performance to divert church funds to pay for large personal purchases. For years, no one confronted his errors, which led to compounding the issue. If your friends always agree with you, then you may not experience spiritual growth in meaningful ways. Proverbs 27:17 (NIV) describes: "Iron sharpens iron, so one person sharpens another." This doesn't sound like a cookie baking contest but more like a toe-to-toe or a nose-to-nose experience full of passion and concern for each other.

While traveling with a friend, I heard her taking God's name in vain. I had not heard her do this before. After a few days of praying and contemplating what to do, I decided to mention it to her. She was not happy about this conversation, and in her defense, I might have been somewhat awkward during the process. She informed me it was OK to bring certain things to God's attention and that no one else had noticed it or confronted her, not even her parents. I felt heavy hearted and hoped it wouldn't harm our friendship. However, because of my "user error" mentality, I began to examine my personal habits. Matthew 7:3 came to mind: "Why do you look at the speck in your brother's eye, but do not consider the plank in your own eye?" I began to examine my habits and prayed not only for her but for conviction of any habit which might be harming my spiritual journey. The most amazing thing happened, although it didn't happen overnight. I became convicted of several similar detrimental habits which had crept into my daily discourse. Also, over the next several months I began to realize she was not using this phrase anymore. Truly a humbling experience.

The Bible is deep, full of endless nuances and facets, declarations of love, hardcore reality, and new lessons for every stage of life. As previously mentioned, take the time to read and study Jude 1:9. This verse tells us that as the archangel Michael argued with the devil over the body of Moses [for taking to heaven], he did not dare to condemn or slander Satan, but instead said, "The Lord rebuke you!" This verse contains deep wisdom. Just as Jesus in the wilderness could have turned the rocks into bread, He could have debated with Satan over the body of Moses, but He knew this was dangerous territory and could lead to the original sin, Lucifer's distortion of God's character by undermining His love-based kingdom. Satan can and does lie; Jesus does not. Sometimes Satan's lies are so appealing we would rather believe a lie than accept a difficult truth. Heeding the intent of this verse could prevent many needless and damaging arguments. We should daily contemplate this verse. Instead of rebuking others and engaging in fruitless arguments, avoid all arguments and accusations.

A new term has entered our vernacular, but it is as old as Satan's fall from heaven—gaslighting. It is a virulent type of gossiping. It is a form of psychological manipulation in which a person or group, covertly or not so covertly, sow seeds of doubt about a targeted individual or situation. Compassion is weaponized for the perpetrator and absent for the victim, when in reality, it is a misunderstanding between two individuals that could have been avoided if they had followed biblical conflict resolution principles. Instigators cloud reality with their slyly twisted version of events. They often recruit others to join in their harassment of an individual or group using social media. Most of the recruits have no firsthand knowledge of the event and only serve to inflame and complicate the situation. People using this technique spread lies, contradictions, and misinformation solely to destroy an innocent person with whom they may disagree. As previously mentioned, Jude 1:9 speaks directly against psychological manipulation. We are not to participate in it. It is demonic and will only destroy those involved, even if it is used only to defend one's actions.

> Our contentious behaviors never win over true converts.

Christians should exercise restraint from setting up controversial discussions and then wondering what happened when a disagreement ensues and friends won't speak to each other. No one person or church is the repository of complete truth. This includes parents, teachers, doctors, pastors, and even the leaders of religious organizations. We need to be mindful of our blind spots and weaknesses. There are souls to pluck from destruction. Our contentious behaviors will never win over true converts. This will only serve to widen the gap between Christians and those in the world. They will see Christians as hypocrites and not as true Christ followers.

Instead of arguing with others, pray for them. When we rebuke others, even when we defend orthodox views, we stand in direct opposition to Christ's example. Instead, pray for your "enemies." Instead of complaining about our leaders, pray for them. Prayer is the most powerful tool we have to effect changes in ourselves and in others.

The anatomy and physiology of gaslighting; here is a modern postmortem of how Lucifer's fall from heaven may play out in our lives:

1. Begin by comparing yourself to someone else who has something you do not have.

2. Manufacture a threat. Blame God for your unhappiness and poor choices.

3. Choose to be unhappy with your station in life (no matter how good it may be), resulting in pathological jealousy—I deserve what someone else has.

4. Divert honor and praise from the true object of such (i.e., God).

5. Set up yourself as deserving of praise and honor; set up a false idol or self-worship.

6. Esteem yourself as impeccable and above reproach (believing you are better than others). Satan fooled the angels into believing him when he (the great deceiver) was no better than they were.

7. Secretly and openly be unwilling to worship and direct all praise and glory to God.

8. Recruit others to join your campaign. Use every avenue of communication to push your false narrative. Create fear and panic. This has the end result of increasing and broadening the effect and influence of evil. This is done under the guise of labeling something inherently good as "evil."

9. Recruit others who have no direct relationship to the original event, which is a hallmark of gaslighting. It has the effect of spreading discomfort, lies, and fear.

10. Completely flip the dialogue to be dishonest and misleading, ignoring the reality of competing facts, and making it less likely to reach a successful resolution. This requires overstating or even twisting the facts of the situation (i.e., altering the reality enough to skew it toward your biases). The skew is always toward taking your eyes off Jesus and putting the emphasis on self-development, self-aggrandizement, self-enlightenment, self-importance, self-righteousness, self-pity, etc. The lure is to believe God is withholding something from us. There is always an attack on some aspect of God's character.

11. Promote corruption and lies. Vilify goodness as being evil and selfish.

12. Promote evil as being normal and desirable. In the garden of Eden, as the serpent approached Eve, he normalized and even glamorized sin (i.e., separation from God in mind and action). He appealed to the highest realm of self-development, the enlightened mind, or the attainment of unique knowledge. The serpent promoted evil as nothing more than wanting to enlighten your mind and become like God (i.e., normalizing evil).

13. Once you begin to participate in evil, your physiology changes. You no longer desire fellowship with Jesus. Spending time with Christians is boring. Darkness is preferable to Light. Instead of thriving in Christ, we suffer in darkness. This is a terrible road to choose. Choose the Light – the True and Faithful one and not darkness.

Instead of defending ourselves, we should consider using Jesus' response to Satan as Satan attempted to get Him to stoop to his level. Jesus replies in Jude 1:9, "The Lord rebuke you."

One aspect of Satan's deception is to entice us into revering his role as the first to fall.

He wants to take as many people with him as possible in a rebuke to Christ and to Christ's atonement for our sins. Satan wants to instill panic, fear, and urgency to motivate people to think they must immediately react instead of thinking and using their frontal lobes. Believing Satan's lies requires one to trade frontal lobe function for self-righteous indignation (i.e., "how dare you . . .") and a false sense of moral outrage, ultimately manifesting as evil itself. Honor, dignity, and human tenderness toward others figuratively leaves the one who participates in gaslighting. Everyone is susceptible to gaslighting another person. Those with minimal social support and those who have an intense concern for self, are particularly susceptible. Christians do no view the Bible through a social, cultural and societal lens, rather, Christians view society and culture through the lens of the Bible. The Bible is always the standard.

> Believing Satan's lies requires one to trade frontal lobe function for self-righteous indignation...

In this age of social media, the need to be seen as relevant increases (i.e., extreme judgmentalism) our susceptibility to this phenomenon. When a pastor is arrested for possession of child porn, or the university president is charged with embezzlement, we are quick to ride the "high horse" and call them out. By publicly offering a distinction between their "badness" to our apparent "goodness," we unwittingly adopt Satan's tactics. We are all susceptible to the Luciferian paradox of the outward appearance of purity (e.g., being a pastor) but having inward self-worship, self-deception, and a desire to recruit as many people as possible to one's viewpoint.

When we are tempted to criticize a fellow traveler who has taken a spectacular fall, we instead need to repeat a thousand times, "by the grace of God, there go I." 1 Corinthians 15:7–10 (VOICE translation) describes this wildly crazy and incredible thing called God's grace: "Soon He appeared to James, His brother and the leader of the Jerusalem church, and then to all the rest of the emissaries He Himself commissioned. Last of all, He appeared to me; I was like a child snatched from his mother's womb. You see, I am the least of all His emissaries, not fit to be called His emissary because I hunted down and persecuted God's church. Today I am who I am because of God's grace, and I have made sure that the grace He offered me has not been wasted. I have worked harder, longer, and smarter than all the rest; but I realize it is not me, it is God's grace with me that has made the difference."

Keep in mind the incredible moment we will be with the Lord in heaven and cast our crowns at His feet. Even in heaven, we will honor and give all the glory to God! There is no place in heaven for self-aggrandizement and self-love. Do not trade your heavenly crown for earthly accolades. Our only hope is in Christ and following in His footsteps.

Memorize and recall Jude 1:9 when you are tempted to criticize others or denounce others as dangerous. Matthew 7:1–5 (ESV) gives us advice about how we should speak to others: "Judge not, that you be not judged. For with the judgment you pronounce you will be judged, and with the measure you use it will be measured to you. Why do you see the speck that is in your brother's eye, but do not notice the log that is in your own eye? Or how can you say to your brother, 'Let me take the speck out of your eye,' when there is the log in your own eye? You hypocrite, first take the log out of your own eye, and then you will see clearly to take the speck out of your brother's eye."

James 4:11, 12 (WEB) advises us: "Do not speak evil against one another, brothers. The one who speaks against a brother or judges his brother, speaks evil against the law and judges the law. But if you judge the law, you are not a doer of the law but a judge. There is only one lawgiver and judge, he who is able to save and to destroy. But who are you to judge your neighbor?"

Matthew 12:36,37 reads: "Every idle word that men shall speak, they shall give account thereof in the day of judgment. For by thy words thou shalt be justified, and by thy words thou shalt be condemned."

1 Corinthians 4:5 states: "Therefore judge nothing before the time, until the Lord come, who both will bring to light the hidden things of darkness, and will make manifest the counsels of the hearts: and then shall every man have praise of God."

Ecclesiastes 12:13, 14: "Let us hear the conclusion of the whole matter: Fear God, and keep his commandments: for this is the whole duty of man. For God shall bring every work into judgment, with every secret thing, whether it be good, or whether it be evil."

Gaslighting has severe consequences. It undermines our fellow humans and degrades us. When we participate in it, even if casually, we participate in Lucifer's original sin of falsely maligning someone's character. Should we expect life to be fair? If anything, we should expect to be treated unfairly and yet remain Christ-like. Life on earth is not about exacting some type of existential equality from highly flawed and sinful human beings, but it is about reforming and conforming our characters to Christ.

Humanity is a level playing field in the sense that our primary purpose in life is to know Christ and to win souls to Him. You can do this whether you have $10 million in the bank or $10. If you read the Bible and believe Christ was treated fairly, you need to reread the Good Book. Christ was homeless, jobless, never attended theology school, owned one set of clothes, never traveled far and wide, never married, received variable emotional support from his family and friends, healed thousands of seriously ill people, practiced extreme love and kindness to all, and managed to "threaten" every single religious leader and politician of his time by claiming to be divine.

In reality, love and kindness are the hallmarks of Christ's followers. This does not preclude taking a stand against moral decay, against broken promises to God and others, and against adopting harmful societal norms. Surround yourself with people invested in your salvation and who are unafraid to confront you in the face of moral compromise. Even if you feel uncomfortable about having a difficult conversation with a friend, you can always praise and pray them to victory. God answers our prayers and we should never believe our smallest request is too insignificant, especially on the behalf of others.

Some people are a pleasure to know and love while others present us with challenges. As pleasurable or painful as this reality might be, every person in our life may be there to teach us a lesson or to help us develop a relational skill. If we kick them out too soon or painfully distort the relationship, we may fail to learn a specific lesson. Don't get me wrong, not everyone will stay in your life. Sometimes, circumstances prevail and some friendships wane while others wax and grow strong. Praise and prayer for those who have come and gone and for those who remain in our lives is important. As we learn more about Christ from the study of Scripture and by establishing a robust prayer life, we become changed. Our change may be the spark for others to make similar changes. Over time, our characters transform from that of a worldly person into a Spirit filled person. We learn how to accept others and walk with them on their journey.

For some of us, refining our character could be compared to the Bill Murray movie, "Groundhog Day." If we fail to learn the lessons required to refine our character, we will continue to experience similar type trials. At the point where we learn the virtue of humility, or we exhibit the fruits of the Spirit, such as patience while driving in heavy traffic, etc., we have gained a great lesson. The next step is growth and further development in this area. Prayer allows us to live a fulfilling life and not to live only for ourselves. We may never know the impact of our prayers until we get to heaven, but there is ample evidence: prayer matters.

Popular twenty-first century cultural norms and practices rarely support Christians. Society rewards secular character traits while downplaying and even mocking Christian character traits. Humility, patience, longsuffering, agape love (i.e., unconditional love), philios love (i.e., affectionate or brotherly love), pragma love (i.e., enduring love and commitments), storge love (i.e., love for family and children), etc., are seen as old-fashioned. Instead, eros love (i.e., love of the body, sexual passion, desire), philautia (i.e., an archaic 16th century word used to describe self-love, self-conceit, undue regard for one's self or one's own interests) and mania love (i.e., obsessive love) are revered and exploited to enhance our pleasure and signal our liberation from boring, old-fashioned norms. (See the Lexico dictionary.)

We are obsessed with certain physical characteristics and not the quality of one's character. The norm becomes manic and debauched lives, with little room left for developing and growing enduring love and commitment. Instead of dealing with depression, we learn to live with it. We value what is secular and not what endures. We learn to virtue signal (i.e., feign righteousness) instead of demonstrating our real value. Expressing one's identity politics is more important than experiencing true happiness. Judgmentalism runs rampant with almost no governor limiting this slow-motion societal disaster.

Postmodernity, with all its entrapments, such as prestigious jobs, lots of spending cash, and constant entertainment demands, often leaves us unfulfilled and empty. We are loyal and devoted to a sports team while our family and friends who desperately need our time, attention, and guidance, observe our twisted priorities. We mindlessly play golf or go shopping while our children roam the streets or explore pathological online attractions. Children learn to use drugs and certain behaviors to ease their depression and feel normal again. These addictions come at the expense of long-term equanimity and peace (i.e., serotonergic stability and good frontal lobe functions). We live in a world where it is acceptable for adult children to live in a mansion while their parents struggle to put food on the table, or vice versa.

Harry Chapin's 1974 folk rock hit, "Cats in the Cradle," eloquently portrays the path of familial detachment and disconnection, prominent characteristics of modern society. With each successive generation, the pattern repeats with increasingly desperate results: "We'll get together then, you know we'll have a good time then" (the melancholic harmony swelling then trailing off).

Determine to not repeat this scenario. Choose to be real. Learn to care about your family, as well as others beyond the confines of your own family. Demonstrate how to love others as Christ loved us, even if it means loving the outcasts (see Philippians 2:4). The answer is not more government but more humanity, more Jesus and less me. Refuse to live with regrets. Live with the greatest degree of liberty and freedom. I like G. K. Chesterton's definition of liberty. He argues liberty is merely the right to choose between one set of limitations or another. He states the limitations we choose create "all the poetry and variety of life." Liberty is knowing your set of limitations and living in a way that honors your commitments.

Many Christians, instead of living a life of liberty and freedom in Christ, live in a virtual prison. We live with and accept various degrees of infirmity, fear, hate, abuse, etc. This is right where Satan wants us. We are within his grasp and sphere of influence. Praise and prayer lift us above society's fray into a heavenly sphere. Some of these promises are found in the following verses: Exodus 14:14; 15:26; 2 Chronicles 7:14; Psalm 18:35–36; 34:16–20; 146:9; Proverbs 3:7, 8; 17:22; Isaiah 46:4; 54:17; 58:11; Jeremiah 17:14; 33:6; Matthew 6:22,

27; 1 Corinthians 9:27; Ephesians 4:16; 2 Timothy 4:18; Revelation 7:16, 17.

Do we resort to speaking praises or curses when bad things happen? If curse words are the first thing you utter when something bad happens, you have not called upon Heaven. You have called upon the spirit and demon world. If you routinely utter the words, "Oh my god!" is it possible you are crying out to a demonic god and not the God of the universe? Our words reflect our thoughts. When we spend time contemplating Bible promises, those words will be the first comments out of our mouth when bad news comes our way. For example, if we trip and fall, and we find ourselves uttering a Bible promise such as, "The Lord protects the bones of the righteous; not one of them is broken!" (Psalm 34:20, NLT) instead of a string of curse words, our mind and habitual thoughts are in line with heaven. (Hat tip to Peggy Joyce Ruth.)

This type of communication with heaven mobilizes the angels to intervene on our behalf and protect us. Every time we claim a promise or offer a sincere prayer, our petitions are laid at Jesus' feet. We need only to pray once to be heard by God. Those petitions for ourselves and our loved ones never expire.

Our prayers for strangers link us together. They demonstrate humanity can rise above its own selfish pursuits and make time during prayer to intervene on behalf of others (1 Corinthians 10:24; Galatians 6:2). The following is a story about how daily prayer for someone by name for over decade unfolded. For many years I prayed for a friend and her family, each member by name. When her son graduated from college, he ended up in my area for advanced flight training. I had not seen him since he was a small child, but now I was on my way to go to dinner with him. He was a tall and handsome young man. We quickly found some common ground and began to forge a friendship.

> Our prayers for strangers link us together...

I saw him several times over the course of his training. It was an honor to get to know him and to see how he had grown into a stable and interesting young adult. The last time we met for breakfast, I confessed to him I had prayed for him almost every single day by name for over a decade. I didn't know if I would ever see him again. He asked if I had prayed for some-thing specific. I said that I prayed only for God to bless him and his parents in meaningful ways. It's amazing how this simple act of praying for someone knits us together in Christ. We finished up breakfast and soon thereafter, he left the area to start a new job. Every now and then we text and provide life updates. This experience enriched my life and hopefully his as well.

Prayer opens the door for all kinds of meaningful interactions. I hope the focus on praise, promises, and prayer is the beginning of new spiritual growth, a new way of thinking, and a new way of living for you too.

The psalmist David wrote about how God keeps track of our sorrows and collects our tears in a bottle, recording each one in His book (Psalm 56:8). We never have to fear our God is a faceless entity, looking down on us with shame and pity. Our God is there with us for every step of our lives. Psalm 86 (NIV) is a beautiful prayer. As you read David's prayer, think about your prayers and how to petition God.

Hear me, Lord, and answer me, for I am poor and needy. Guard my life, for I am faithful to you; save your servant who trusts in you. You are my God; have mercy on me, Lord, for I call to you all day long. Bring joy to your servant, Lord, for I put my trust in you.

You, Lord, are forgiving and good, abounding in love to all who call to you. Hear my prayer, Lord; listen to my cry for mercy. When I am in distress, I call to you, because you answer me.

Among the gods there is none like you, Lord; no deeds can compare with yours. All the nations you have made will come and worship before you, Lord; they will bring glory to your name. For you are great and do marvelous deeds; you alone are God.

Teach me your way, Lord, that I may rely on your faithfulness; give me an undivided heart, that I may fear your name. I will praise you, Lord my God, with all my heart; I will glorify your name forever. For great is your love toward me; you have delivered me from the depths, from the realm of the dead.

Arrogant foes are attacking me, O God; ruthless people are trying to kill me—they have no regard for you. But you, Lord, are a compassionate and gracious God, slow to anger, abounding in love and faithfulness. Turn to me and have mercy on me; show your strength in behalf of your servant; save me, because I serve you just as my mother did. Give me a sign of your goodness, that my enemies may see it and be put to shame, for you, Lord, have helped me and comforted me.

Think about Jesus in the Garden of Gethsemane. Immediately before the rapid succession of events leading up to His death on the cross, Jesus asked His disciples to pray for Him. Jesus knew the power of prayer. Luke 22:39–46 tells us as Jesus and three of His disciples entered the Garden, He commanded them to "Pray that you will not fall into temptation." He then left them and went a little farther into the Garden. After praying for about an hour, Jesus returned to find the disciples asleep. He once again admonished them, "Get up and pray so that you will not fall into temptation." We all know what happened. They fell asleep a second time. But Jesus continued in prayer until large drops of blood rolled down his face. This is a rare condition known as hematohidrosis, or sweating blood. It occurs under great stress which causes the capillaries in or near the sweat glands to rupture and sweat combines with blood.

As Jesus faced certain death, prayer fortified Him for the cross, and it fortifies us against the evil one. The command to pray also applies to us. When we pray for others and ourselves, we are more likely to forge a deep connection with God. This insulates us against temptations, hypocrisy, darkness, evil, and being lukewarm.

As we learn to praise God, claim His promises, and purposefully pray for others, we can expect tremendous victories in our personal lives. Expect a connection with those for whom you pray. Whether or not you ever meet them, you are connected to them by the prayers and requests on their behalf you have laid at the feet of Jesus. This is what matters in life and gives it meaning.

Scriptures about gossip:
- Exodus 20:16; 23:1
- Leviticus 19:11,16
- Deuteronomy 13:14
- Psalm 1:1–6; 15:1–5; 24:1–10; 31:18; 34:13; 41:7; 50:19–23; 58:3; 64:2–4; 91:1–16; 101:5, 7; 119:163; 141:3
- Proverbs 6:16–19; 10:18, 19; 11:9,12, 13; 12:5, 22; 13:3; 14:5; 16:28; 17:4, 9; 18:6–8, 21; 19:5, 9, 14; 20:19; 21:23; 25:23; 26:17, 20–22, 28; 29:12; 30:8
- Isaiah 1:1–31
- Jeremiah 6:28; 9:1–11
- Hosea 7:3; 10:13
- Nahum 3:1
- Zephaniah 3:13
- Matthew 5:1–48; 7:1–29; 12:36; 18:1–35
- Luke 6:31
- John 8:4–10, 44; 10:10
- Romans 1:28–32; 8:1–39
- 1 Corinthians 13:1–13
- 2 Corinthians 12:20
- Ephesians 4:15, 16, 25, 29, 31; 5:11
- Philippians 4:8
- Colossians 3:8, 9; 4:6
- 1 Thessalonians 4:11
- 1 Timothy 3:9–11; 4:2, 3; 5:13, 14, 19
- 2 Timothy 2:16
- Titus 2:2–5; 3:2
- Hebrews 6:18; 11:1–40
- James 1:26; 3:8; 4:11
- 1 Peter 2:1; 3:16; 4:15
- Revelation 2:2; 21:8; 22:11

# Introduction

Christianity compels us to live sacrificially. This book is about taking a year, starting on any day during the year, and praying for others. You may use this book every day, once a week, once a month, or every now and then. You may use it over and over, year after year. (I recommend using a mechanical pencil, #5 lead, which allows you to effectively erase and rewrite). At the end of each month, there is a section dedicated to an epilogue. This is where you write about your praise, promises, and prayer experiences over the past month. Take the time to acknowledge God's guidance, recognize answers to prayer, and describe how daily prayer and praise increased your faith. Use this book over many years. By reusing this book, you will see how God is leading in your life.

Over time and with the near-perfect vision of hindsight, we may see things differently. Frequently, the things and events we prayed for on a specific date worked together for good or God minimized their importance to us. We see how God answered our prayer in an unexpected and yet magnificent manner. We may see how God used a stressful situation to His glory by uniting adversaries, rewarding hard work, or accomplishing a once-perceived impossible task.

Combining praise, claiming promises, and prayer connects us to our loved ones, to the broader community, and even to the world at large. It provides a method and a paradigm shift that gives life inspiration and meaning. These activities broaden our perspective and increase our empathy and faith. Praise and prayer place us in right relation to our heavenly Father.

This book is not about a quick fix for a lackluster prayer life. It is about taking steps to revive your faith. Praise, promises, and prayer reside at the core of our faith. Claiming Bible promises brings us into a holy sphere of energy and power. I have taken Einstein's theory of special relativity formula, seen below (first equation), and have rewritten it to show how faith is a function of claiming Bible promises, praise, and prayer (second equation).

$$E = mc^2$$

$$\text{Faith} = (\text{Promises} \times \text{Prayer})^{\text{Praise}}$$

This book gives you the opportunity to pray for and track 365 to 366 people or groups (depending on the year). Praying for someone will take 5 to 10 minutes of your time. It may seem like a sacrifice because you will not be spending time with your family, or mowing the lawn, or chatting on the phone with your best friend. However, you will be in conversation with God. In this light, it really is not a sacrifice but a privilege. Some months, you may need to do some research to identify appropriate prayer targets. But, most of the months you should have no problem identifying people to target individually during your daily prayer time. It should not be a one-and-done type prayer but a meaningful day-long conversation with God for the identified person, persons or group.

This book is about getting back to the basics. It is about learning to let go of anger, fear, desperation, all the "-isms" that have invaded our psyche, our conversations, and our personal lives. It is difficult to shift gears from being a judgmental, legalistic, severe, harsh, or critical person, to being a loving, understanding, accepting, faithful, righteous-living person. It requires conversion on a daily basis. We often see conversion as a public event, when in reality it is deeply personal. The process of converting to His likeness is sanctification, the work of a lifetime. Daily, we accede our sinful human nature with the tendency to sin, to a new spiritual nature that abhors sin. At some point during the process, we leave behind our critical nature, our addiction to watching TV, taking God's name in vain, gossip, etc. This is when Christian growth and a real relationship with God begins.

It may happen gradually or suddenly, but when we cease to regularly pray for ourselves and our loved ones, we begin to lose our dependence on God. This opens the door for increasing self-sufficiency and self-righteousness. An intellectual knowledge of the gospel truth is not enough. We are advised to pray, and then in peace and confidence, go about our business. "Thou wilt keep him in perfect peace, whose mind is stayed on thee: because he trusteth in thee" (Isaiah 26:3). I like to think about prayer in this way. As we arrive in heaven and begin to meet our friends and family, we will also meet millions of new friends. I believe there will be a special fellowship with those we have prayed for, including complete strangers. At the end of our life, we could easily have prayed not only for our family and loved ones, but for thousands of strangers. Stranger prayers are a special type of co-ministry with heaven and affirm the power and sovereignty of a loving Lord and Savior.

At the end of each month and at the end of the year, take the time to fill out the epilogue section. This is where you describe the conclusions of the matter, etc. Document how prayer has changed you as well as answers to your prayers. Whether you are outwardly stoic or joyful, it should be impossible to hold back the good news of answered prayers. Share your experiences with others and watch your faith grow.

Incorporating virtues into our lives, such as humility, patience, belief, service, sacrifice, bearing your cross, harmonious living, treating animals and the planet with great care, and loving each other, all converge to help us emerge from the ashes of our sinful lives. Our virtues become our greatest gift to God and others! Combine this activity with friends and family to gain the greatest joy. Hopefully, our walk with God may rival that of Enoch. It's my prayer that we all may one day walk together with God and Enoch. Is any among you suffering? Let him pray. Is any cheerful? Let him sing praises.

# Chapter 1
## For whom should we pray?

How many times do you get a request to pray for someone you know? Do these requests give you great joy and anticipation of an amazing outcome? Or do you groan a little bit on the inside, doubting the power of your prayers?

Prayer is one of the great privileges of Christians. But an even greater privilege than praying for our loved ones is to pray for strangers. I used to get slightly annoyed at the requests posted all over social media to pray for this person or that situation, etc. I didn't know them, so why should I take the time to pray for them? And on top of the unknowns of such situations, what exactly should I include in this prayer? Over time, I came to realize that this is a blessing and one of the amazing aspects of social media. We can pray for, and therefore connect with, complete strangers!

For a moment, let's contemplate the impact of our prayers, not only here on earth, but also in heaven. Our praise and prayers are a large contributor to our spiritual health and wellness. Participating in daily and ongoing prayer is a powerful indicator of how well our frontal lobes function. Most people find it easy and even natural to pray for our loved ones, but for others it may feel somewhat unnatural to pray for a complete stranger. Yet, what if our prayers for a complete stranger somehow link us to that person? What if our prayers for a complete stranger lead that person to Christ? Would that not be counted as winning a soul for Christ? For now, we will not know how our prayers may change the trajectory of someone's life and maybe even lead to his salvation. But when we get to heaven, we will see it clearly. If this is true, we should dedicate a few minutes or more of every day for these types of prayers.

In part, I dedicated this book to my grandmother, Hallie Tressie Spraggins Whitten. For almost 100 years, she prayed for her wild and oftentimes crazy family. She married young and never desired a driver's license. After her husband died in the 1970s, she lived by herself almost until the day she died in 2012, just a few months shy of being 100 years old. She had seven children, twenty-four grandchildren, and I have lost count of how many great-grandchildren, nieces, and nephews. She lived most of her life within a 100-mile radius of where she was born and grew up. Even though she lived alone, her house was frequently full of family. Each of us grandkids thought we were her favorite.

When one of us went to jail, she wrote him a letter every day for the entire time he was there. Her letters described various aspects of farm life, who visited, that she killed a rattlesnake with a shovel, etc. Her letters to him also contained a short Bible verse or two and a brief Bible study or story. Every day while in jail, my cousin read her letters to his fellow inmates. My Mimi became somewhat of a "rock star" with them. They loved to hear him read her letters. When he got out of jail, they asked him if he would leave behind her letters so they could reread them. We may never know the specifics of the impact her letters had on the inmates, but someday it will be clear.

Another aspect I appreciated about Mimi was her cool head. She never yelled or said hurtful things to her children. She never over-emotionalized or fell apart when bad things happened. To put it in modern day terms, she was not a drama queen. She knew the greatest power came from God. She knew the only way to defeat the enemy was through reading the Bible, claiming its promises, praising God, and praying for her flock. And while she never shied away from speaking biblical truths, she never made anyone angry, alienated a family member with legalistic comments, and yet managed on her meager income to feed and house us when we visited her. It is rare that a family as large as ours did not have major interpersonal conflict and drama. Believe me, we were never perfect, but Mimi came close! I cannot think of a greater legacy than her kind, soft words of encouragement—and her prayers.

While architects design skyscrapers, salespeople sell things, and engineers build advanced technological feats, my grandmother won the hearts and souls of her family and their friends. I believe her dedication and influence will win every member of her family to Christ. This story highlights the importance of praise, promises, and prayer. This is her legacy.

If you are experiencing the worst crisis of your life, how would you want your family and friends to respond?

Option A: "I'm so worried about you! Let's go eat ice cream and go shopping or golfing and take your mind off your problems."

Option B: "I just want you to know I am praising the Lord for you and claiming Bible promises on your behalf as well as lifting you up in prayer every day. Can we pray together?"

Option C: "I'm not doing anything. It is none of my business."

I hope Option B is the obvious choice. This does not negate helping others with physical, social, emotional, and financial support. There is nothing wrong with shopping and golfing. However, when we or our loved ones are under attack, it is important to engage in real-time spiritual warfare. Fun times and outings, while oftentimes necessary, do not preclude spiritual warfare on someone's behalf. Prioritize your life in a way that protects your family against the powers which seek to destroy you and your loved ones. Praise, claiming Scripture promises, and prayer are the most powerful tools in a Christian's toolbox. Is any among you suffering? Let him pray. Is any cheerful? Let him sing praises.

# Chapter 2
## When should we pray?

This question is personal. Some may pray almost continuously, while others set aside specific times to pray. As each of us grows in Christ, our prayer life will also grow and evolve. Think of prayer as a conversation we are having with an influential and important person in our life. There is never a "bad" time to pray.

From time to time, as I interact with an agnostic or God-skeptic, I feel the need to pray. A furious debate goes on inside my head. Should I offer to pray or not? I admit that I have gone both ways. Sometimes I end up asking if she would mind if I prayed with her. No one has ever turned me down. We should never hesitate to pray at any time, although it is understandable that as Christians we would not want to offend someone. If we see prayer as petitioning the most powerful, positive, and loving force in the universe, I think we would never hesitate to pray anywhere, at any time!

The regular habit of initiating a conversation with our powerful and loving God always improves our mental state, gives us great joy and equanimity, provides us with deep spiritual insights, and brings to our side the greatest retinue of angelic warriors. I cannot think of a single reason not to pray, whether silently, privately, or corporately. Is any among you suffering? Let him pray. Is any cheerful? Let him sing praises.

The following are verses which describe when we should pray.

- When we desire to return to God (Deuteronomy 4:25–29)
- In distress, turmoil, and battle (2 Chronicles 13:13–16)
- When our enemies threaten us (Psalm 3:5, 6)
- Early in the morning (Psalm 5:3; 119:146, 147; Mark 1:35)
- In the day of trouble (Psalm 50:15)
- Three times per day (Psalm 55:16, 17; Daniel 6:10)
- When we reach the end of human help (Psalm 60:11)
- When our heart is overwhelmed (Psalm 61:2)
- Day and night (Psalm 88:1)

- As long as we live (Psalm 116:1, 2)
- When depressed (Psalm 130:1)
- When we face battles (Proverbs 21:31)
- While He is near (Isaiah 55:6)
- When we need mercy (Daniel 1:5)
- When death is near (Jonah 2:2)
- When our soul is in jeopardy (Jonah 2:7)
- When we are alone (Matthew 14:23; Luke 6:12)
- In the evening (Matthew 14:23; Luke 1:10)
- Always pray, do not give up (Luke 18:1)
- When assembling with believers (John 17:1)
- In the afternoon (Acts 3:1; 10:30)
- Before eating a meal (1 Corinthians 10:30, 31)
- In private (1 Timothy 4:4, 5)
- When we need wisdom (Proverbs 4:6, 7; Ecclesiastes 2:26; James 1:5)
- All the time; pray without ceasing (Luke 18:1; Ephesians 6:18; 1 Thessalonians 5:17)

# Chapter 3
## Where should we pray?

Many of us are blessed to live in a country with the liberty and freedom to pray anywhere and anytime. I enjoy watching others bless their food in a restaurant or pray before a meeting. I admire health professionals who offer to pray with their patients.

Most Christians do not impose their beliefs on others. Our prayer neither interrupts others nor requires special consideration. It is immediate, simple, and direct communication with God. We do not need to be on our knees to pray. We can say a silent prayer or we can verbalize our petitions to heaven. When necessary, we can pray with our eyes open, such as when we are driving, on a prayer walk, or even while in conversation. Keep in mind, the earth is God's creation. He is OK with prayer on any part of it.

If you feel God is tugging at your heart for a prayer, do not hesitate to stop what you are doing and pray. Closing our eyes allows us to focus on the words and the communication with God without being distracted. It is a sign we are focused on Him and nothing else. When possible, demarcate your prayers by kneeling in reverence to God. This sets prayer time apart from everything else that goes on throughout the day.

On occasion while growing up, I would accidentally walk in on my mother when she was on her knees praying. I am almost certain I was the object of her prayers, or at least I had a prominent role in them. These visuals remain with me. I appreciate her witness and want to be more diligent with my prayers. You may pray alone or as part of a group. Is any among you suffering? Let him pray. Is any cheerful? Let him sing praises.

The following Bible texts offer guidance on where to pray:

- At the well, while getting refreshed (Genesis 24:12,13)
- On the battlefield (Joshua 10:12, 13)
- In a secret, private place (Matthew 6:6)
- In large groups (Matthew 14:19; Acts 1:14; 2:1-12)
- In the mountains (Matthew 14:23)
- In a solitary place (Mark 1:35, Luke 5:16)
- In God's house (Luke 2:36, 37)
- Amongst believers (Luke 11:1)

- At the river (Acts 16:13)
- In prison (Acts 16:25)
- At the beach (Acts 21:5)
- In the presence of unbelievers (Acts 27:35)

# Pray anywhere

# Pray everywhere

-1 Timothy 2:8

# Chapter 4
## Types of prayers

It was March 2011, and I had just arrived in Moldova. At the time of my visit, the average monthly household income was approximately $20. Most "homes" were not much different than what we would use as a chicken coop here in the States. Some homes had thicker walls, but many were just a compilation of various types of building materials cobbled together. It was bitterly cold.

I arrived on a Thursday, and when Sabbath arrived, we bundled up and drove to the local church. As the parishioners entered at the back of the church transept, almost everyone arriving walked into the sanctuary area at the back and knelt on a prayer bench and prayed before finding their seat in the main sanctuary. Some knelt on the bench for just a few seconds while others spent several minutes on the bench. I had seen prayer benches in grand cathedrals throughout Europe, but I had never seen one used in a Christian church. Around 55 to 60 people gathered in the small church.

As the service began, I noticed a real reverence and joy among those in attendance. When it came time to collect the offering, the elder noted it would be going to the mission field. He encouraged everyone to give as much as possible. As the offering plate was passed around, almost every person put something in it. It boggled my mind how these poverty-stricken people would give of their meager funds to help others. In my mind, they should have been the recipients of the church's offerings. It was at that moment that I realized I was in church and amongst some truly admirable and genuine Christians.

For years, this experience has humbled me and provided insight as to how the early church may have operated. Christianity is not about an outward "form of godliness" (2 Timothy 3:5) but a genuine relationship with the Lord. Ever since this experience, I have wondered if our corporate worship might not benefit from prayer benches to prepare our hearts and minds for corporate worship. So often, our weekday concerns and issues follow us into the sanctuary as we corporately worship. We discuss our cares and concerns with our fellow worshippers, taking our eyes off of God and focusing on our faithless struggles in life.

Prayer is a genuine conversation with God. Prayer is not a "quickie" or "drive-through" experience. While it is OK to offer up a short prayer, hopefully our normal prayer practices are private and meaningful. "But you, when you pray, go into your room, and when you have shut your door, pray to your Father who is in the secret place; and your Father who sees in secret will reward you openly" (Matthew 6:6, NKJV).

The Bible is clear about how we should approach prayer. If our prayers are rote, and we just go through the motions for the sake of meeting someone's expectations, we will likely not experience the incredible power of prayer. Some professed Christians may go for years without truly connecting with God through prayer. First John 3:22 provides insight: "Whatsoever we ask, we receive of him, because we keep his commandments, and do those things that are pleasing in his sight." According to this verse, successful prayer hinges on keeping the commandments. In Revelation 14:12, John emphasized the importance of keeping the commandments: "Here is the patience of the saints: here are they that keep the commandments of God, and the faith of Jesus." In Isaiah 59:1, 2, we read that God can do anything but chooses not to cooperate with humans when we separate ourselves from Him. "Behold, the Lord's hand is not shortened, that it cannot save; neither his ear heavy, that it cannot hear: but your iniquities have separated between you and your God, and your sins have hid his face from you, that he will not hear." "If you want to enter into life, keep the commandments" (Matthew 19:17, NKJV).

This is not an exhaustive chapter on the many types of prayer. It is just enough to barely cover the basics — "bikini" coverage, if you will. Many types of prayers, for various purposes, exist. The Bible gives hundreds of examples of how to pray, and I suggest you study those examples. Prayer may be short and simple, long and detailed (private and personal prayers), regal and profound, but when words fail us, God understands even our tears. "You keep track of all my sorrows. You have collected all my tears in your bottle. You have recorded each one in your book" (Psalm 56:8, NLT).

Below are brief descriptions of various types of prayer. This list may be helpful because it guides us when we participate in corporate prayers as well as in personal prayers. We may not pray a benediction prayer at home, but if asked to pray the benediction at church, here is a guide. And the Lord said, "Let them pray" (James 5:14).

### Benediction, or blessing, prayers.
These are often the last act of a formal worship service before the congregation disperses or participates in koinonia. The benediction tradition is traced back to the high priest, Aaron, and his sons, who spoke this blessing for the Israelites:

The Lord bless you and keep you; the Lord make His face shine upon you, and be gracious to you; the Lord lift up His countenance upon you, and give you peace (Numbers 6:24–26, NKJV).

Other Scripture-based benediction verses include: Psalm 23:6; Romans 1:7; 15:33; Ephesians 3:16–21; 6:23, 24; 2 Thessalonians 3:16; 1 Timothy 1:2; 2 Timothy 4:22; Colossians 3:15–17; Hebrews 13:20, 21; 1 Peter 5:14; 2 Peter 1:2; Revelation 1:4, 5.

**Chain prayers.** These are initiated when a troubling and apparently impossible situation or dilemma emerges. It could be a prayer for healing, for deliverance, or for some other dire situation. Oftentimes, prayer chains target public figures, Christians under persecution, life-and-death matters, or environmental disasters, such as prayers to end a drought, for rescue, or for current social concerns. A chain of earnest, praying believers encircling the world may claim the promise of God: "Where two or three are gathered together in my name, there I am in the midst of them" (Matthew 18:20).

Rarely a day passes when I don't see prayer requests on social media. Sometimes, the prayer request is revealed to be several years old. This always makes me wonder about the outcome. But, no matter the outcome, God is always glorified and praised, and claiming promises and prayer is always the answer.

Hebrews 12:1 (NIV) tells us, "Therefore, since we are surrounded by such a great cloud of witnesses, let us throw off everything that hinders and the sin that so easily entangles." Chain prayers connect hundreds if not thousands of Christians in seeking God's intervention on behalf of a complete stranger.

Over the years, I have come to believe the Creator put a small piece of His being into every aspect of creation. DNA is considered a rapid retrieval bio-information library for every living process. When the body needs to make insulin, the 3630 gene (gene ID) provides instructions.

Certain features of DNA, also known as the genotype, manifest as a phenotype, or a physical manifestation of the arrangement of DNA base pairs. One has a unique genotype, but the expression of the genotype or the phenotype is influenced by both endogenous (originating within the body) and exogenous (originating from outside the body) influences.

It is the exogenous influences that create a slightly different version of you on a daily basis. It may be compared to Claude Monet's water lily paintings. There are 250 versions of Monet's water lilies, and while each painting includes water, water lilies, and reflections on the water, each one is unique and beautiful in its own way. These paintings are similar to how we experience thousands of emotions, eat thousands of chemicals, drink a variable amount of water, process millions of visual cues, and make zillions of synaptic connections. Each data point over our lifetime will serve to either strengthen or weaken our constitution. For example, the most common diagnosis before being diagnosed with breast cancer is depression. If you are sad, angry, disconnected from others, marginalized from society, or experience any number of negative emotional states, you are more likely to acquire health concerns.

Our internal dialogue about ourselves informs our mind how to act. If we have a negative dialogue, we will more likely paint a dark, even grotesque, painting (e.g., Guernica by Picasso painted in reaction to Nazi Germany's war atrocities). However, if we are happy, joyful, full of praise for God, helping others, praying every day, and relying on the Lord for our strength, our life painting might reflect something like a beautiful majestic mountain range or pastoral picture of content children playing with their dogs. The same principle applies to our connection to God. If we praise Him, serve Him, love Him, want to please Him, live for Him, our body will reflect this in several significant ways. When we are confronted with challenging circumstances, we will not fall into depression; we learn to rely on God for all our needs. When we are presented with discouraging news, we do not dwell on it and lose sleep but give it to the Lord in prayer. The adjustments Christians make to their lives positively reflects on their physical state.

In addition to DNA, there are epigenetic influences on DNA. Epigenetic means "above genetics" or "outside of genetics." Epigenetic effects are similar to "on" and "off" switches. When you go on a two-hour bike ride, epigenetic influences are switched "on" or "off" to protect some aspect of your physiology. Two hours of sunlight exposure will turn off a number of genes known to predispose you to developing cancer. These genes may be turned off for two hours, two days, or two weeks. As a scientist, I suspect prayers for strangers (as well as for our loved ones) also have an epigenetic effect on us. We are learning that every experience, every choice we make, every word we speak, and every thought we process, impacts our epigenetics. When we praise God, claim Bible promises and pray for someone, epigenetic effects occur. Whether we pray alone or join with others to participate in chain prayers, the benefits go beyond the recipient(s) of our prayers, the benefits favorably impact us.

Chain prayer scriptures: Matthew 18:19; 18:20; Acts 1:14; 2:46; 4:24, 31; 2:42; 12:5, 12; Romans 15:30; 2 Corinthians 1:11; Colossians 4:3; 2 Thessalonians 3:1; 1 Timothy 2:8; James 5:16; 1 Peter 3:7

**<u>Claiming promises prayers</u>.** These prayers cause us to stand on the promises of God! Search the Scriptures for God's promises. Make praise and Scriptural promises your prayers. God's promises have power, and claiming those promises in prayer increases faith. As we see God working out His promises in our lives, we have great certainty He will finish His work in us. Let's join David in Psalm 13:6 (MSG) as he praises God for answered prayer: "I've thrown myself headlong into your arms, I'm celebrating your rescue. I'm singing at the top of my lungs, I'm so full of answered prayers." First Kings 8:56 (NKJV) states: "Blessed be the Lord, who has given rest to His people Israel, according to all that He promised. There has not failed one word of all His good promise, which He promised through His servant Moses." Below is just a small sampling of some of my favorite Bible promises. Take the time to claim a promise from every book of the Bible. (See Chapter 10.)

Promise scriptures: Psalm 34:17; 50:15; Isaiah 40:29, 31; 43:2; 54:17; Mark 11:24; Romans 8:28; James 1:5; 4:7; 1 John 1:9; Revelation 3:5

**<u>Communing with God through praise, thanksgiving, and prayer</u>**. This is something we do all day long. We wake up and thank the Lord for our rest and for waking us up one more time. We shower and thank the Lord for water. We dress the kids and thank the Lord for family. We eat and thank the Lord for creating plants that deliver such tasteful nutrients. We drive to our appointments and thank the Lord for transportation. We speak with a friend and thank the Lord for friends. We finish a report and thank the Lord for an organized and methodical mind. We arrive home and thank the Lord for a roof over our head. We open our mail and thank the Lord we have enough. We read a book and thank the Lord for creative authors. We go to bed and thank the Lord for another day. This is how we commune with God in praise and thanksgiving.

This type of continual communing with God explains how Enoch was welcomed into heaven without seeing death. I'm not the first to say this, but what if we woke up and had access only to the things we thanked the Lord for the previous day? Would our home disappear? Would the car be in the garage? How about our relatives and friends? What about food and water?

This reminds me of a pastor named Glen Coon. He visited our church when I was a very young child. Even as a child, he made a huge impact on me. He taught us how to pray. He advocated for thanking God for our fingers and toes, our teeth and bones, our toothbrush and toothpaste. It's a good thing he was not a biologist, because his prayers would have never ended, thanking the Lord for our cartilage, ligaments, muscles, cells, mitochondria, electrons, etc. Everything he could think of, he thanked the Lord for providing. This was a seminal concept in my early life, learning how to be thankful for everything. It also includes praising the Lord for everything, both the good and the bad.

When we praise the Lord for our hardships, we immediately join Team Heaven, and God can provide an endless supply of power and energy to those in His kingdom. Even short of heaven, we have access to the power behind every word of His promises. Communing with God's scriptures: Psalm 119:11; John 1:1–3; 6:67–71; 14:20; Acts 2; Hebrews 4:16

**<u>Consecration and praise prayers</u>**. These allow us to consecrate our soul, body, and spirit to God every day. A morning prayer of consecration serves to purify our thoughts. It gives us a burst of physical and mental power to discern spiritual things. Consecration cultivates spirituality and provides us a window to the beauty and grandeur of living a holy life. Consecrate your life, home, family, job, resources, time, activities, etc. Consecration praise and prayer connects every aspect of your life into one prayer. It links your hopes and desires with those of heaven; this opens the way for God's leading. Consecration leads to right living.

The Bible labels several historical figures as being righteous, including God (Ezra 9:15; Psalm 11:7), Abel (Matthew 23:35; Hebrews 11:4), Enoch (Hebrews 11:5), Abraham and Sarah (Hebrews 11:8–12, 17–19), Melchizedek (Hebrews 7:1, 2), Joseph (Matthew 1:19), Noah (Genesis 6:9; 7:1), Moses (Hebrews11:23–30), Job (Job 1:1, 8; 2:3), Rahab (James 2:25), Elizabeth and Zacharias (Luke 1:5, 6), John the Baptist (Mark 6:20), Jesus (Isaiah 53:11; Zechariah 9:9; Matthew 27:19, 24; Acts 3:14; 7:52; 1 John 2:1, 29), and Anna and Simeon (Luke 2:25–38). We too can get special mention in heaven as we cooperate with God and consecrate our lives to the Lord.

**<u>Continual prayers for awareness and watchfulness.</u>** These prayers answer the question of how much time we should spend in prayer. David, describing a blessed person, wrote in Psalm 1:2, "His delight is in the law of the LORD; and in his law doth he meditate day and night."

This type of prayer lifts up everyone entering our stream of consciousness. When an ambulance races by, we pray for the victim and the first responders. When we drive by a prison, we pray for the inmates, for their families, and for their keepers. When a person's name pops into our consciousness, we pray for them. We pray for events, for family, and for friends, for the checkout clerk at the market, for the young boy we see stealing from the sporting goods store. We pray for events, before they occur, as they occur, and after they occur. As the pandemic rages and the flu season worsens, we pray for those with weakened immune systems. As our aging parents begin to exhibit signs of frailty, we pray. This type of prayer continually puts our concerns before the Lord. If you haven't come to this conclusion yet, praise and prayer are always the answer to all of our concerns, issues, problems, and life circumstances! Watchfulness prayer scripture: 1 Thessalonians 5:16–18

**<u>Conversational prayers</u>**. These remind me of Enoch walking with God, which means the two of them had many conversations. Imagine the intriguing and thought-provoking discussions between those two. I doubt they gossiped or made cavalier comments about others. They genuinely enjoyed conversing with each other. God must have enjoyed hearing Enoch's stories about life on earth. Imagine Enoch asking God to re-tell how He formed the earth and the planets making up our solar system, how He placed the water over the ground, how He designed the elements to sustain us, how He designed each type of plant and animal for our delight, etc. I can hear Enoch inquiring of God to explain the incredible design of the human eye and how vision works. I imagine they had deep conversations about physics, biology, chemistry, psychology, and more.

God desires our thoughts and focus to be on Him. When we learn to converse with Him as we would our best friend, we become more like Him. Conversational prayer scriptures: Psalm 51:7, 10–12; Matthew 6:9–13; Luke 21:36; Ephesians 3:14–20; Philippians 1:9–11; Hebrews 11:6

**Corporate or public prayers.** These prayers include The Lord's Prayer, given to us as a model. In Matthew 6, Jesus instructs His disciples to pray in the following manner:

Our Father which art in heaven, Hallowed be thy name. Thy kingdom come. Thy will be done in earth, as it is in heaven. Give us this day our daily bread. And forgive us our debts, as we forgive our debtors. And lead us not into temptation, but deliver us from evil: For thine is the kingdom, and the power, and the glory, forever. Amen.

It is not a long prayer but a simple conversation with God our Father. In these few sentences, we praise the Father, acknowledge His power and authority, and anticipate His Son's return and our subsequent close association with Him. We admit everything we have and need comes from Him. We state our intent to cooperate with and further His kingdom by forgiving others when they fail us, because we too are faulty and commit the same type of offenses. We then express our desire to live holy and acceptable lives according to His will. We finish strong with offering up the ultimate in praise and devotion to Him, not because it will actually help Him, but because we link ourselves to His kingdom when we do this. How much better to unite our voices in prayer to God than to unite our voices in fear or anger toward our fellow men.

Corporate prayer unites all those who willingly and consciously pray together. Corporate prayers in Scripture: 2 Chronicles 7:14; Esther 4:16; Nehemiah 9; Isaiah 56:7; Joel 1:14; 2 Thessalonians 1

**Dedication prayers.** These are oftentimes offered for new events, transitions, and renewals, such as dedicating a building or a baby, engagement, marriage, beginning a new life in Christ, appointing leaders, entering into a new school year, starting out on a new career, and moving into a new home. A prayer of dedication acknowledges the past while giving praise and thanks for how the Lord has led. "Rejoice always, pray continually, give thanks in all circumstances; for this is God's will for you in Christ Jesus" (1 Thessalonians 5:16–18, NIV). By prayer and supplication, with thanksgiving, make your requests known" (Philippians 4:6, ESV). These are just a few short verses that direct us to dedicate everything we own, everything that has value, and everything that has blessed us, to the Lord.

Even when we are far from whole, we dedicate ourselves to His kingdom, thus linking our tattered, rickety lives to the one who makes us whole. According to James 4:14 (NKJV), our lives are but "a vapor that appears for a little time and then vanishes away." If we live for

Christ, we can expect to be redeemed. Events on earth are nearing their completion. Christ will soon return. The dead in Christ will arise and will be caught up with those who are living at the time of His second coming. Our lives are reconstituted as we join Him forever. We will not live as diaphanous spirits floating around on a cloud, but as fully recovered and restored humans, living out our humanity as originally intended.

Dedication events require long-term commitment. Many Christian couples choose to dedicate their children. This takes place during the main church service with family and loved ones. All involved commit to loving and supporting the child from infancy onward. Over the decades of attending church, you see hundreds of parents dedicating their young ones to the Lord. Rarely, but it happens, a couple or a parent will go on and do deplorable things causing grave emotional or physical harm to their children. They may berate their children, speak poorly of them, divorce their spouse, have affairs, go to jail, etc. What happened? How did the parents and corporate church fail the family and child?

This is relevant because these abused children grow up and see their abusive parent(s) lead out in church. This level of hypocrisy causes them to leave the church. The church family should assist the parents by supporting Christian values. When church members go astray, many of the children, teens, and young adults attending church observe the older members' childish, rebellious, and impertinent behaviors. What does this convey to the church's youth? It shows hypocrisy, a personal characteristic that many young people cite as a reason they leave the church or reject biblical living. Commitments last a lifetime not until we get bored or find something more exciting.

The public dedication of a child does not end when the child turns eighteen, when the parents turn fifty, when the parents get divorced, or when the child grows up and becomes a parent. A parent's immediate mission field remains their family and close friends for their entire life. Parents should never give up on their children until they are safely in the hands of God.

Dedication prayers offer all church members the opportunity to reaffirm their commitment to God and to the corporate church family. Dedication prayers: 1 Kings 8:28; Psalm 103:2; Romans 12:2; Hebrews 11:6; James 1:5–7; 4:7

<u>**Desperation prayers**</u>. These prayers have been prayed by many Bible authors, including Moses, Job, David, Jonah, and Jeremiah. When your life is folded into God's will, you and your loved ones likely will be targeted, criticized, challenged, and attacked for your beliefs and practices. During these intense experiences, it is critical to stay connected to God through praise and prayer. As our lives or a family member's life hangs by a thread, we oftentimes offer up a prayer of desperation.

A prayer of desperation should never be offered without also praising God for His wisdom and sovereignty. Praising allows God to work out amazing things for us. Remember Job, as he suffered and played out the controversy between good and evil? Job was the pawn in a chess game, who because of his great faith, cooperated with God and placed a checkmate on evil. In the end, Job had the most incredible communication from God ever recorded in the Bible. The Lord speaks to Job beginning in chapter 38 and ends in the beginning of chapter 40 (NIV) by saying, "Will the one who contends with the Almighty correct Him? Let him who accuses God answer him!" Job replies in verses 3–5, and then the Lord challenges Job in the remaining verses of chapter 40 and through the end of chapter 41. In the first six verses of Job 42, Job answers the Lord and repents. This is where we read how the Lord blessed Job in his latter days more than in his beginning.

Prayers of desperation are common, but instead of blaming and criticizing God, praise Him, claim His promises, and keep praying. In Romans 8:28–30, Paul writes, "And we know that all things work together for good to them that love God, to them who are called according to his purpose. For whom he did foreknow, he also did predestinate to be conformed to the image of his Son, that he might be the firstborn among many brethren. Moreover, whom he did predestinate, them he also called: and whom he called, them he also justified: and whom he justified, them he also glorified."

No matter our circumstances, God has chosen us. While prayers of desperation may be offered, a new day dawns every twenty-four hours. We do not have to remain in a desperate condition if we choose praise, promises, and prayer instead of fear, desperation, and anxiety. Pray a prayer of desperation and then praise the Lord for his sovereignty and for the good news that awaits all of His children.

<u>**Healing prayers**</u>. These play a significant role in healing. Studies have shown those who regularly pray for twenty or more minutes experience less anxiety, more positive moods, greater spiritual insights, and greater pain tolerance (PubMedID 16049627). Other studies have shown decreases in blood pressure, lower cortisol, and activation of various areas of the brain. Praise and prayer, when part of everyday life, lead to changes in the general tone of the nervous system. Instead of remaining in overdrive, the sympathetic system's fight or flight mode, praise and prayer help the body shift into high gear and cruising mode, the parasympathetic system's rest and digest mode.

Prayer for healing honors what God loves to do. When Jesus lived amongst us, He spent more time healing than preaching. We are healed by His stripes. When Christ died on the cross, He died for our diseases as well as for our sins. Many Scripture verses describe this, including: Exodus 15:26; 23:25; Deuteronomy 32:39; 2 Chronicles 7:14, 15; Proverbs 4:20–22; 17:22; Ecclesiastes 3:1–8; Isaiah 33:2; 38:16, 17; 41:10; 53:4, 5; 57:18, 19; Jeremiah 17:14;

30:17; 33:6; Philippians 4:19; James 5:6, 14, 15; 3 John 1:2; Revelation 21:4 Claim these verses and others in your prayers for healing.

**Imprecatory prayers.** These prayers are prayed against Satan, against our own sinful nature, against corruption in high places, against oppression, against genocide, against God's enemies. This type of prayer was used by David to affirm God's actions over evil forces. It is not asking or seeking revenge on a person or group that has hurt you or someone you love, but it is recognizing God's sovereignty over evil, such as harm to children, murder, genocide, etc. It is prayed by the oppressed and the persecuted.

Imprecatory prayer should not be used lightly, in a hateful or bitter manner or as a way to exact revenge or seek retribution. Imprecatory prayer is seeking victory against the spirit realm of evil forces, written about in Ephesians 6:12 (ESV): "We do not wrestle against flesh and blood, but . . . against the spiritual forces of evil in the heavenly places." We pray against Satan and the evil angels. The following scriptures are examples of imprecatory prayers: Gen 12:3; Ps 69:24; 103:6; Romans 12:14, 19; Galatians 1:9; Rev 6:10

**Intercessory prayers.** These prayers are on the behalf of others, whether or not they know you are praying for them. Intercessory prayer is a privilege and serves to unite us with the objects of our prayer. Chain prayers are usually intercessory in nature but include large numbers of people offering up a similar prayer on behalf of someone else.

Pray for the lost, the lonely, the hurting, the hungry, those at war, and the sick, that in their lives the power of Satan will be bound. Pray for children, parents, teachers, and leaders. Intercessory prayer is powerful and can be done at many levels, including on national and international platforms. Examples of intercessory prayer in the Bible: Luke 6:38; John 6:63; Revelation 5:8

**Jericho prayers or prayer walks.** A group of people get together and surround a meeting or a place of work, a court house, a prison, a home of a troubled family, a neighborhood, etc., with a group of people who are praying. Be sure everyone knows the purpose of the prayers. Start with reading scripture passages and pray using scripture promises.

**Prayers of agreement and unity.** These point us to Matthew 18:20 (VOICE): "When two or three gather together in My name, I am there in the midst of them." I love this translation because it shows how much God loves us to pray together. Prayers of agreement are usually focused on one thing: to spread the burden and therefore bond with others. This type of prayer is described in Acts 2:1 (NKJV), where the believers prayed "with one accord." Each person present may choose to pray a few short lines, or several people may pray longer prayers of agreement and represent the corporate gathering. Examples of prayers of agreement: 1 Chronicles 16:11; 2 Chronicles 7:14; Psalm 66:18; 145:18; Isaiah 53:5; 59:2; Jeremiah 29:11,12; 33:31; Ezekiel 22:30; Matthew 21:22; Mark 11:24; John 14:14; 15:7; James 4:3; 5:16; 1 John 1:9; 5:14

**Private prayers.** These prayers occur during alone time, between spouses, between a parent and their child, between friends, and even between strangers. Private prayers are when we pour out our heart to the Lord. There is no required formula or reference for offering up private prayers. I have observed the most significant times in my prayer life are when I pray alone or when I pray with one other person. In my experience, praying in nature magnifies the presence of God.

The Bible recommends our private prayers be in a secret place. In Matthew 6:5, 6, we read it is better to avoid hypocritical public prayers and pray in our rooms where we shut the door and then pray to the Father. When the Father sees in secret, He will reward openly. Examples of private prayers: Mark 1:35; Romans 8:26, James 5:16, Ephesians 6:18

**Spiritual warfare prayers.** These are the type Paul wrote about in Ephesians 6:12: "We wrestle not against flesh and blood, but against principalities, against powers, against the rulers of the darkness of this world, against spiritual wickedness in high places."

We are not safe unless we are praying spiritual warfare prayers for spiritual discernment, for the armor of God, for continual protection against the dark forces of evil, and to overcome the darkness, etc. Unless we are willing to acknowledge the enemy and claim our victory in Christ Jesus, we will fail to fully comprehend the basic human struggle: to know and accept the Lord as our Savior and Redeemer. Spiritual warfare prayers and related praises are essential for spiritual growth. Examples of spiritual warfare prayers: Isaiah 54:17; Zechariah 4:6; Luke 9:18; 2 Corinthians 10:3–5; Ephesians 6:11–17; Philippians 4:6, 7; 1 John 4:4

**Supplication prayers.** These prayers are such as we find in Philippians 4:6 (NIV): "Be anxious for nothing, but in everything by prayer and supplication, with thanksgiving, let your requests be made known to God."

A prayer of supplication functions as a petition to God to lift up our needs. This prayer is humble and earnest. It may be a prayer for specific guidance, wisdom, or to spare a life. Examples of supplication prayers: 1 Kings 8:45; Psalm 28:2; 30:8; 86:6; 143:1; Jeremiah 36:7; Jeremiah 42:2; Daniel 6:11

**Tears-are-a-language-God-understands prayers.** These are for those times when words do not come but tears flow down our cheeks and onto our pillowcases. God understands our tears in the same way he understands auditory prayers. Tears are a

Language God Understands, is a song composed by Gordon Jenson in 1971. Here are a few lines from the song:

> Often you wonder why tears come into your eyes and burdens seem to be much more than you can bear, but God is standing near, He sees your tears and hears them when they fall. God weeps along with man and He takes him by the hand... Tears are a language God understands...

Examples of tears-are-a-language-God-understands prayers: Psalm 6:6; Psalm 42:3; Psalm 56:8; Psalm 126:5; Isaiah 25:8; Ecclesiastes 4:1; 2 Kings 20:5; Esther 8:3; Job 16:20

**Thanksgiving prayers.** These prayers indicate God sustains us every second of every minute of our existence. Acknowledging this every day and at every age provides us with a renewed freshness in our religious lives. While we were growing up, every evening at the dinner table, my dad would ask my brother and me what we learned that day. Parents, in addition to asking what their kids learned, could also ask what they are thankful for.

Praise and thanksgiving should flow from our lips to God. A marvelous transformation takes place in our lives when we learn to praise and give thanks to God. "Don't worry about anything; instead, pray about everything. Tell God what you need, and thank him for all he has done. Then you will experience God's peace, which exceeds anything we can understand. His peace will guard your hearts and minds as you live in Christ Jesus. And my God will fully satisfy every need of yours according to his riches in glory in Christ Jesus" (Philippians 4:6, 7, 19, NLT). Scriptures of thanksgiving: Psalm 28:7; 50:14; Jonah 2:9; Philippians 4:6, 7; 1 Timothy 4:4, 5

**Worship prayers.** These include adoration, praise, thanksgiving, and requests. I remember one of my childhood pastors, Gary Rustad, Sr., would begin every sermon by speaking, and within several minutes he was praying. I never quite knew when he transitioned from speaking to praying, but it was his sermon trademark. I don't know if he planned it or if it just naturally flowed in that direction. I do know I intently listened to each sermon, trying to mark the beginning of the prayer. Looking back, it is possible that his entire sermon was more of a prayer-like conversation with God that included the congregation.

Ideally, worship prayers include prayer requests and praises. They often make mention of current events. Worship prayers and all public worship should be largely apolitical. Praying for our leaders is biblical, but this should be done privately or done in the most judicious and apolitical way possible when done as a call to worship or corporately. In addition, call to worship prayers should always include those who were not specifically mentioned in the prayer requests. The following scriptures set the tone for call to worship prayers: Psalm 5:7, 8; 66:1–4; 96:8–13; 100; Matthew 11:28, 29. Is any among you suffering? Let him pray. Is any cheerful? Let him sing praises.

# Chapter 5
## Prayer formulas

Prayer does not have to be a formula, but you may find one or more of the following prayer formulas to be helpful.

ABC = Ask, Believe, Claim

ACTS = Adoration, Confession, Thanksgiving, Supplication

BLESS = Body (a healthy body), Labor (job and finances), Emotional, Social, Spiritual

PRAY = Praise, Repent, Ask, and Yield


My prayer formula:

To: Dear Father in heaven,

From: Identification
This is Crystal, your harmless little fuzzball from Texas, USA, Earth who is hanging out on the most beautiful planet you created, Earth, rotating at 863.8 miles per hour, speeding around the sun at 67,000 miles per hour, and orbiting around the Milky Way at 448,000 miles per hour. Thank You that 99.99999% of the time this does not cause me to be dizzy!

Thanks and praises:
Thank You for waking me up this morning and for the rest You provided. Thank You for my bed and sheets and blankets, for a roof over my head, for clean water running through a showerhead and faucets all over the house. Thank You for my friends and family scattered around the planet, for my dog Jack and the rest of the lovely animals on the planet (excluding the mean ones and the annoying ones, such as spiders and snakes), for clothes, for a job, for my colleagues, for daily tasks You have given, for complexity in life to make it interesting, for cars, for a functional body habitus, for a sound mind, for funny friends, for grapefruit and all the other delicious edible plants, for delicious and nutritious food for breakfast and throughout the day, for rain, for sunlight, for oceans, for mountains, for sandy dunes, for forests, for beautiful rock formations, for long and winding roads that lead to incredible adventures, for the skies and airplanes that take us to far-away places, for oceans, rivers, lakes, waterfalls, for the quiet place in the wilderness to contemplate Your glory, for grass, for dirt, for plants, for trees and flowers, for the ability to travel and appreciate far-away places. Thank You for the valleys which make the peaks so much more meaningful. Thank You for

difficult challenges — You must know I can handle them. Most of all, thank You for sending Jesus to redeem us.

Failings and weaknesses:
Lord, I am sorry for every action, word, or thought that crucifies You anew. Forgive me for being pathetic, weak, judgmental, prideful, and lacking in mercy. Have mercy on me, O God, according to Your unfailing love. According to Your great compassion blot out my transgressions. Wash away my iniquity and cleanse me from my sin. Create in me a clean heart and renew a right spirit within me. Cast me not away from thy presence and take not thy Holy Spirit from me. Restore unto me the joy of thy salvation. Uphold me with thy free spirit. Convert me to your ways. Deliver me from my guilt and be the God of my salvation. Please forgive my sins and bring to my awareness any unfinished business or someone who might need my help. Help me not to call people "dummies," because I too am a "dummy." Convict me of my unrighteous ways so I may confess and learn to rely on You for everything. May I bear my cross with humility and without too many complaints. May no sacrifice for You seem too great or unreasonable.

Promises claimed:
Today I claim Your promises, including that You will freely love us, if we confess our sins. You are faithful and just to cleanse us from all unrighteousness. You will heal our backsliding. You will never leave nor forsake us. You will hold my right hand while encouraging me not to fear. No weapon formed against us will prosper. You will give knowledge and skill and understanding, to make me part of the head and not the tail. You will keep us from the hour of temptation. You will bring all things to our remembrance.

May I not walk in the counsel of the ungodly. May I be fervent in serving You. The presence of God is with us, so we may dwell in the shelter of the Most High, for deliverance from the snares of the enemy and from the deadly plagues, that the plagues will be turned away at my door. Your faithfulness will form a shield around me, so I will not fear the terror of the night nor the arrows that fly by day. No evil will befall me when a thousand fall on my left and ten thousand die on my right. These horrors will not come near me, my angels will guard me, my angels will bear me up lest I graze my food against a stone, and I will walk on the lion and cobra and trample the lion and serpent under my foot.

You answer when I call to You. Our salvation is secure. You provide us with what we need and give us rest. None of Your words will fail us. You hear our cries. You keep us in perfect peace whose minds are steadfastly on You, because we trust in You. You will give us wisdom and understanding for today, provide us a way out of temptation, and will not let the righteous go hungry. Yea though we walk through the valley of the shadow of death, no harm will come to us. May we not add or subtract from your word but clearly understand both your word and the witness of your creation.

Strengthen my witness:
I ask for nothing that would detract from Your glory and honor. I ask that throughout the day ahead I must decrease and You must increase. I ask a blessing for those who struggle, for those who experience great hardship, and even more for those who have material goods but lack a knowledge of You!

Prayers on behalf of specific people, situations, and issues:
I would like to lift up these people, these situations, these issues before heaven (insert names, situations, and issues here). Please hear this petition on the behalf of myself and others. Also, be with all the animals who are needlessly ripped from their families and needlessly die a harsh and cruel death to satisfy our ways.

Our most precious and deepest desires:
Lord, You have placed certain desires in my heart. I thank You and praise You for meeting and exceeding those expectations.

Looking forward:
I have confidence in You and in Your ability to be with me through whatever happens in life.

Signing off:
Lord, we cannot wait to meet You in person, to see the river of pure living waters brilliantly shimmering and flowing from Your throne. We look forward to eating from the tree of life and experiencing the healing of all the nations. We look forward to continually worshipping You, to throwing down our crowns at Your feet, to hug and kiss You, and to spending eternity with You. We love You and thank You in Jesus' name for hearing and answering this prayer. Looking forward to checking in again with You soon. Yours forever, love, Crystal.


What is Your Prayer Formula?

Is any among you suffering? Let him pray. Is any cheerful? Let him sing praises.

# Chapter 6
## Prayer activity

The next two pages include a number of Bible verses. Each verse is its own paragraph. The activity is to copy these pages, cut each prayer into a strip, and then combine various verses to make a single prayer. If done as a group, each person reads his version, compares with the others, and asks them what they found to be the most meaningful phrases. For example, one person's prayer could look like example A and another person's prayer could look like example B. Is any among you suffering? Let him pray. Is any cheerful? Let him sing praises.

Example A

Praise ye the Lord. We are thankful you Lord, are near to us all who call upon You. We confess our sins to You and to one another and pray to be healed. We humbly ask for our prayers to have great power. We reject being conformed to this world. We ask for the renewing of our mind through praise and communing with you. We claim your promise that You will prove what is Your perfect good and acceptable will for our lives.

Example B

Let everything that hath breath praise You, Lord. We give thanks to You, Lord; for You alone are good. We ask that our prayers be righteous. We are so thankful Your mercy endures forever. We thank You for the times we come together and break bread together with our loved ones. We praise You and claim Your favor. We claim our spot at Your family's Heavenly table. We ask to be merchants of Your will as we go through our time here on earth, claiming souls for Your Kingdom. We sing songs of praise exalting You! We celebrate and pray all the time, taking joy in knowing You. We claim Your peace and are untroubled by fear and harm that threaten us on every side. We thank You for Your faithfulness and know You have already answered our unspoken requests. We thank and praise the King of Glory forever and ever! Amen.

Let everything that hath breath praise the Lord. Praise ye the Lord (Psalm 150:6).

It shall come to pass, before they call, I will answer; and while they are yet speaking, I will hear (Isaiah 65:24).

I urge then, first of all, that petitions, prayers, intercession and thanksgiving be made for all people, for kings and all those in authority, that we may live peaceful and quiet lives in all godliness and holiness (1 Timothy 2:1, 2, NIV).

Is anyone among you in trouble? Let them pray. Is anyone happy? Let them sing songs of praise (James 5:13, NIV).

O give thanks unto the Lord; for he is good; for his mercy endureth for ever (1 Chron 16:34).

Have no anxiety about anything, but in everything by prayer and supplication with thanksgiving let your requests be made known to God (Philippians 4:6, RSV).

Let my mouth be filled with thy praise and with thy honour all the day (Psalm 71:8).

Pray in the Spirit on all occasions with all kinds of prayers and requests. With this in mind, be alert and always keep on praying for all the Lord's people (Ephesians 6:18, NIV).

Then you will call to me. You will come and pray to me, and I will answer you (Jer 29:12).

I say to you, Love your enemies and pray for those who persecute you (Matt 5:44, ESV).

When you pray, do not babble repetitiously like the Gentiles, because they think that by their many words they will be heard (Matthew 6:7, NET).

Do not be conformed to this world, but be transformed by the renewing of your mind, that you may prove what is that good and acceptable and perfect will of God (Romans 12:2).

The Lord is near to all who call upon Him, to all who call upon Him in truth (Ps 145:18).

Confess your sins to one another and pray for one another, that you may be healed. The prayer of a righteous person has great power (James 5:16, ESV).

I can do all things through Christ who strengthens me (Philippians 4:13, NKJV).

If we confess our sins, he is faithful and just and will forgive us our sins and purify us from all unrighteousness (1 John 1:9, NIV).

Wherefore thou art great, O Lord God: for there is none like thee, neither is there any God beside thee, according to all that we have heard with our ears (2 Samuel 7:22).

O give thanks unto the Lord; call upon his name: make known his deeds! (Ps 105:1, ESV).

There is none holy as the Lord: there is none beside thee: neither is there any rock like our God (1 Samuel 2:2).

Now I Nebuchadnezzar praise, extol and honour the King of heaven, all whose works are truth, and his ways judgement: and those that walk in pride, he is able to abase (Dan 4:37).

Who is this King of glory? The Lord of hosts, he is the King of glory. Selah (Psalm 24:10).

Why, my soul, are you downcast? Why so disturbed within me? Put your hope in God, for I will yet praise him, my Saviour and my God (Psalm 42:11).

I will give thanks to you, Lord, with all my heart; I will tell of your wonderful deeds (Ps 9:1.)

I heard every creature in heaven and on earth and under the earth and in the sea, and all that is them, saying, "To him who sits on the throne and to the Lamb be blessing and honor and glory and might forever and ever!" (Revelation 5:13, ESV).

As surely as I live, says the Lord, every knee will bow before me; every tongue will acknowledge God (Romans 14:11, NIV).

Finally, brothers and sisters, whatever is true, whatever is noble, whatever is right, whatever is pure, whatever is lovely, whatever is admirable, if anything is excellent or praiseworthy, think about such things (Philippians 4:8, NIV).

Every day they met together in the temple courts. They broke bread in their homes and ate together with glad and sincere hearts, praising God and enjoying the favor of all the people. And the Lord added to their number daily those who were being saved (Acts 2:46, 47).

And this same God who takes care of me will supply all your needs from his glorious riches, which have been given to us in Christ Jesus (Philippians 4:19, NLT).

But all who listen to me will live in peace, untroubled by fear and harm (Prov 1:33, NLT).

If you declare with your mouth, "Jesus is Lord," and believe in your heart that God raised him from the dead, you will be saved (Romans 10:9, NIV).

Make sure no one returns evil for evil, but always pursue what is good as it affects one another in the church but also all people. Celebrate always, pray constantly, and give thanks to God no matter what circumstances you find yourself in. (This is God's will for all of you in Jesus the Anointed.) Don't suppress the Spirit. Don't downplay prophecies. Take a close look at everything, test it, then cling to what is good. Put away every form of evil. May the God of peace make you His own completely and set you apart from the rest. May your spirit, soul, and body be preserved, kept intact and wholly free from any sort of blame at the coming of our Lord Jesus the Anointed. For the God who calls you is faithful, and He can be trusted to make it so (1 Thessalonians 5:15–24).

Rejoice always, pray continually, give thanks in all circumstances; for this is God's will for you in Christ Jesus (1 Thessalonians 5:16-18).

Commit to the Lord whatever you do, and he will establish your plans (Proverbs 16:3).

But those who hope in the Lord will renew their strength. They will soar on wings like eagles; they will run and not grow weary, they will walk and not be faint (Isaiah 40:31).

# Chapter 7
## Praises for victory

Praise is a powerful force which, when combined with an avid prayer life, leads to victory in Christ. It thwarts Satan's efforts to distract us from our real blessings. If we faithfully praise God for what we have, there is no time to get discouraged. Satan likes to point out what we do not have so he can get us busy breaking the Ten Commandments (e.g., envying, coveting, lusting, worshipping other gods, deceiving, gaslighting). By choosing to focus on the things we lack, we fail to gain the advantage our heavenly Father offers to all those who believe in Him.

We learn to believe what others say about us. When we say someone is a "godly" person, this debases God to a human level. There is no one on the earth who is godly. In Isaiah 55:8, 9 (NLT), we read: " 'My thoughts are nothing like your thoughts,' says the Lord. 'And my ways are far beyond anything you could imagine. For just as the heavens are higher than the earth, so my ways are higher than your ways and my thoughts are higher than your thoughts.' " The only safe praise and adoration belongs to God. Many are ruined by receiving constant praise and honor. Gratuitous praise may cause the recipient to believe s/he is infallible and above reproach. "Great," "awesome," and "amazing" are the types of praises that belong to God!

This is hard to practice. A specific compliment or targeted praise is better than blanket praise. For example, if you enjoyed the preacher's message, you could say something such as, "I really connected with the content of your sermon." This takes the general praise element out of the conversation and provides a more accurate comment versus heaping praise on the preacher. Almost anyone, when heaped with praise and adoration, will begin to believe in their own greatness. This oftentimes leads to our ruin. It may or may not immediately affect our life, but eventually we become impossible to live and work with. Even though we are made in God's image, we cannot fully comprehend God. No matter how many people write books about God, research the "God" particle (some say the Higgs boson particle is the "God" particle, discovered in 2012), and preach about God's character, no one person has cornered the market on understanding God and His ways. Each person must come to know God through the avenues of Scripture reading, praise, prayer, spending time in nature, studying physical and natural laws, the witness of others, fellowship with others, practicing hospitality, random acts of kindness, etc.

We can, however, know God through His Son Jesus Christ, who assumed humanity, lived a sinless life, died, and was raised up to atone for our sins. We can read the accounts written about Jesus, and we can even read His words and emulate His ways. He is worthy of our praise. When He is lifted up, all men are drawn to him.

When we are lifted up and used as a standard of righteousness, some may run and scream in fright, not because we are bad people, but because we will never be free of a sinful past that directly bears on our biological blueprint. We will retain an always-present sinful nature until we are translated and glorified. This does not negate the possibility we may gain the victory over sin; it means we have a sinful past which has altered the course of our biological, social, spiritual, and mental nature.

Not only is sin manifest as a spiritual consequence, it epigenetically alters every aspect of our biological, social, and thought processes. Sin leaves an indelible mark to be removed only when Christ physically comes to redeem us. While our sins will be erased and the biological blueprint of sin removed, Christ's physical scars will remain, a tribute to the everlasting gospel of redemption.

When we shift our focus from the current crisis or crises in our lives to Christ, we connect with God in a way that places the emphasis on Christ and Christ alone, with absolutely no focus on our efforts to achieve perfection. This does not negate the fact that we as Christians become more like Christ as we grow in Him. This is illustrated through acts of graciousness, kindness, and gratitude toward others. These acts are not to earn salvation but they are the benefit of a growing and burgeoning Christ-centered life.

The point of this discussion is to direct our most magnificent and eloquent praises and prayers to heaven, not to our fellow humans. At the appropriate time, we deserve various modicums of praise, but not the excessive and grandiose praise given gratuitously and to gain influence and standing with others. We should always strive to place God in the right relation to mankind. As Christ gains standing in our lives and we exhibit the fruits of the Spirit, such as humility, we will begin to see the praises of man as ostentatious and will seek to redirect this type of praise to the Creator. Scripture praises may include:

Isaiah 43:18, 19 (VOICE) – Eternal One: Don't revel only in the past [referring to the exodus] or spend all your time recounting the victories of days gone by. Watch closely: I am preparing something new; it's happening now, even as I speak, and you're about to see it. I am preparing a way through the desert; waters will flow where there had been none.

Isaiah 65:21, 22 (RSV) – They shall build houses and inhabit them; they shall plant vineyards and eat their fruit. They shall not build and another inhabit; they shall not plant and another eat; for like the days of a tree shall the days of my people be, and my chosen shall long enjoy the work of their hands.

Exodus 14:14 (NIV) – The Lord will fight for you; you need only to be still.

Exodus 20:12 (NIV) – Honor your father and your mother, so that you may live long in the land the Lord your God is giving you.

Isaiah 40:29–31 – He giveth power to the faint; and to them that have no might he increaseth strength. Even the youths shall faint and be weary, and the young men shall utterly fall: But they that wait upon the Lord shall renew their strength; they shall mount up with wings as eagles; they shall run, and not be weary; and they shall walk, and not faint.

Isaiah 41:10 (VOICE) – So don't be afraid. I am here, with you; don't be dismayed, for I am your God. I will strengthen you, help you. I am here with My right hand to make right and to hold you up.

# Chapter 8
## My blessings

You are the author of this chapter. This could be your greatest written work ever! Write this chapter to God. What has God provided for you? What are your blessings?

Below, you will see a few examples of things to be thankful for and after that, use the blanks on the next page to list your greatest blessings!

- God, Jesus, the Holy Spirit, and my life.
- God is love and has provided an example of love for me to follow.
- God is always with me.
- My family and friends.
- God woke me up this morning.
- Promise of a new day to earn my daily bread.
- For the command to have a lovely dominion over the animals which honors and respects their life and their social, physical, mental and environmental needs.
- I strive to do my best in all endeavors.
- Many conveniences of life not available to our ancestors.
- Liberty and the freedom to worship, freedom of religion, freedom of movement, etc.
- Life challenges to make me appreciate His sovereignty over my life.
- Great and inspired musicians to compose and play beautiful music.
- Enough money to get by and enough money to help others.
- People in my life who offer me an alternative view of myself.
- A beautiful planet to explore and protect.

My blessings

- 
- 
- 
- 
- 
- 
- 
- 
- 
- 
- 
- 
- 
- 
- 
- 
- 
- 
- 
- 
- 
- 
- 
- 
- 
- 
- 
- 
- 
- 
- 
- 
-

# Chapter 9
## Demonstrating gratitude

Take the palm of your hand and place it just above your eyebrows. You are touching your frontal lobes. This region of the brain is responsible for gratitude. It is how we connect with God. It houses spirituality, spiritual discernment, morality, generosity, and gratitude. Moses describes how gratitude, as manifested in kind and loving actions, is connected with frontal lobes. Deuteronomy 11:18, 19 reads, "So commit yourselves wholeheartedly to these words of mine. Tie them to your hands and wear them on your forehead as reminders. Teach them to your children. Talk about them when you are at home and when you are on the road, when you are going to bed and when you are getting up." See Figure 1.

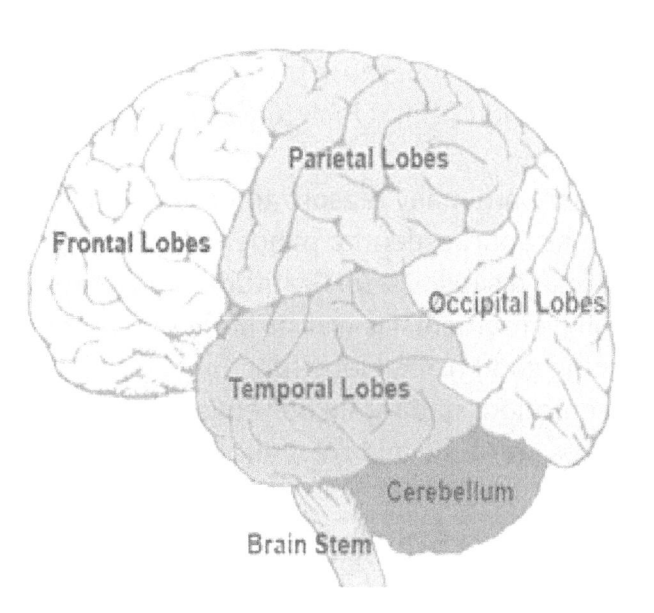

Figure 1. Frontal lobes and other regions of the brain

The Bible connects our hands, a symbol of how we serve and help others, to our forehead, a symbol of being connected to Christ. Let's turn from the beginning of the Bible to the last book. Revelation 7:3 says, "Hurt not the earth, neither the sea nor the trees, till we have sealed the servants of God in their foreheads." The redeemed bear a seal on their foreheads. This seal indicates we are connected to Christ. Our actions reflect those of the Savior in gentleness, meekness, humility, patience, love, long-suffering, etc. The seal on our forehead is the opposite of the mark of the beast. In contrast, Revelation 13:11–18 describes those who receive the mark of the beast, being found on their right hands or forehead. How does the mark of the beast differ from the mark Christ's servants will receive?

Metaphorically speaking, John connects our hands to our foreheads. Revelation 14:9–11 (NIV) reads: "A third angel followed them and said in a loud voice: If anyone worships the beast and its image and receives its mark on their forehead or on their hand, they, too, will drink the wine of God's fury, which has been poured full strength into the cup of his wrath." The mark of a Christian is gratitude, which is manifest as a spiritual connection, spending time in prayer, and being the hands of Christ by helping others. The mark of a Christian is gratitude, which is manifest as a spiritual connection and spending time in prayer. Both indicate good frontal lobe function, as well as being the hands of Christ and helping others.

Gratitude is the outpouring of loving and benevolent actions. Oftentimes these actions are spontaneous in nature. Our hearts fill with constant gratitude as we contemplate the gift from God to us, of Christ, our personal Savior. Theoretically, we can be intellectually thankful for something without there being a corresponding action; however, gratitude requires actions and good frontal lobe function.

There are many reasons to be grateful, even when we face the darkest moments in life, such as unprecedented pandemics, unfair and unjust actions, financial collapse, death of a loved one, disability, etc. Gratitude is a gift and is evident as we experience life's exciting and thrilling moments as well as life's low moments. Both highs and lows are critical to developing good frontal lobe function. This allows us to experience the entire range of human emotions and retain our equanimity. Good frontal lobe function allows us to experience gratitude and treat all of God's creatures with dignity and respect.

A long list of symptoms indicates our frontal lobes may not be optimally functioning. This does not necessarily affect the intellect. One or two symptoms may not indicate frontal lobe impairment, especially if temporary. However, the more symptoms you have and the longer they persist, the more likely you have frontal lobe issues.

These signs include: increase in sweets and carbohydrate cravings, dramatic changes in personality, loss of empathy, poor insight, poor judgment, loss of social graces, decline in personal hygiene and grooming, mental rigidity, inflexibility, distractibility, hyper-orality (talking too much), frequent risk-taking behaviors, lack of behavioral restraint, compulsive behaviors, ritualistic behaviors, loss of emotional recognition, inappropriate sexual behaviors, confabulation, apathy, loss of motivation, changes in moral beliefs, perseveration (cannot end a task), loss of interest in helping others, frequently yelling and screaming at family and friends, lack of sensitivity to other people's feelings, unable to sustain meaningful relationships, loss of spontaneity, lack of concern, addictions, disorganization, inability to properly use language, dementia, and deception.

How do we lose our frontal lobe functions? Stress builds and multiplies if not checked by a healthy lifestyle, adequate intake of protein and B vitamins, good thyroid functions, and a meaningful devotional life. Chronic unrelenting stress, as well as other conditions, compromise frontal lobe functions. If as a Christian you find yourself yelling at your family, "living on the edge," finding faults with everyone, unable to disconnect from the stresses of life, etc., you may have compromised frontal lobe functions.

Good frontal lobes require corresponding actions of gratitude, even when dealing with angry and difficult people. This might be the best time to witness to someone. You can be grateful they released their energy toward you and not toward their spouse or child. For example, if someone yells at you while having to wait to fill up with gas, buy their gas. If someone cuts in line while waiting to order at the fast food restaurant, buy their meal. This act of gratitude may change their life. At a minimum, it will start a meaningful conversation. You have a witnessing opportunity which would have been lost if you responded in kind to their aggression. For this reason, creativity and gratitude are correlated with good frontal lobe function.

We can be intellectually thankful for a loving God who cares for every aspect of our life; however, gratitude toward a loving God manifests as individual actions, such as feeding the hungry, sheltering the needy, paying an unpaid bill for a friend, passing along your old washing machine to someone who needs one, etc. Gratitude cannot be legislated nor required. It spills over from having more than enough, even if you are money-poor.

If you are always needy and wanting others to serve you and give you things, you are not be able to experience the beauty of gratitude. It is easy to identify those who exhibit gratitude. They don't complain about social or even economic inequities, but they show gratitude to the Savior in countless ways. They are a pleasure to know and bless everyone around them. Christians should experience gratitude toward God and their fellow men on a daily basis.

Praise and prayer place us on heaven's playground where huge entourages of heavenly angels eagerly await a new assignment to uplift the human race. As Christians, our first response to any life situation should be to find something to praise God about, claim a Scripture promise, and a dedicate a time to speak with Him in prayer. At any time, we can engage in a two-way conversation with heaven. Make your words and sentiments align with God's purposes as revealed in Scripture and with how He has already led in your life. We are on a journey, and the "best practice" is to live a life full of thankfulness and gratitude. Is any among you suffering? Let him pray. Is any cheerful? Let him sing praises.

Texts mentioning the forehead (i.e., frontal lobes) for study: Exodus 13:16; 28:36–38; Leviticus 13:41–43; Numbers 24:17; Deuteronomy 6:8; 11:18, 19; 1 Samuel 17:49; 2 Chronicles 26:19, 20; Jeremiah 48:45; Ezekiel 3:8, 9; 9:4; Revelation 7:3; 9:4; 13:6; 14:1; 14:9; 17:53; 20:4, 22:4

Using the rest of the blank pages in this chapter, write out ways you can show gratitude to God and others. A few examples are provided:
- When your parent or spouse works late, show gratitude by doing extra chores around the house.

- When your friends go on vacation, offer to keep their pets, keep up their yard, pick up newspapers, etc.
- Care for the children of friends while they welcome a new baby or require a hospital stay. Keep your corner of the environment clean and tidy.
- Care for the beautiful animals God has given us to protect. Provide beautiful music for others to enjoy.
- Participate in sacrificial relationships where you may give more than you receive.
- Exercise the fruits of the Spirit, such as joy, patience, longsuffering, peace, kindness, forbearance, gentleness, faith, modesty, self-control, speaking words of wisdom and knowledge, etc.
- Choose peaceful thoughts over fear. Serve others.
- Participate in random acts of kindness.
- Exercise logic and the ability to reason from cause to effect.
- Avoid hateful thoughts and attitudes.
- Avoid conflict.
- Listen to others.
- Spend time with others.
- Prepare and serve food to others.
- Do the dishes and other housekeeping tasks. Build up others.
- Show appreciation.
- Write letters of encouragement.
- Raise respectful and well-behaved children. Share your talents.
- Visit the elderly, prisoners, lonely people, etc.
- Learn how to say "thank you" when someone does something for you, no matter how small.
- Respect other people's time (i.e., avoid wasting their time).
- Respect other people's accomplishments and views.

Ways to show gratitude…

- _____
- _____
- _____
- _____
- _____
- _____
- _____
- _____
- _____
- _____
- _____
- _____
- _____
- _____
- _____
- _____
- _____
- _____
- _____
- _____
- _____
- _____
- _____
- _____
- _____
- _____
- _____
- _____
- _____
- _____

# Chapter 10
## Bible promises: from Genesis to Revelation

This chapter contains selected promises of God in order of the books of the Bible. Reading through some of the promises contained in each chapter is uplifting and refreshing. We have so much to be thankful for. There are more than 31,000 verses in the Bible and at least 10% of those verses are promises.

Take the time to make your own list of promises from each book of the Bible. Read through them every day and especially at times of discouragement and fear. When you see the sweep of history through the promises of God, we have nothing to fear and everything to hope for and claim in Christ!

### Genesis
So now you see how the Creator swept into being the spangled heavens, the earth, and all their hosts in six days. On the seventh day, with the canvas of the cosmos completed, God paused from His labor and rested. Thus, God blessed day seven and made it special, an open time for pause and restoration, a sacred zone of Sabbath-keeping, because God rested from all the work He had done in creation that day (2:1–3, VOICE). [The first thing God blessed was the Sabbath day.]

And I will put enmity between you and the woman, and between your offspring and hers; he will crush your head, and you will strike his heel. (3:15, NIV; the John 3:16 of the Old Testament)

I will surely multiply (1) your sorrowful toil in fieldwork and (2) your conception. With effort you will bring forth children Your [loving] desire [is] to your husband but he [is rebelliously ruling over himself and] will rule over you. (3:16, Bruce C. E. Fleming, tru316.com)

Then the angel of the Lord called again to Abraham from heaven. "This is what the Lord says: Because you have obeyed me and have not withheld even your son, your only son, I swear by my own name that I will certainly bless you. I will multiply your descendants beyond number, like the stars in the sky and the sand on the seashore. Your descendants will conquer the cities of their enemies. And through your descendants all the nations of the earth will be blessed, all because you have obeyed me. (22:15–18, NLT)

### Exodus
Then the people complained and turned against Moses. "What are we going to drink?" they demanded. So Moses cried out to the Lord for help, and the Lord showed him a piece of wood. Moses threw it into the water, and this made the water good to drink. It was there at Marah that the Lord set before them the following decree as a standard to test their faithfulness to him. He said, "If you will listen carefully to the voice of the Lord your God and do what is right in his sight, obeying his commands and keeping all his decrees, then I will not make you suffer any of the diseases I sent on the Egyptians; for I am the Lord who heals you. (15:24–26, NLT)

Now if you will obey me and keep my covenant, you will be my own special treasure from among all the peoples on earth; for all the earth belongs to me. (19:5, NLT)

### Leviticus

You shall therefore keep my statutes and my ordinances, by doing which a man shall live: I am the Lord (18:5, RSV).

### Numbers

Then you will remember to obey all my commands, and you will be God's holy people. I am the Lord your God, who brought you out of Egypt to be your God. I am the Lord your God (15:40, 41, NIV).

### Deuteronomy

Look at what I've done for you today: I've placed in front of you, life and good, death and evil. And I command you today: Love God, your God. Walk in his ways. Keep his commandments, regulations, and rules so that you will live, really live, live exuberantly, blessed by God, your God, in the land you are about to enter and possess. But I warn you: If you have a change of heart, refuse to listen obediently, and willfully go off to serve and worship other gods, you will most certainly die. You won't last long in the land that you are crossing the Jordan to enter and possess. I call Heaven and Earth to witness against you today: I place before you, life and death, blessing and curse. Choose life so that you and your children will live. And love God, your God, listening obediently to him, firmly embracing him. Oh yes, he is life itself, a long life settled on the soil that God, your God, promised to give your ancestors, Abraham, Isaac, and Jacob (30:15–20, MSG).

### Joshua

This Book of the Law shall not depart from your mouth, but you shall meditate in it day and night, that you may observe to do according to all that is written in it. For then you will make your way prosperous, and then you will have good success (1:8, NKJV).

For what great nation is there that has a god so near to it as the Lord our God is to us, whenever we call upon him? (4:7, RSV).

Behold, this day I am going the way of all the earth. And you know in all your hearts and in all your souls that not one thing has failed of all the good things which the Lord your God spoke concerning you. All have come to pass for you; not one word of them has failed (23:14, NKJV).

### Judges

Thus let all Your enemies perish, O Lord! But let those who love Him be like the sun when it comes out in full strength (5:31, NKJV).

### Ruth

Stop pushing me away, insisting that I stop following you! Wherever you go, I will go. Wherever you live, I will live. Your people will be my people. Your God will be my God. Wherever you die, I will also die and be buried there near you. May the Eternal One punish me, and even more so, if anything besides death comes between us. When Naomi heard this and saw Ruth's resolve, she stopped trying to talk her out of returning to Judah (1:16–18, VOICE).

### 1 Samuel

He will guard the feet of His saints, but the wicked shall be silent in darkness. For by strength no man shall prevail (2:9, NKJV).

Then all this assembly shall know that the Lord does not save with sword and spear; for the battle is the Lord's, and He will give you into our hands (17:47, NKJV).

## 2 Samuel
Therefore you are great, O Lord God. For there is none like you, and there is no God besides you, according to all that we have heard with our ears (7:22, ESV).

## 1 Kings
When David's time to die approached, he charged his son Solomon, saying, "I'm about to go the way of all the earth, but you—be strong; show what you're made of! Do what God tells you. Walk in the paths he shows you: Follow the life-map absolutely, keep an eye out for the signposts, his course for life set out in the revelation to Moses; then you'll get on well in whatever you do and wherever you go (2:1–3, MSG).

## 2 Kings
But to the king of Judah, who sent you to inquire of the Lord, thus shall you say to him, Thus says the Lord, the God of Israel: Regarding the words that you have heard, because your heart was penitent, and you humbled yourself before the Lord, when you heard how I spoke against this place and against its inhabitants, that they should become a desolation and a curse, and you have torn your clothes and wept before me, I also have heard you, declares the Lord (22:18, 19, ESV).

## 1 Chronicles
Then you will succeed, if you carefully obey the rules and regulations which the Lord ordered Moses to give to Israel. Be strong and brave! Don't be afraid and don't panic! (22:13, NET).

## 2 Chronicles
When I shut up the heavens so that there is no rain, or command locusts to devour the land or send a plague among my people, if my people, who are called by my name, will humble themselves and pray and seek my face and turn from their wicked ways, then I will hear from heaven, and I will forgive their sin and will heal their land. Now my eyes will be open and my ears attentive to the prayers offered in this place (7:13–15, NKJV).

## Ezra
We are the servants of the True God of heaven and earth; we are rebuilding His house, a house that was originally crafted by one of the greatest kings of Israel early in our nation's history. Our ancestors disobeyed the True God of heaven and provoked His anger. He empowered Nebuchadnezzar, the Chaldean king of Babylon, to capture our rebellious ancestors, deport them to Babylon, and destroy His temple. We languished in captivity for more than a generation, until King Cyrus, in his first year as king over Persia and Babylon, allowed us to rebuild the True God's temple (5:11–13, VOICE).

Our True God takes care of anyone who follows Him, but He uses His power and anger against anyone who abandons Him (8:22, VOICE).

## Nehemiah
And he said to them, Go your way, eat the fat, and drink the sweet, and send portions to them for whom nothing is prepared; for the day is holy to our Lord; and be not grieved, for the joy of Jehovah is your strength (8:10, DARBY).

## Esther
If you keep quiet at a time like this, deliverance and relief for the Jews will arise from some other place, but you and your relatives will die. Who knows if perhaps you were made queen for just such a time as this? (4:14, NLT).

### Job
Besides, I know my Redeemer lives, and in the end He will rise and take His stand on the earth. And though my skin has been stripped off, still, in my flesh, I will see God. I, myself, will see Him: not some stranger, but actually me, with these eyes. Toward this end, my deepest longings pine away within my chest (19:25–27, VOICE).

### Psalms
Because he has set his love upon Me, therefore I will deliver him; I will set him on high, because he has known My name (91:14, NKJV).

You who love the Lord, hate evil! He preserves the souls of His saints; he delivers them out of the hand of the wicked (97:10, NKJV).

The Lord is my best friend and my shepherd. I always have more than enough. He offers a resting place for me in his luxurious love. His tracks take me to an oasis of peace, the quiet brook of bliss. That's where he restores and revives my life. He opens before me pathways to God's pleasure and leads me along in his footsteps of righteousness so that I can bring honor to his name. Lord, even when your path takes me through the valley of deepest darkness, fear will never conquer me, for you already have! You remain close to me and lead me through it all the way. Your authority is my strength and my peace. The comfort of your love takes away my fear. I'll never be lonely, for you are near. You become my delicious feast even when my enemies dare to fight. You anoint me with the fragrance of your Holy Spirit; you give me all I can drink of you until my heart overflows. So why would I fear the future? For your goodness and love pursue me all the days of my life. Then afterward, when my life is through, I'll return to your glorious presence to be forever with you! (23, TPT).

### Proverbs
I, Solomon, David's son and Israel's king, pass on to you these proverbs, a treasury of wisdom, so that you would recognize wisdom and value discipline; that you would understand insightful teaching and receive wise guidance to live a disciplined life; that you would seek justice and have the ability to choose what is right and fair. These proverbs teach the naive how to become clever; they instruct the young in how to grow in knowledge and live with discretion. The wise will pay attention to these words and will grow in learning, and the discerning will receive divine guidance, and they will be able to interpret the meaning of a proverb and a puzzle, the twists and turns in the words of the wise and their riddles. Let us begin. The worship of the Eternal One, the one True God, is the first step toward knowledge. Fools, however, do not fear God and cannot stand wisdom or guidance (1:1–7, VOICE).

Love overlooks the mistakes of others, but dwelling on the failures of others devastates friendships (17:9, TPT).

### Ecclesiastes
That's the whole story. Here now is my final conclusion: Fear God and obey his commands, for this is everyone's duty (12:13, NLT).

### Song of Solomon
He has brought me to his banquet hall, and his banner over me is love (2:4, NASB).

## Isaiah

He has swallowed up death forever! The Lord Yahweh will wipe away tears from off all faces. He will take the reproach of his people away from off all the earth, for Yahweh has spoken it. (25:8, WEB)

You will keep in perfect peace those whose minds are steadfast, because they trust in you. (26:3 NIV)

The grass withereth, the flower fadeth: but the word of our God shall stand for ever. (40:8, KJV)

So do not fear, for I am with you; do not be dismayed, for I am your God. I will strengthen you and help you; I will uphold you with my righteous right hand (41:10, NIV).

For the mountains shall depart, and the hills be removed; but my kindness shall not depart from thee, neither shall the covenant of my peace be removed, saith the LORD that hath mercy on thee. (54:10, KJV)

"Afflicted city, storm-battered, unpitied: I'm about to rebuild you with stones of turquoise, Lay your foundations with sapphires, construct your towers with rubies, Your gates with jewels, and all your walls with precious stones. All your children will have GOD for their teacher — what a mentor for your children! You'll be built solid, grounded in righteousness, far from any trouble — nothing to fear! far from terror — it won't even come close! If anyone attacks you, don't for a moment suppose that I sent them, and if any should attack, nothing will come of it. I create the blacksmith who fires up his forge and makes a weapon designed to kill. I also create the destroyer — but no weapon that can hurt you has ever been forged. Any accuser who takes you to court will be dismissed as a liar. This is what GOD's servants can expect. I'll see to it that everything works out for the best." GOD's Decree. (54:11-17, MSG)

The sun shall be no more thy light by day; neither for brightness shall the moon give light unto thee: but the LORD shall be unto thee an everlasting light, and thy God thy glory. Thy sun shall no more go down; neither shall thy moon withdraw itself: for the LORD shall be thine everlasting light, and the days of thy mourning shall be ended. (60:19,20, KJV)

Thus saith the LORD, The heaven is my throne, and the earth is my footstool: where is the house that ye build unto me? and where is the place of my rest? For all those things hath mine hand made, and all those things have been, saith the LORD: but to this man will I look, even to him that is poor and of a contrite spirit, and trembleth at my word. (66:1,2, KJV)

## Jeremiah

For I know the thoughts that I think toward you, saith Jehovah, thoughts of peace, and not of evil, to give you in your latter end a hope (29:11, DARBY).

## Lamentations

The Lord's loving kindnesses indeed never cease, for His compassions never fail. They are new every morning; great is Your faithfulness. "The Lord is my portion," says my soul, "Therefore I have hope in Him." The Lord is good to those who wait for Him, to the person who seeks Him. It is good that he waits silently for the salvation of the Lord (3:22–26, NASB).

## Ezekiel

And I will give you a new heart, and I will put a new spirit in you. I will take out your stony, stubborn heart and give you a tender, responsive heart (36:26, NLT).

## Daniel
Shadrach, Meshach, and Abednego answered and said to the king, "O Nebuchadnezzar, we do not need to give you an answer in this matter. If it be so, our God whom we serve is able to deliver us from the burning fiery furnace, and He will deliver us out of your hand, O king. But even if He does not, be it known to you, O king, that we will not serve your gods, nor worship the golden image which you have set up (3:16-18, MEV).

## Hosea
I will heal their backsliding, I will love them freely; for mine anger is turned away from him (14:4, DARBY).

## Joel
And it will come about that whoever calls on the name of the Lord Will be delivered; for on Mount Zion and in Jerusalem there will be those who escape, as the Lord has said, Even among the survivors whom the Lord calls (3:22, NASB).

## Amos
Surely the Lord God will do nothing, but he revealeth his secret unto his servants the prophets (3:7, KJV).

## Obadiah
The day of the Lord is near for all nations. As you have done, it will be done to you; your deeds will return upon your own head (1:15, NIV).

## Jonah
He issued a proclamation and said, "In Nineveh, by the decree of the king and his nobles: No human or animal, cattle or sheep, is to taste anything; they must not eat and they must not drink water. Every person and animal must put on sackcloth and must cry earnestly to God, and everyone must turn from their evil way of living and from the violence that they do. Who knows? Perhaps God might be willing to change his mind and relent and turn from his fierce anger so that we might not die (3:7–9, NET).

## Micah
He hath shewed thee, O man, what is good; and what doth the Lord require of thee, but to do justly, and to love mercy, and to walk humbly with thy God? (6:8).

## Nahum
The Lord is good indeed, he is a fortress in time of distress, and he protects those who seek refuge in him (1:7, NET).

## Habakkuk
Yet I will rejoice in the Lord, I will joy in the God of my salvation. The Lord God is my strength, and he will make my feet like hinds' feet, and he will make me to walk upon mine high places (3:18, 19, KJV).

## Zephaniah
Yahweh, your God, is among you, a mighty one who will save. He will rejoice over you with joy. He will calm you in his love. He will rejoice over you with singing (3:17, WEB).

## Haggai

According to the word that I covenanted with you when ye came out of Egypt, so my spirit remaineth among you: fear ye not. For thus saith the Lord of hosts; Yet once, it is a little while, and I will shake the heavens, and the earth, and the sea, and the dry land; and I will shake all nations, and the desire of all nations shall come: and I will fill this house with glory, saith the Lord of hosts (2:5–7, KJV).

## Zechariah

So he said to me, "This is the word of the Lord to Zerubbabel: 'Not by might nor by power, but by my Spirit,' says the Lord Almighty' " (4:6, NIV).

And thou shalt say unto them, Thus saith Jehovah of hosts: Return unto me, saith Jehovah of hosts, and I will return unto you, saith Jehovah of hosts (1:3, DARBY).

Return to your walled cities, safe and secure, O hostages of hope. I announce today that I will restore to you twice as much as what was taken (9:12, VOICE).

## Malachi

But for you who revere my name, the sun of righteousness will rise with healing in its rays. And you will go out and frolic like well-fed calves (4:2, NIV).

## Matthew

Come to me, all you who labor and are heavily burdened, and I will give you rest. Take my yoke upon you and learn from me, for I am gentle and humble in heart; and you will find rest for your souls. For my yoke is easy, and my burden is light (11:28–30, WEB).

## Mark

Jesus looked at them and replied, "With people it is impossible, but not with God; God makes all things possible! (10:27, TPT).

## Luke

But the angel reassured them, saying, "Don't be afraid. For I have come to bring you good news, the most joyous news the world has ever heard! And it is for everyone everywhere! For today in Bethlehem a rescuer was born for you. He is the Lord Yahweh, the Messiah (2:10, 11, TPT).

## John

For God expressed His love for the world in this way: He gave His only Son so that whoever believes in Him will not face everlasting destruction, but will have everlasting life. Here's the point. God didn't send His Son into the world to judge it; instead, He is here to rescue a world headed toward certain destruction (3:16, 17, VOICE).

## Acts

You have made known to me the paths of life; you will fill me with joy in your presence (2:28).

## Romans

Therefore, there is now no condemnation for those who are in Christ Jesus, because through Christ Jesus the law of the Spirit who gives you life has set you free from the law of sin and death (8:1-2, NIV).

You have not received a spirit that makes you fearful slaves. Instead you received God's Spirit when he adopted you as his own children. Now we call him, "Abba, Father" (8:26)

So, we are convinced that every detail of our lives is continually woven together to fit into God's perfect plan of bringing good into our lives, for we are his lovers who have been called to fulfill his designed purpose (8:28, TPT).

So, what does all this mean? If God has determined to stand with us, tell me, who then could ever stand against us? For God has proved his love by giving us his greatest treasure, the gift of his Son. And since God freely offered him us as the sacrifice for us all, he certainly won't withhold from us anything else he has to give (8:31-32, TPT).

So, now I live with the confidence that there is nothing in the universe with the power to separate us from God's love. I'm convinced love with triumph over death, life's troubles, fallen angels, or dark rulers in the heavens. There is nothing in our present or future circumstances that can weaken his love. There is no power above us or beneath us – no power that could ever be found in the universe that can distance us from God's passionate love, which is lavished upon us through our Lord Jesus, the Annointed One (8:38-39, TPT)!

## 1 Corinthians
We all experience times of testing, which is normal for every human being. But God will be faithful to you. He will screen and filter the severity, nature, and timing of every test or trial you face so that you can bear it. And each test is an opportunity to trust him more, for along with every trial God has provided for you a way of escape that will bring you out of it victoriously (10:13, TPT).

## 2 Corinthians
But he answered me, "My grace is always more than enough for you, and my power finds its full expression through your weakness." So, I will celebrate my weaknesses, for when I'm weak I sense more deeply the mighty power of Christ living in me (12:9, TPT).

## Galatians
And we no longer see each other in our former state, Jew or non-Jew, rich or poor, male or female, because we're all one through our union with Jesus Christ with no distinction between us (3:28, TPT).

## Ephesians
Now to the God who can do so many awe-inspiring things, immeasurable things, things greater than we ever could ask or imagine through the power at work in us, to Him be all glory in the church and in Jesus the Anointed from this generation to the next, forever and ever. Amen (3:20, 21, VOICE).

## Philippians
Don't be anxious about things; instead, pray. Pray about everything. He longs to hear your requests, so talk to God about your needs and be thankful for what has come (4:6, VOICE).

## Colossians
And whatsoever ye do, do it heartily, as to the Lord, and not unto men; knowing that of the Lord ye shall receive the reward of the inheritance: for ye serve the Lord Christ (3:23, 24, KJV).

## 1 Thessalonians
Resist revenge, and make sure that no one pays back evil in place of evil but always pursue doing what is beautiful to one another and to all the unbelievers. Let joy be your continual feast. Make your life a prayer. And in the midst of everything be always giving thanks, for this is God's perfect plan for you in Christ Jesus (5:15–18, TPT).

## 2 Thessalonians
And pray that we'll be rescued from these scoundrels who are trying to do us in. I'm finding that not all "believers" are believers. But the Master never lets us down. He'll stick by you and protect you from evil (3:2, 3, MSG).

May the Master of Peace himself give you the gift of getting along with each other at all times, in all ways. May the Master be truly among you! (3:16, MSG).

## 1 Timothy
Be quick to abstain from senseless traditions and legends, but instead be engaged in the training of truth that brings righteousness (4:7, TPT).

## 2 Timothy
For God will never give you the spirit of fear, but the Holy Spirit who gives you mighty power, love, and self-control (1:7, TPT).

## Titus
And remind them of this: respect the rulers and the courts. Obey them. Be ready to do what is good and honorable. Don't tear down another person with your words. Instead, keep the peace, and be considerate. Be truly humble toward everyone because there was a time when we, too, were foolish, rebellious, and deceived, we were slaves to sensual cravings and pleasures; and we spent our lives being spiteful, envious, hated by many, and hating one another (3:1–3, VOICE).

## Philemon
Your love has given me great joy and encouragement, because you, brother, have refreshed the hearts of the Lord's people (1:7, NIV).

## Hebrews
Therefore, since we are surrounded by such a great cloud of witnesses, we must get rid of every weight and the sin that clings so closely, and run with endurance the race set out for us, keeping our eyes fixed on Jesus, the pioneer and perfecter of our faith. For the joy set out for him he endured the cross, disregarding its shame, and has taken his seat at the right hand of the throne of God (12:1, 2, NET).

## James
Confess and acknowledge how you have offended one another and then pray for one another to be instantly healed, for tremendous power is released through the passionate, heartfelt prayer of a godly believer! (5:16, TPT).

Is any among you suffering? Let him pray. Is any cheerful? Let him sing praises. (James 5:13)

## 1 Peter
But this is so that the true value of your faith may be discovered. It is worth more than gold, which is tested by fire even though it can be destroyed. The result will be praise, glory and honour when Jesus the Messiah is revealed. You love him, even though you've never seen him. And even though you don't see him, you believe in him, and celebrate with a glorified joy that goes beyond anything words can say, since you are receiving the proper goal of your faith, namely, the rescue of your lives (1:7–9, NTE).

## 2 Peter
The Lord is not slack concerning his promise, as some men count slackness; but is longsuffering to us-ward, not willing that any should perish, but that all should come to repentance (3:9, KJV).

## 1 John
But if we walk in light, as also he is in light, we have fellowship together; and the blood of Jesus Christ, his Son, cleanseth us from all sin (1:7, WYC).

## 2 John
This love means living in obedience to whatever God commands us. For to walk in love toward one another is the unifying commandment we've heard from the beginning (1:6, TPT).

## 3 John
Beloved, don't imitate that which is evil, but that which is good. He who does good is of God. He who does evil hasn't seen God (1:11, WEB).

## Jude
To him who is able to keep you from stumbling and to present you before his glorious presence without fault and with great joy, to the only God our Savior be glory, majesty, power and authority, through Jesus Christ our Lord, before all ages, now and forevermore! Amen (1:24, 25, NIV).

## Revelation
And I heard a voice from heaven saying, "Write this: Blessed are the dead who die in the Lord henceforth." "Blessed indeed," says the Spirit, "that they may rest from their labors, for their deeds follow them!" 14:13 (RSV)

Blessed and holy is he who shares in the first resurrection! Over such the second death has no power, but they shall be priests of God and of Christ, and they shall reign with him a thousand years. 20:6 (RSV)

Then the angel showed me the river of the water of life, as clear as crystal, flowing from the throne of God and of the Lamb down the middle of the great street of the city. On each side of the river stood the tree of life, bearing twelve crops of fruit, yielding its fruit every month. And the leaves of the tree are for the healing of the nations. No longer will there be any curse. The throne of God and of the Lamb will be in the city, and his servants will serve him. They will see his face, and his name will be on their foreheads. There will be no more night. They will not need the light of a lamp or the light of the sun, for the Lord God will give them light. And they will reign for ever and ever (22:1–5, NIV).

"Behold I come quickly! Wonderfully blessed is the one who carefully guards the words of the prophecy of this book (22:7)."

And he said to me, "Don't keep secret the prophetic words of this book, for the time is near. Let the evildoers be at their worst and the morally filthy continue in their depravity – yet the righteous will still do what is right, and the holy will still be holy." "Behold, I am coming quickly! I bring my reward with me to repay everyone according to their works. Am the Aleph and Tav, the First and the Last, the Beginning and the Completion." Wonderfully blessed are those who wash their robes while so they can access the Tree of Life and enter the city of bliss by its open gates. Those not permitted to enter are outside: the malicious, hypocrites, the sexually immoral, sorcerers, murderers, idolaters, and every lover of lies. "I, Jesus, sent my angel to you to give you this testimony to share with the congregations. I am the bright Morning Star, both David's spiritual root and his descendant." "Come," says the Holy Spirit and the Bride in divine duet. Let every who hears this duet join them in saying, "Come." Let everyone gripped with spiritual thirst say, "Come." And let everyone who craves the gift of living water come and drink it freely. "Come." I testify to everyone who hears the prophetic words of this book: If anyone adds to them, God will add to him the plagues described in this book. And if anyone subtracts from the prophetic words of this book, God will remove his portion from the Tree of Life and in the holy city, which are described in this book. The one who testifies to these things says, "Yes, I am coming quickly." Amen! Come, Lord Jesus! May the grace of the Lord Jesus be with all the holy believers. Amen! (22:10-21)

# Chapter 11
## Prayer connects strangers

Everyone has someone he or she calls "family." I hope you are blessed with many wonderful family members. If you are not blessed with a large family, you have likely "chosen" your family. A "chosen" family is just as legitimate as blood relatives. However wonderful our family, many of us wish our family included more people, different people, famous people, fun and exciting people, physicians, dentists, rich people, etc. Yet, in reality, we are all one family and one race. In God's eyes, we are all His children.

Let's try to view the human race from God's perspective. When Adam and Eve were expelled from Eden, they propagated the earth with children. These children intermarried. At that time, no prohibition existed against intermarrying. The prohibition against intermarriage was not given for another 2,500 years when God through Moses, gave specific guidelines to the Israelites. These guidelines are found in Leviticus 18 and 20 and in Deuteronomy.

We get so caught up in our nuclear family we oftentimes miss opportunities to minister to others, even to complete strangers. Many societal problems stem from tribalism. If we could see everyone as our "family," we would treat each other with more care. We are all equal in God's eyes. If the stranger is important to God, the stranger should be important to us. We should pray for "non-family" as passionately as we would pray for our own family.

The possibilities for "stranger prayers" (SPs) are innumerable. I have come to believe stranger prayers are just as important as prayers for our loved ones. Growing up, our church family prayed for missionaries. Almost every week at church we listened to incredible miraculous stories about the missionaries. I am sure our prayers for the missionaries were answered many times even though we never knew how and when. Sometimes it appeared evil prevailed and the worst actually happened, such as a missionary being slain. However, we eventually learned how the Lord used the situation for His heavenly purposes.

Because we serve a loving God, one who is 100% trustworthy and vested in our salvation, I think our God also has a few surprises planned for us. The Bible claims we cannot understand God's ways, purposes, and methods. All we can do is trust in Him and work to further His kingdom.

Let's examine SPs more closely. Let's start with several assumptions as we examine the spiritual phenomenon we call prayer. These assumptions provide the framework for seeing prayer as an outreach. The following are some of the assumptions we make about prayer.

- We should pray as directed by the Bible.
- Prayer is a direct line of communication with God and heaven.

- Prayer is a two-way communication, and God takes actions.
- Prayer is effective.
- Prayer is in the spirit realm.
- We pray to a heavenly God, and in a similar manner we can also contact evil spirits.
- Not all prayer requests are answered as requested, but all prayers are answered.
- Our heavenly Father has our best interests at heart.
- Heavenly angels assist in actionable prayer requests.
- God keeps a record of our prayers.
- Prayers for others are a form of ministry.
- The prayers of the righteous avail much!
- What we think we need from God might not be the same as what He has prepared for us. Sometimes we must wait for God to fulfill His promises to us.
- Prayer for a stranger or someone who does not know we are praying for her, links us to that person, although we may not discover it until we get to heaven.

It is the last assumption which makes this book exciting. I propose our SPs powerfully link us to the object of our sincere prayers. As Christians, our prayers give heaven "permission" to send heavenly hosts to intervene on behalf of the object of our prayers.

Let's use a celebrity as an example. Most people around the world have heard of Madonna, the pop queen of the 1980s. Her popularity remains high, even after four decades in the entertainment business. She has sold more than 300 million records worldwide. According to Wikipedia, Madonna is the highest-grossing solo touring artist of all time. She is known for her on-stage avant-garde behaviors and for dating much younger men. I do not know Madonna or even listen to her music, but let's use her as an example of the last assumption. If I were to sincerely pray for Madonna, that she would come to appreciate biblical values, accept Christ as her personal Savior, and devote 100% of her talents to helping others accept Christ, you might get a good chuckle at my expense, or you might be intrigued with the idea. If you are intrigued by this idea, let's go further.

Tonight, before going to bed, I will say my prayers and include Madonna. Many items on my prayer list have been there for years. Does this mean God has not heard my prayers? Absolutely not. Our expectations of God are frequently different than His expectations for us. Instead of feeling disappointed that our prayers seemingly go unanswered, it is better to hope and wait for the fulfillment of His promises in His time. Some promises are conditional while others are not. Let's read Matthew 6:30–33:

> "Wherefore, if God so clothe the grass of the field, which today is, and tomorrow is cast into the oven, shall he not much more clothe you, O ye of little faith? Therefore, take no thought, saying, What shall we eat? or, What shall we drink? or, Wherewithal shall we be clothed? (For after all these things do the Gentiles seek:) for your heavenly Father knoweth that ye have need of all these things. But seek ye first the kingdom of God, and his righteousness; and all these things shall be added unto you."

As we pray, God informs the angels of our prayer and an angelic contingent is assigned to respond to the prayer. In the case of the Madonna example, if she is open to heavenly influences, she may feel a tug on her heart strings. She may feel her life is empty and without meaning; maybe she longs for "something better" or a life filled with spiritual meaning and relevance. Then, as fast as she feels a brief "tug on her heart strings," she ignores it and goes back to her old habits and ways of thinking. This may go on for years, but at some point, she may be in exactly the right place in life where she is open to hearing God's calling on her life. She may be willing to accept the truth and not work at cross-purposes with God.

Every time we pray for someone, there is a heavenly response. Stranger prayers are powerful, but God especially loves it when our prayers are accompanied by supportive actions, especially for those living at the margins. When we get to heaven, we will be linked through our prayers, with many people. We can count on one thing: there will be a lot of surprises about who is in heaven. I hope every person reading this book and the objects of their prayers are in heaven.

It seems possible that our prayers, in cooperation with God, may even be responsible for others being in heaven. If true, we have a huge mission right at the tip of our tongues: praying for others! This is illustrated by the whimsical poem, "Folks in Heaven," by J. Taylor Ludwig. My grandmother framed this prayer and it sat on her dresser for many years. I believe it gave her hope and encouragement as she contemplated her family.

**Folks in Heaven**

I was shocked, confused, bewildered as I entered Heaven's door.
Not by the beauty of it all, nor the lights or it's decor
But it was the folks in Heaven who made me sputter and gasp.
The thieves, the liars, the sinners, the alcoholics and the trash.
There stood the kid from seventh grade who swiped my lunch money twice.
Next to him was my old neighbor who never said anything nice.
Herb, who I always thought was rotting away in hell
Was sitting pretty on cloud nine, looking incredibly well.
I nudged Jesus, "What's the deal? I would love to hear your take.
"How'd all these sinners get up here? God must've made a mistake "
And why's everyone so quiet, so somber, give me a clue.
"Child," He said, "they're all in shock,
They never thought they'd be seeing you!"

# Chapter 12
## Answers to prayer build faith

Align your life and prayers with Scripture. God will never provide you with an answer contrary to biblical principles. Some people mistakenly perceive common life events as an answer to a prayer. You pray for a spouse and you meet someone the next day. You pray for a sign to move to a certain city and the sign materializes. You pray for a sunny day in the face of 100 percent chance of rain, and it turns out to be sunny. These are not always from God. It may take some time to determine whether or not an event is an answer to prayer or within God's will for your life.

Every aspect of our life should depend on God. What we eat, wear, speak, seek, everything should be placed before the Lord in prayer. Study to show yourself approved. This is what leads to understanding God's will for your life. When we study, pray, claim promises, praise God, get involved in outreach, love others as Christ loves us, our faith grows. As our faith grows, we are not exhausted by doing the right thing but are full of grace and love for others. Our lives are not compartmentalized but seamless. We do not gossip about our best friend. We do not yell and scream at our mother and then show up at church and lead out in song service and prayer. We do not use pejorative language toward our spouse while claiming the title of "elder." While God can work with anyone alive on the planet, we must align our purposes with His. Otherwise our Christian walk will seem more like Sisyphus, pushing the boulder up the hill.

Many of us are predisposed to agree with those we like or with whom we have much in common. This tendency creates "strange bedfellows" when it comes to finding love, choosing a business partner, and even establishing friendships. Most people have tendencies to look for superficial, positive attributes. This tends to impair judgment when it comes to deeper matters. A superficial impression of a person often changes over time and with subsequent interactions. This is why we should build each new relationship on biblical principles, such as avoiding gossip, being hospitable, reaching out, regular communication, etc. Proverbs 17:17 (NIV) speaks about friendship: "A friend loves at all times, and a brother is born for a time of adversity."

The tendency to establish superficial relationships may cloud our ability to perceive God's will for us. Oftentimes chemistry, readiness, timing, agreement, conformity, and religiosity converge to set the stage for fertile agreement or even merging of similar ideologies. However, ideology without God and biblical principles at the center can lead to disappointment and may even be dangerous. In every relationship, the true character of a person will eventually emerge, leading to either confirmation of the initial impression or disappointment. What does this have to do with building faith?

We often go astray when we rely on ourselves and not on Christ. When we first meet a person we really like, we usually seek to find common ground. One person loves classical guitar and the other loves heavy metal electric guitar. Finding common ground may take ten minutes or sometimes it may take up to a year or more. However, "chemistry" should not always determine our destiny. God created chemistry to "start the engine," but He also gives us the ability to either rev up or turn off the engine. Sometimes the chemistry is strong, and other times, the lack of chemistry is misperceived or overlooked. This is important because we want to find and marry someone who is the best possible option. In other words, we project onto our belief system that God wants us to find a "perfect" spouse. I am not sure this is true. Read the book of Hosea or follow the example of Christ, who remained single for his entire human existence.

When looking for a spouse, the tendency is to believe our desire converges with God's will. We are prone to believe that outwardly positive circumstances surrounding specific interactions are from God, and negative interactions are seen as the devil trying to spoil something which God predestined. When it comes to love, some couples get engaged prematurely and then marry when they should have taken more time to pray, study Scripture, and wait for God's will to become evident. Almost every couple I know has at one time claimed God brought them together. However, after ten or fifteen years of marriage, some couples are fighting, calling each other names, abusing one another, and eventually separating and divorcing. This might be a bitter pill to swallow, but a sovereign God would not express His will for you to marry someone when He knows your union will eventually fail. This does not necessarily provide a justification for staying in an abusive marriage. Sometimes bad relationships turn around.

The failure comes on our part. Psychologists call this cognitive bias. Cognitive bias is defined as a systematic error in thinking, which affects decision-making and judgment. This occurs more easily when we deviate from a normal response or adopt an irrational belief. There are always signs to the contrary leading us back to safety. We often miss these signs, even when they are, figuratively speaking, huge flashing red lights. Sometimes friends and family warn us, but most of the time, such warnings are shrugged off. If we are highly motivated, over-stressed, desperate or even depressed, we are more likely to experience cognitive bias.

Cognitive bias keeps psychologists in business. It provides the entertainment business with content for snarky sitcoms and lovable comedies. The entertainment industry has normalized cognitive bias within relationships to the extent it is considered normal, if not desirable. It has almost obscured the ability to reason from cause to effect. No level of education or training exempts one from experiencing cognitive bias. Take a few minutes to do an Internet search on the types of cognitive bias. Be prepared to laugh and cry while reading about cognitive bias. This area of psychology is sometimes referred to as "The Psychology of Human Misjudgment."

Cognitive bias, in combination with the Baader-Meinhof Phenomenon, is a very good example of why sometimes, Christians make poor choices. Baader-Meinhof occurs when we meet someone or learn something new. Now we see aspects of this person or concept everywhere and in everything. In reality, Satan completely understands and exploits our human weaknesses, especially in regard to how we think and process information.

Vigilance and commitment to the truth are requisites for making major, as well as minor, life decisions. For some, this may require a new way of approaching life. Faith is not based on spiritual apprehension but is based on spiritual discernment and good frontal lobe function. The Bible offers abundant proof we can totally rely on God for all of our needs. We should base every decision, no matter how small or large, on the Word and apply diligent study and our intellect to problem solving. Faith is not jumping the gun. Faith moves forward, not based on the expectation of a godly magic trick, but on our applied intellect and understanding of biblical principles. It is based on our gifts, intellect, and life story. Faith is confidence in God to lead and guide us along the biblical principles.

The example of "God-ordained failed marriages" may make it difficult for some people to develop faith. It may lead others to reject a god that would give them a sexually deviant father or an abusive spouse. Mislabeling something as God's will, ultimately makes it more difficult to understand and intellectually process events that turn out not to be "God's will" (i.e., a bad decision that had nothing to do with God's will and was a human decision with no detectable amount of stepping out in faith). We all like to believe we are exercising faith when it comes to making decisions. We like to believe God is leading us in one direction or another. Some people base their decisions on a "gut" feeling while mingling the decision with a hefty dose of cognitive bias and a fascination with new faces and new facts.

While some are finding ways to justify their decisions, others search the Scriptures for how to live. Decisions where we must step out in faith require careful rendering of Scripture, along with adequate time to process relevant data. When making major life decisions, we must realize the tremendous subconscious bias we face. Instead of saying things such as, "God brought us together," or "God found us this property," or, "God opened the door for this opportunity," it might be better to say something such as, "After a long and prayer-filled season of petitioning God, I have peace with this decision. Even if this decision does not turn out as I anticipated, I know God will be with me/us through this process." This takes the God "magic" out of the equation. It acknowledges we are fallible and cannot always know God's will for our lives. It acknowledges that even if our decision is not ideal, we choose to go through the experience with God at the helm.

Oftentimes, quick and whimsical decisions do not allow for the exercise of faith. We commit early and sometimes fail to take the time and effort to study and align our decisions with Scripture. This distorts our ability to act in faith, as we expect God to support our decisions by answering our prayers in the affirmative. Aligning our decisions with Scripture puts us in harmony with God's will for us and makes exercising faith easier. When we read Scripture, pray, praise, claim promises, and then engage in thoughtful conversations with wise associates, we are in a better place to exercise and grow our faith.

We make decisions every day, decisions to move, buy a house, accept a new job, marry a certain person, etc. Most of the time we make decisions without directly praying, consulting Scripture, or talking with trusted associates. We don't even determine whether or not we want our decisions to be based in Scripture and be used to develop faith. We frequently act on impulse and then retrospectively attribute the decisions to "faith." Our decisions might be an exercise of faith in chance, faith in fate, or even faith in change of status; however, it is not an exercise of faith in the sovereign and almighty God.

In most cases, society does not help Christians make faith-based decisions. Society romanticizes relationships, buying a house, choosing a job, and even what to have for lunch. We learn from societal norms that we should be impulsive and happy, as opposed to being reflective, studious, prayerful, and watchful. The latter traits take time and much greater effort and include delayed gratification.

However, it is possible to make decisions that require faith and for these decisions to be 100% within God's hopes and desires for us. This is when our faith grows. God-based faith will never grow if it is based on anything but God's Word. Combine searching the scriptures with praise, prayer, the informed opinions of your respected loved ones, with intelligent discourse with your friends and family, with your historical context, and with giving faith the benefit of adequate time for God's will to manifest.

Appropriately placed faith, memorizing Scripture, claiming Scripture promises, praising God for His goodness, and an avid prayer life, are just some of the components of spiritual growth. As we align our purposes to His stated purposes, we gain an incredible tailwind. This helps to grow and mature our Christian faith. This walk is what is known as sanctification, the work of a lifetime. It is a privilege to walk with other Christians going down the same path toward the same goal. We are not always at the same mile marker, but as our faith grows, we begin to help others behind us and appreciate those ahead of us.

As the answers to our prayers begin to accumulate, we grow in grace and gain favor with the Lord. This leads to further growing our faith and to better understanding God's character and how He communicates with us. This book is designed to grow your faith and to assist you in recording the outcomes of your praises and prayers.

# Chapter 13
## Last words before signing off

God wants to hear from us! We pray to learn dependence on God. We pray because it provides us with the greatest opportunity to express the highest ideals known to man. When we praise God and speak His promises in prayer to Him, we move the heart of God. In a sense we become co-laborers with God in redeeming the human race. Each time we pray we learn to rely less on our resources and more on heaven's resources. Fear and anxiety are replaced with peace and increasing faith. We pray to buttress ourselves against evil forces in the world.

Evil is unmasking in postmodern society. It no longer shyly flirts as a minority voice luring young people to their moral demise, but it is emboldened by increasing numbers as it threatens to overtake us as the majority voice. Evil has invaded every corner of society. Even institutions once considered impenetrable to cultural folly and madness now willingly cooperate with evil. Society has so completely adapted to evil that those who retain their Christian values are mocked and ridiculed for their beliefs.

Instead of equanimity, joy, happiness, patience, longsuffering, and the rest of the fruits of the Spirit, we experience the negative effects of affairs, divorce, hedonism, drugs, alcohol, embezzlement, lying, idolatry, greed, selfishness, addictions, slavery to the amoral entertainment industry, addiction to highly paid sports teams, slavery to fashion, as well as many other actions which characterize postmodern society.

The lure of these vices is powerful. We are groupies to complete strangers, and worse, to a social media system which pits our lives against others: my team is better than yours; your team is a bunch of cheaters. There will always be someone having more fun, with more money, and with more friends, compared to what we have. It is important to recognize that our value is not based on how much we have but on our heritage as God's children. We have more than enough when we see ourselves as God sees us.

Our beliefs and preferences in life define us. If we believe the earth is flat, we will seek to associate with others who also believe the earth is flat. If you want to live only in Idaho or Montana, you should not interview for a job in Florida. If you believe war is morally wrong, you should not marry someone in the military. In other words, when you link yourself to someone else, whether through friendship, marriage, or business interests, you need to consider how your association with this person or this company will affect your beliefs and preferences.

Today it is common for spouses, friends, and parents to adopt or adapt to things their spouse, friends, or kids are doing, things they never would have condoned before. If an adult child takes up drinking or hardcore partying, the parents have the choice of either accepting their behaviors or encouraging them to do differently. The latter option almost always carries the risk of estrangement. Instead of co-piloting our children, siblings, parents, friends, or colleagues to safe waters, we go along to get along. There is another option. We can pray and praise our friends and loved ones to safety. If we believe we are God's children, we will treat others as we would want to be treated.

Comparing ourselves to others will always lead to dissatisfaction. Christ never encouraged humanity to wallow in self-pity, jealousy, etc.; He admonished new converts to "go and sin no more." When our zeal for God wanes or when we consciously choose to leave a saving relationship with Him, we enter the realm of eternal loss. Without a continuous connection in the face of ingrained habits and harmful behaviors, we have no hope.

With God we have hope and light. Isaiah described this phenomenon: "The people walking in darkness have seen a great light; on those living in the land of deep darkness a light has dawned" (9:2, NIV). Without God we have desperation, loneliness, and darkness. However, Light overcomes darkness. Light always wins out. Choose Light over darkness.

# Chapter 14
## The 10 commandments

The 10 Commandments are a direct communication from God to His people. They are not old-fashioned and out of date. They have direct relevance to the quality of our lives. I know of a family whose Friday evening ritual is to eat tacos and read the 10 Commandments. Their ritual cements these words into their hearts:

- "And these words, which I command thee this day, shall be in thine heart: and thou shalt teach them diligently unto thy children, and shalt talk of them when thou sittest in thine house, and when thou walkest by the way, and when thou liest down, and when thou risest up. And thou shalt bind them for a sign upon thine hand, and they shall be as frontlets between thine eyes (Deuteronomy 6:6–8).

- Then God began to speak directly to all the people.

- I am the Eternal your God.

- I led you out of Egypt and liberated you from lives of slavery and oppression.

- You are not to serve any other gods before Me.

- You are not to make any idol or image of other gods. In fact, you are not to make an image of anything in the heavens above, on the earth below, or in the waters beneath.

- You are not to bow down and serve any image, for I, the Eternal your God, am a jealous God.

- As for those who are not loyal to Me, their children will endure the consequences of their sins for three or four generations.

- But for those who love Me and keep My directives, their children will experience My loyal love for a thousand generations.

- You are not to use My name for your own idle purposes, for the Eternal will punish anyone who treats His name as anything less than sacred.

- You and your family are to remember the Sabbath Day; set it apart, and keep it holy. You have six days to do all your work, but the seventh day is to be different; it is the Sabbath of the Eternal your God. Keep it holy by not doing any work, not you, your sons, your daughters, your male and female servants, your livestock, or any outsiders living among you. For the Eternal made the heavens above, the earth below, the seas, and all the creatures in them in six days. Then, on the seventh day, He rested. That is why He blessed the Sabbath Day and made it sacred.

- You are to honor your father and mother. If you do, you and your children will live long and well in the land the Eternal your God has promised to give you.

- You are not to murder.

- You are not to commit adultery.

- You are not to take what is not yours.

- You are not to give false testimony against your neighbor.

- You are not to covet what your neighbor has or set your heart on getting his house, his wife, his male or female servants, his ox or donkey, or anything else that belongs to your neighbor.

- As all the people witnessed the signs of God's presence, the blast of the ram's horn, the roaring thunder, the flashing lightning, and the smoke-covered mountain, they shook with fear and astonishment and wisely kept their distance (Exodus 20:1–18, VOICE).

# Chapter 15
## My current prayer list

This book is about being more specific when praying for others. It is about combining praises, promises, and prayer. You may already be praying for a number of people on a daily basis. Many of you may have a separate prayer journal. This section of the book is to record the names of those you already pray for on a daily basis. These names may or may not fit into the rest of the book, but it is a place to acknowledge each valuable person in your life.

This book is for our loved ones, but it also stretches our comfort zone to include complete strangers. This way of praying is meant to increase our faith and to connect us to those who need prayer. It may be helpful to fill in the following blanks with the names of people on your prayer list.

People, Events, Situations I Pray for by Name Every Day

- _____
- _____
- _____
- _____
- _____
- _____
- _____
- _____
- _____
- _____
- _____
- _____
- _____
- _____
- _____
- _____
- _____
- _____
- _____
- _____

- _____
- _____
- _____
- _____
- _____
- _____
- _____
- _____
- _____
- _____
- _____
- _____
- _____
- _____
- _____
- _____
- _____
- _____
- _____

The remaining pages of this book are dedicated to each day of the year. The Bible verse(es) for each day come from one of 26 different Bible translations. Each verse or verses are chosen for their clarity, beauty, or prose.

# January

## Pray for those who have made your life more difficult.

Just past midnight on 3 January 1982, my cousin Dennis' car broke down on a Dallas freeway. He stopped on the side of the road to wait for his friend to show up with some tools. As his friend drove up and parked behind his car, a drunk driver crashed into his friend's car and crushed Dennis who was standing between the two cars. Several days later, Dennis died. It was the second time this drunk driver had taken a life. Dennis' case went to court, and ultimately, the drunk driver walked free. For many years I rehearsed how I would have prosecuted his case and won, how the drunk driver, named Ricky, would go to the electric chair. I am ashamed to say that it was only recently that I stopped hating this man and started praying for him. He never showed remorse, he never apologized, and he continues to live in the area. He's alive and Dennis is dead, completely unfair. But I feel sorry for Ricky. He still has a chance to repent and ask for forgiveness. Will he? I don't know. But I do know that God hears my prayers for him.

January is the month we learn to pray for our enemies and those who have hurt or damaged our loved ones. This includes the drunk driver who killed your wife and two children, the doctor who missed a diagnosis, the surgeon who botched your surgery, the former boss who made your life miserable, your cheating ex-spouse, your former employee who embezzled money from your medical office, the friend who stole your spouse, your father who abused you, your sister who won't talk with you, your mom's or dad's second spouse that lies to you and about you, etc. Even if you have a near perfect life with no enemies and no caustic adversaries, you likely know people who struggle with relational issues. We all know someone who is going through a rough patch, or even a tumultuous time, with an acquaintance, friend, or relative.

These difficult experiences serve to increase our faith and refine our character. Instead of reacting out of fear and hate toward the instigators and participants, use these experiences to learn how to respond in a way which shows concern, not just for your side of the issue, but also for their character and their salvation. Learn how to help others grow while you also gain valuable lessons in developing the fruits of the Spirit. This month is about identifying individuals or groups who have targeted you, your family, your friends, or even your community, with harsh or unfair actions.

# January Ideas

Pray to be able to forgive.
Pray for a change of heart.
Pray for healthy boundaries.
Pray your adversaries encounter God.
Pray for others as you would pray for yourself.
Pray to repair broken relationships and repair the breach.
Pray to love others as Jesus loved us – enough to die for us.
Pray for God's love on those who cause you pain and suffering.
Pray to not hold resentment against people disloyal to you and your family.

1. _____
2. _____
3. _____
4. _____
5. _____
6. _____
7. _____
8. _____
9. _____
10. _____

19.
20.
21.
22.
23.
24.
25.
26. Pray for those who have made your life, or the lives of your loved
27. ones, more difficult.
28.

## 1 January

*Pray for your enemies and those who persecute you and / or your family.*

You have heard it was said, "Love your friends, hate your enemies." But now I tell you: love your enemies and pray for those who persecute you, so you may become the children of your Father in heaven. For he makes his sun to shine on bad and good people alike, and gives rain to those who do good and to those who do evil. Why should God reward you if you love only the people who love you? Even the tax collectors do that! And if you speak only to your friends, have you done anything out of the ordinary? Even the pagans do that! You must be perfect, just as your Father in heaven is perfect. Matthew 5:43–48, GNT

Person or situation you are praying for:
Praises and promises:
Prayer:

## 2 January

*Pray for those who target your community with emotional or physical harm.*

But to you who are listening I say: Love your enemies, do good to those who hate you, bless those who curse you, pray for those who mistreat you. Luke 6:27, 28, LEB

Person or situation you are praying for:
Praises and promises:
Prayer:

## 3 January

*Pray for the ability to treat your enemies as you would want to be treated.*

Therefore, whatever you would have men do to you, even so do to them. For this is the Law and the Prophets. Matthew 7:12, RGT

Person or situation you are praying for:
Praises and promises:
Prayer:

## 4 January
*Pray to be a loving, kind and compassionate person to those who mistreat you.*

Summing up: Be agreeable, be sympathetic, be loving, be compassionate, be humble. That goes for all of you, no exceptions. No retaliation. No sharp-tongued sarcasm. Instead, bless, that's your job, to bless. You will be a blessing and also get a blessing. Whoever wants to embrace life and see the day fill up with good, here is what you do: say nothing evil or hurtful; snub evil and cultivate good; run after peace for all you're worth. God looks on all this with approval, listening and responding well to what he's asked; but he turns his back on those who do evil things. If with heart and soul you're doing good, do you think you can be stopped? Even if you suffer for it, you're still better off. Don't give the opposition a second thought.

Through thick and thin, keep your hearts at attention, in adoration before Christ, your Master. Be ready to speak up and tell anyone who asks why you're living the way you are, and always with the utmost courtesy. Keep a clear conscience before God so that when people throw mud at you, none of it will stick. They will end up realizing that they are the ones who need a bath. It's better to suffer for doing good, if that is what God wants, then to be punished for doing bad. That's what Christ did definitively: suffered because of others' sins, the Righteous One for the unrighteous ones. He went through it all, was put to death and then made alive, to bring us to God. 1 Peter 3:8–13, MSG

Person or situation you are praying for:
Praises and promises:
Prayer:

## 5 January
*Pray for a change of heart toward someone who has hurt you.*

Do not seek revenge or bear a grudge against anyone among your people, but love your neighbor as yourself. I am the LORD. Leviticus 19:18, NIV

Person or situation you are praying for:
Praises and promises:
Prayer:

## 6 January
*Pray for those who have taken a loved one from you.*

Therefore, whatever you would have men do to you, even so do to them. For this is the Law and the Prophets. Matthew 7:12, RGT

Person or situation you are praying for:
Praises and promises:
Prayer:

## 7 January
*Pray to treat your enemies' property as you would your own and to treat animals with loving kindness.*

If you are walking along and come across your enemy's ox or donkey that has wandered away, then you must return it to its owner. If you see the donkey of someone you know who hates you and it has fallen beneath its load, you must not leave it there. You must stop and help the donkey recover the load. Exodus 23:4, 5, VOICE

Person or situation you are praying for:
Praises and promises:
Prayer:

## 8 January
*Pray to be the person who overlooks petty offenses.*

Good sense makes a man slow to anger, and it is his glory to overlook an offense. Proverbs 19:11, RSV

Person or situation you are praying for:
Praises and promises:
Prayer:

## 9 January
*Pray to reflect the servanthood and humility of Christ's ministry by returning kindness for the hateful and spiteful actions of others toward you.*

You have heard that it was said, "An eye for an eye and a tooth for a tooth." But I say to you, do not resist the evildoer. But whoever strikes you on the right cheek, turn the other to him as well. And if someone wants to sue you and take your tunic, let him have your coat also. And if anyone forces you to go one mile, go with him two. Give to the one who asks you, and do not reject the one who wants to borrow from you. Matthew 5:38–42, NET

Person or situation you are praying for:
Praises and promises:
Prayer:

## 10 January
*Forgiveness is at the core of Christianity and is a spiritual discipline that must be practiced and mastered.*

Then Peter came to Jesus. "Master," he said, "how many times must I forgive my brother when he sins against me? As many as seven times?" "I wouldn't say seven times," replied Jesus. "Why not seventy times seven?" Matthew 18:21, 22, NTE

Person or situation you are praying for:
Praises and promises:
Prayer:

## 11 January
*Pray to forgive others so God will forgive us.*

When you pray, if you remember anyone who has wronged you, forgive him so that God above can also forgive you. Mark 11:25, VOICE

Person or situation you are praying for:
Praises and promises:
Prayer:

## 12 January
*Pray to see others through the eyes of Jesus.*

Do for others what you want them to do for you. Luke 6:31, GNT

Person or situation you are praying for:
Praises and promises:
Prayer:

## 13 January

*Christ forgives us, and likewise, we must forgive others.*

Pay attention and always be on your guard [looking out for one another]. If your brother sins (misses the mark), solemnly tell him so and reprove him, and if he repents (feels sorry for having sinned), forgive him. And even if he sins against you seven times in a day, and turns to you seven times and says, I repent [I am sorry], you must forgive him (give up resentment and consider the offense as recalled and annulled). Luke 17:3, 4, AMPC

Person or situation you are praying for:
Praises and promises:
Prayer:


## 14 January

*Not everyone should be trusted with our confidences; be astute and use good judgment when discussing personal matters with others.*

You cannot trust gossipers with a secret; they'll just go blab it all. Put your confidence instead in a trusted friend, for he will be faithful to keep it in confidence. Proverbs 11:13, TPT

Person or situation you are praying for:
Praises and promises:
Prayer:


## 15 January

*Pray to have a heart to include everyone and to not give payback when others knowingly exclude you.*

Work at getting along with each other and with God. Otherwise you'll never get so much as a glimpse of God. Make sure no one gets left out of God's generosity. Keep a sharp eye out for weeds of bitter discontent. A thistle or two gone to seed can ruin a whole garden in no time. Watch out for the Esau syndrome: trading away God's lifelong gift in order to satisfy a short-term appetite. You well know how Esau later regretted that impulsive act and wanted God's blessing, but by then it was too late, tears or no tears. Hebrews 12:14–17, MSG

Person or situation you are praying for:
Praises and promises:
Prayer:

## 16 January

*Witness to others, even when persecuted for right / righteous positions.*

But in our time something new has been added. What Moses and the prophets witnessed to all those years has happened. The God-setting-things-right that we read about has become Jesus-setting-things-right for us. And not only for us, but for everyone who believes in him. For there is no difference between us and them in this. Since we've compiled this long and sorry record as sinners (both us and them) and proved that we are utterly incapable of living the glorious lives God wills for us, God did it for us. Out of sheer generosity he put us in right standing with himself. A pure gift. He got us out of the mess we're in and restored us to where he always wanted us to be. And he did it by means of Jesus Christ. God sacrificed Jesus on the altar of the world to clear that world of sin. Having faith in him sets us in the clear. God decided on this course of action in full view of the public, to set the world in the clear with himself through the sacrifice of Jesus, finally taking care of the sins he had so patiently endured. This is not only clear, but it's now—this is current history! God sets things right. He also makes it possible for us to live in his rightness Romans 3:21–26, MSG

Person or situation you are praying for:
Praises and promises:
Prayer:

## 17 January

*Pray to forgive others, even under extreme and difficult circumstances.*

*This unlocks our ability to know Christ and be His follower.*

About midnight Paul and Silas were praying and singing hymns to God, and the prisoners were listening to them, and suddenly there was a great earthquake, so that the foundations of the prison were shaken. And immediately all the doors were opened, and everyone's bonds were unfastened. When the jailer woke and saw that the prison doors were open, he drew his sword and was about to kill himself, supposing that the prisoners had escaped. But Paul cried with a loud voice, "Do not harm yourself, for we are all here." And the jailer called for lights and rushed in, and trembling with fear he fell down before Paul and Silas. Then he brought them out and said, "Sirs, what must I do to be saved?" And they said, "Believe in the Lord Jesus, and you will be saved, you and your household." And they spoke the word of the Lord to him and to all who were in his house. And he took them the same hour of the night and washed their wounds; and he was baptized at once, he and all his family. Then he brought them up into his house and set food before them. And he rejoiced along with his entire household that he had believed in God. Acts 16:25–34, ESV

Person or situation you are praying for:
Praises and promises:
Prayer:

## 18 January
### Pray to be kind to everyone.

And be kind to one another, tender hearted, forgiving each other, just as God also in Christ forgave you. Ephesians 4:32, WEB

Person or situation you are praying for:
Praises and promises:
Prayer:

## 19 January
### Pray to treat others how Jesus would treat them.

See that no one renders evil for evil to anyone. But always seek to do good to one another and to all. 1 Thessalonians 5:15, MEV

Person or situation you are praying for:
Praises and promises:
Prayer:

## 20 January
### Pray for those who tell lies, half-truths, or outright slander against you or others.

What this adds up to, then, is this: no more lies, no more pretense. Tell your neighbor the truth. In Christ's body we're all connected to each other, after all. When you lie to others, you end up lying to yourself. Ephesians 4:25, MSG

Person or situation you are praying for:
Praises and promises:
Prayer:

## 21 January
### Pray for those who have deeply wounded you.

You do well when you complete the Royal Rule of the Scriptures: "Love others as you love yourself." But if you play up to these so-called important people, you go against the Rule and stand convicted by it. You can't pick and choose in these things, specializing in keeping one or two things in God's law and ignoring others. The same God who said, "Don't commit adultery," also said, "Don't murder." If you don't commit adultery but go ahead and murder, do you think your non-adultery will cancel out your murder? No, you're a murderer, period. James 2:8–11, MSG

Person or situation you are praying for:
Praises and promises:
Prayer:


## 22 January
### Pray to love difficult people.

Your calling is to fulfill the royal law of love as given to us in this Scripture: "You must love and value your neighbor as you love and value yourself!" For keeping this law is the noble way to live. Matthew 6:14, 15 TPT

Person or situation you are praying for:
Praises and promises:
Prayer:


## 23 January
### Pray that brotherly love for others permeates and animates our lives.

Let brotherly love continue. Do not forget to entertain strangers, for thereby some have entertained angels unknowingly. Remember those who are in chains, as if imprisoned with them, and those who are ill-treated, since you are also in the body. Marriage is to be honored among everyone, and the bed undefiled. But God will judge the sexually immoral and adulterers. Let your lives be without love of money, and be content with the things you have. For He has said: "I will never leave you nor forsake you." Hebrews 13:1–5, MEV

Person or situation you are praying for:
Praises and promises:
Prayer:

## 24 January

*Pray for those who have persecuted or have used harsh words against you.*

Bless those who persecute you, bless and do not curse. Romans 12:14, TLV

Person or situation you are praying for:
Praises and promises:
Prayer:


## 25 January

*Pray to overcome spite and the need to exact revenge on others.*
*Pray for the person upon whom you would like to exact revenge.*

Don't ever spitefully say, "I'll get even with him! I'll do to him what he did to me!" Proverbs 24:29, TPT

Person or situation you are praying for:
Praises and promises:
Prayer:


## 26 January

*Pray for the salvation of those who have harmed you or your loved ones.*

Beloved, don't be obsessed with taking revenge, but leave that to God's righteous justice. For the Scriptures say: "If you don't take justice in your own hands, I will release justice for you," says the Lord. Romans 12:19, TPT

Person or situation you are praying for:
Praises and promises:
Prayer:

## 27 January
*Pray to see others through Christ's eyes.*

I pray that the Father of glory, the God of our Lord Jesus Christ, would impart to you the riches of the Spirit of wisdom and the Spirit of revelation to know him through your deepening intimacy with him. I pray that the light of God will illuminate the eyes of your imagination, flooding you with light, until you experience the full revelation of the hope of his calling, that is, the wealth of God's glorious inheritances that he finds in us, his holy ones! I pray that you will continually experience the immeasurable greatness of God's power made available to you through faith. Then your lives will be an advertisement of this immense power as it works through you! This is the mighty power that was released when God raised Christ from the dead and exalted him to the place of highest honor and supreme authority in the heavenly realm! Ephesians 1:17–20, TPT

Person or situation you are praying for:
Praises and promises:
Prayer:

## 28 January
*Practice the habits of benevolence, goodness, and holiness in how you treat others.*

I pray with great faith for you, because I'm fully convinced that the One who began this glorious work in you will faithfully continue the process of maturing you and will put his finishing touches to it until the unveiling of our Lord Jesus Christ! Philippians 1:6, TPT

Person or situation you are praying for:
Praises and promises:
Prayer:

## 29 January
*Pray to be sustained by a divine power.*

Hatred keeps old quarrels alive, but love draws a veil over every insult and finds a way to make sin disappear. Proverbs 10:12, TPT

Person or situation you are praying for:
Praises and promises:
Prayer:

## 30 January
*Pray to avoid misrepresentations and falsehoods.*

If you cover up your sin you'll never do well. But if you confess your sins and forsake them, you will be kissed by mercy. Proverbs 28:13, TPT

Person or situation you are praying for:
Praises and promises:
Prayer:

## 31 January
*Pray that the most distressful and negative situations provide an opportunity to reflect the grace and love of Christ.*

Let every word you speak be drenched with grace and tempered with truth and clarity. For then you will be prepared to give a respectful answer to anyone who asks about your faith. Colossians 4:6, TPT

Person or situation you are praying for:
Praises and promises:
Prayer:

# January's Epilogue

Your written epilogue, is a way of rounding out a literary work, bringing closure, or summarizing the final scene of a dramatic play. In this case, it is a summary of your prayer life and walk with God during the month of January. This page is for you to record your comments and write a few summary statements as you have prayed for those who have hurt you and / or your family. Use this page to wrap up loose ends, write a satisfying end to the story or at least propose a satisfying ending.

An epilogue also includes what might lie ahead or what happens next in your story. Writing an epilogue requires you understand your purpose in life and how prayer, praise and Bible promises have impacted you and those around you. At this time, you may not understand the impact of your prayers but don't let this stop you from daily bowing before God, arguing, confessing, praying, praising and singing before Him.

_____
_____
_____
_____
_____
_____
_____
_____
_____
_____
_____
_____
_____
_____
_____
_____
_____
_____
_____
_____
_____

# February

## Pray for your family and loved ones.

We are linked to God through prayer. Pray for a life of constant grace and love. Pray for a character that will express love in all actions. Pray to say words that inspire those around you and give them hope and courage. Pray for the person who uplifts you and others in their daily prayers. Pray for the genuine loving people in your life. Pray for your beloved friends. Pray for the friend who refreshes you. Pray for those with whom you have endured many trials together. Encourage and show gratitude for how the Lord has provided you with lovely family and friends. Unconditional love is the ultimate gift you can give to someone.

It is always a good time to offer up an earnest petition to God. The more we pray, the lovelier His character will appear. Prayer is opening your heart to God. It is through prayer we are speaking to God and our prayer is heard. As we pray, our hearts are melted as we contemplate His great sacrifice and His love toward us. Loving one another should be our way of life! Let your reputation be of one who loves everyone.

# February Ideas

Pray that our cup may be full.
Pray to be filled with God's love.
Pray to strengthen important relationships.
Pray for both specific and general blessings.
Pray that your loved ones experience the love of Christ.
Pray to keep Christ at the center of all your relationships.
Pray for spiritual insight into how best to pray for loved ones.
Pray for unconditional love to permeate all your relationships.

1. _____
2. _____
3. _____
4. _____
5. _____
6. _____
7. _____
8. _____
9. _____
10. _____

19.
20.
21.
22.
23.
24.

Pray for your family and loved ones.

# 1 February

Pray for a life of constant grace and love.

Pray for the person who uplifts you and others in their daily prayers.

But you, my delightfully loved friends, constantly and progressively build yourselves up on the foundation of your most holy faith by praying every moment in the Spirit. Fasten your hearts to the love of God and receive the mercy of our Lord Jesus Christ, who gives us eternal life. Jude 1:20, 21, TPT

Person or situation you are praying for:
Praises and promises:
Prayer:

# 2 February

Show gratitude for how the Lord has provided you with lovely family and friends.

For God has not destined us to experience wrath but to possess salvation through our Lord Jesus, the Anointed One. He gave his life for us so that we may share in resurrection life in union with him whether we are awake or asleep. Because of this, encourage the hearts of your fellow believers and support one another, just as you have already been doing. 1 Thessalonians 5:9–11, TPT

Person or situation you are praying for:
Praises and promises:
Prayer:

# 3 February

Pray for a character that will express love in all actions.

This is my command: Love each other deeply, as much as I have loved you. For the greatest love of all is a love that sacrifices all. And this great love is demonstrated when a person sacrifices his life for his friends. John 15:12, 13, TPT

Person or situation you are praying for:
Praises and promises:
Prayer:

## 4 February
*We are linked to God and others through prayer. Pray for your beloved friend.*

Love is large and incredibly patient. Love is gentle and consistently kind to all. It refuses to be jealous when blessing comes to someone else. Love does not brag about one's achievements nor inflate its own importance. Love does not traffic in shame and disrespect, nor selfishly seek its own honor. Love is not easily irritated or quick to take offense. Love joyfully celebrates honesty and finds no delight in what is wrong. Love is a safe place of shelter, for it never stops believing the best for others. Love never takes failure as defeat, for it never gives up. Love never stops loving. It extends beyond the gift of prophecy, which eventually fades away. It is more enduring than tongues, which will one day fall silent. Love remains long after words of knowledge are forgotten. 1 Corinthians 13:4–8, TPT

Person or situation you are praying for:
Praises and promises:
Prayer:

## 5 February
*It is through prayer we are speaking to God and our prayer is heard. Pray for the genuine loving person in your life.*

Let the inner movement of your heart always be to love one another, and never play the role of an actor wearing a mask. Despise evil and embrace everything that is good and virtuous. Be devoted to tenderly loving your fellow believers as members of one family. Try to outdo yourselves in respect and honor of one another. Romans 12:9, 10, TPT

Person or situation you are praying for:
Praises and promises:
Prayer:

## 6 February
*Pray for the friend who refreshes you.*

Some friendships don't last for long, but there is one loving friend who is joined to your heart closer than any other! Proverbs 18:24, TPT

Person or situation you are praying for:
Praises and promises:
Prayer:

## 7 February
### Prayer is opening your heart to God.

When the extraordinary compassion of God our Savior and his overpowering love suddenly appeared in person, as the brightness of a dawning day, he came to save us. Not because of any virtuous deed that we have done but only because of his extravagant mercy. He saved us resurrecting us through the washing of rebirth. We are made completely new by the Holy Spirit, whom he splashed over us richly by Jesus, the Messiah, our Life Giver. So as a gift of his love, and since we are faultless, innocent before his face, we can now become heirs of all things, all because of an overflowing hope of eternal life. How true and faithful is this message! Titus 3:4–8, TPT

Person or situation you are praying for:
Praises and promises:
Prayer:

## 8 February
### Pray for those with whom you have endured many trials.

A dear friend will love you no matter what, and a family sticks together through all kinds of trouble. Proverbs 17:17, TPT

Person or situation you are praying for:
Praises and promises:
Prayer:

## 9 February
### It is always a good time, through prayer, to offer up an earnest petition to God.

Greet one another with a kiss of peace. Peace to all who are in life union with Christ. Amen. 1 Peter 5:14, TPT

Person or situation you are praying for:
Praises and promises:
Prayer:

## 10 February
### Pray for a friend who appears to be misinformed or misled.

Lovers of God give good advice to their friends, but the counsel of the wicked will lead them astray. Proverbs 12:26, TPT

Person or situation you are praying for:
Praises and promises:
Prayer:


## 11 February
### Let gratitude to God fill our hearts and prayers.

Don't owe anything to anyone, except your outstanding debt to continually love one another, for the one who learns to love has fulfilled every requirement of the law. Romans 13:8, TPT

Person or situation you are praying for:
Praises and promises:
Prayer:


## 12 February
### Pray to say words that inspire those around you and give hope and courage.

Look at how much encouragement you've found in your relationship with the Anointed One! You are filled to overflowing with his comforting love. You have experienced a deepening friendship with the Holy Spirit and have felt his tender affection and mercy. So, I'm asking you, my friends, that you be joined together in perfect unity, with one heart, one passion, and united in one love. Walk together with one harmonious purpose and you will fill my heart with unbounded joy. Be free from pride-filled opinions, for they will only harm your cherished unity. Don't allow self-promotion to hide in your hearts, but in authentic humility put others first and view others as more important than yourselves. Abandon every display of selfishness. Possess a greater concern for what matters to others instead of your own interests. And consider the example that Jesus, the Anointed One, has set before us. Let his mindset become your motivation. Philippians 2:1–5, TPT

Person or situation you are praying for:
Praises and promises:
Prayer:

## 13 February
*As we pray and contemplate His love toward us, our hearts fill with gratitude.*

I give you now a new commandment: Love each other just as much as I have loved you. For when you demonstrate the same love I have for you by loving one another, everyone will know that you're my true followers. John 13:34, 35, TPT

Person or situation you are praying for:
Praises and promises:
Prayer:


## 14 February
*Pray that peace like a river flows through our life as we contemplate His great sacrifice.*

As Moses lifted up the serpent in the wilderness, even so must the Son of Man be lifted up, that whoever believes in him should not perish, but have eternal life. For God so loved the world, that he gave his one and only Son, that whoever believes in him should not perish, but have eternal life. For God didn't send his Son into the world to judge the world, but that the world should be saved through him. He who believes in him is not judged. He who doesn't believe has been judged already, because he has not believed in the name of the one and only Son of God. This is the judgment, that the light has come into the world, and men loved the darkness rather than the light; for their works were evil. For everyone who does evil hates the light, and doesn't come to the light, lest his works would be exposed. But he who does the truth comes to the light, that his works may be revealed, that they have been done in God. John 3:14–21, WEB

Person or situation you are praying for:
Praises and promises:
Prayer:


## 15 February
*No concern of ours, even the most insignificant, escapes His notice.*

Above all, constantly echo God's intense love for one another, for love will be a canopy over a multitude of sins. 1 Peter 4:8, TPT

Person or situation you are praying for:
Praises and promises:
Prayer:

## 16 February

*The more we pray, the lovelier His character appears.*

This is how we know we're living steadily and deeply in him, and he in us: He's given us life from his life, from his very own Spirit. Also, we've seen for ourselves and continue to state openly that the Father sent his Son as Savior of the world. Everyone who confesses that Jesus is God's Son participates continuously in an intimate relationship with God. We know it so well, we've embraced it heart and soul, this love that comes from God. 1 John 4:13–16, MSG

Person or situation you are praying for:
Praises and promises:
Prayer:

## 17 February

*Pray for a genuine heart, one that shuns materialism and worldliness.*

Going through the motions doesn't please you, a flawless performance is nothing to you. I learned God-worship when my pride was shattered. Heart-shattered lives ready for love don't for a moment escape God's notice. Psalm 51:17, MSG

Person or situation you are praying for:
Praises and promises:
Prayer:

## 18 February

*Let love reign supreme in your life.*

Let love and kindness be the motivation behind all that you do. 1 Corinthians 16:14, TPT

Person or situation you are praying for:
Praises and promises:
Prayer:

## 19 February
### Jesus is not tribalistic.
### His family circle is defined by those who accept and follow Him.

Then one said to him, "Behold, your mother and your brothers stand outside, desiring to speak with you." But He answered and said to him that told Him, "Who is My mother, and who are My brothers?" And He stretched forth His hand toward His disciples and said, "Behold My mother, and My brothers. For whoever shall do My Father's will (Who is in Heaven), the same is My brother and sister and mother." Matthew 12:47–50, RGT

Person or situation you are praying for:
Praises and promises:
Prayer:


## 20 February
### We are God's people.

This is what the Eternal has to say: Eternal One: There will come a time when I will be the God of all the clans and families of Israel, and they will be My people. This is what I, the Eternal One, declare to you: My people who survived the sword found grace as they wandered in the wilderness; When Israel went in search of rest, I appeared to them from far away and said: "I have loved you with an everlasting love; out of faithfulness I have drawn you close. Jeremiah 31:1–3, VOICE

Person or situation you are praying for:
Praises and promises:
Prayer:


## 21 February
### Loving one another should be a way of life.

Delightfully loved ones, if he loved us with such tremendous love, then "loving one another" should be our way of life! 1 John 4:11, TPT

Person or situation you are praying for:
Praises and promises:
Prayer:

## 22 February
### Let your reputation be of one who loves everyone.

For love is supreme and must flow through each of these virtues. Love becomes the mark of true maturity. Let your heart be always guided by the peace of the Anointed One, who called you to peace as part of his one body. And always be thankful. Let the word of Christ live in you richly, flooding you with all wisdom. Apply the Scriptures as you teach and instruct one another with the Psalms, and with festive praises, and with prophetic songs given to you spontaneously by the Spirit, so sing to God with all your hearts! Colossians 3:14–16, TPT

Person or situation you are praying for:
Praises and promises:
Prayer:


## 23 February
### Love is supreme.

This is my command: Love each other deeply, as much as I have loved you. For the greatest love of all is a love that sacrifices all. And this great love is demonstrated when a person sacrifices his life for his friends. John 15:12, 13, TPT

Person or situation you are praying for:
Praises and promises:
Prayer:


## 24 February
### Wrap your mind and your heart in the ways of God.

Jesus answered him, "Love the Lord your God with every passion of your heart, with all the energy of your being, and with every thought that is within you." This is the great and supreme commandment. And the second is like it in importance: "You must love your friend in the same way you love yourself." Matthew 22:37–39, TPT

Person or situation you are praying for:
Praises and promises:
Prayer:

## 25 February
### Loyalty is a virtue.

But Ruth replied, "Don't try to make me leave you and go back. Where you go I'll go. Where you stay I'll stay. Your people will be my people. Your God will be my God. Where you die I'll die. And there my body will be buried. I won't let even death separate you from me. If I do, may the LORD punish me greatly." Naomi realized that Ruth had made up her mind to go with her. So she stopped trying to make her go back. Ruth 1:16, 17, NIRV

Person or situation you are praying for:
Praises and promises:
Prayer:

## 26 February
### Unconditional love is the ultimate gift you can give to someone.

Fasten me upon your heart as a seal of fire forevermore. This living, consuming flame will seal you as my prisoner of love. My passion is stronger than the chains of death and the grave, all-consuming as the very flashes of fire from the burning heart of God. Place this fierce, unrelenting fire over your entire being. Rivers of pain and persecution will never extinguish this flame. Endless floods will be unable to quench this raging fire that burns within you. Everything will be consumed. It will stop at nothing as you yield everything to this furious fire until it won't even seem to you like a sacrifice anymore. Song of Solomon 8:6, 7, TPT

Person or situation you are praying for:
Praises and promises:
Prayer:

## 27 February
### Great friends are a joy.

Sweet friendships refresh the soul and awaken our hearts with joy, for good friends are like the anointing oil that yields the fragrant incense of God's presence. So never give up on a friend or abandon a friend of your father—for in the day of your brokenness you won't have to run to a relative for help. A friend nearby is better than a relative far away. Proverbs 27:9, 10, TPT

Person or situation you are praying for:
Praises and promises:
Prayer:

## 28 February
### Guard your heart.

So above all, guard the affections of your heart, for they affect all that you are. Pay attention to the welfare of your innermost being, for from there flows the wellspring of life. Proverbs 4:23, TPT

Person or situation you are praying for:
Praises and promises:
Prayer:

## 29 February
### Love everyone!

Everyone will know you as My followers if you demonstrate your love to others. John 13:35, VOICE

Person or situation you are praying for:
Praises and promises:
Prayer:

# February Epilogue

Your written epilogue, is a way of rounding out a literary work, bringing closure, or summarizing the final scene of a dramatic play. In this case, it is a summary of your prayer life and walk with God during the month of February. This page is for you to record your comments and write a few summary statements as you have prayed for your dear ones. Use this page to wrap up loose ends, write a satisfying end to the story or at least propose a satisfying ending.

An epilogue also includes what might lie ahead or what happens next in your story. Writing an epilogue requires you understand your purpose in life and how prayer, praise and Bible promises have impacted you and those around you. At this time, you may not understand the impact of your prayers but don't let this stop you from daily bowing before God, arguing, confessing, praying, praising and singing His praises!

# March

## Pray for the poor, oppressed, and downtrodden.

If you want to experience a jolting reality check, go to www.worldmeters.info and check out their real-time monitors. You will find a number of indices monitored such as seasonal flu death, deaths of children under five years of age, abortions, deaths of mothers during birth, people infected with HIV/AIDS, deaths caused by HIV/AIDS, deaths caused by cancer, deaths caused by alcohol, suicides, etc. The data are continuously updated by the current day and year. These data show how many people are in dire need of prayer. Our planet is in the ICU. We need an intervention. The best intervention we have is prayer.

Every day around the world, one out of seven people is hungry; this number is rapidly approaching one billion. One out of six children in developing countries is underweight and malnourished. Hundreds of thousands of teenage girls get pregnant and hundreds of thousands of children suffer abuse. Thousands develop drug addictions and thousands of children are abducted from their homes. The numbers are staggering and on the rise.

Off and on for a year or so I attended two predominantly black churches in Mississippi. One church was located in one of the poorest counties in the USA – Yazoo county. I saw what it meant to be very poor. Giving just a dollar was sacrificial for some. There is no doubt everyone should be involved in helping others who have less. Some people believe this is the role of their government while they completely shun any personal attempt to help others. In reality, it is everyone's role, no matter your economic standing. It is also specifically the role of the church, to help the poor. There will always be someone with less than what you have. We need to not only pray for these people, but also to help them in meaningful ways.

Always do what is right in God's eyes. This means when someone is struggling, we offer our services. Maybe we bake them bread or prepare for them a pot of soup. Maybe we can drop off a bag of groceries, help them find a job, employ them, help them register for classes at a community college, or find a spot at a trade school, etc.

This reminds me of family friends who lost their four-year old girl about twenty years ago. She died suddenly, leaving her parents in shock and grief. They had two older boys and had made no preparations for the upcoming Christmas season. A friend of my mother's had given her a beautifully decorated Christmas tree, but because Mother had already put up a tree, she decided to see if the couple who had lost their daughter needed one. Here is an excerpt from their memory of the event:

"One day a couple from our church knocked on our door and wanted to know if we needed a Christmas tree. 'Why, yes! We haven't picked one up yet!' I will never forget their kindness or the many other acts of kindness that kept coming our way in the dense fog of that Christmas season.'" We can pray for a couple that loses their four-year old daughter, but prayer combined with acts of kindness ministered to their needs.

How can we pray for the poor, the oppressed, and the downtrodden? When it comes to family and friends, always err on the side of mercy and love. Help those in need. Remember how God carried the Israelites through the exodus, liberated them from oppression, and destroyed the armies that would have destroyed them. God will do no less for us and for those in great need.

# March Ideas

Pray to be the hands of Jesus.
Pray to be generous with the poor.
Pray to live a life of grace and charity towards others.
Pray for those who are unable to protect themselves.
Pray that God opens our eyes to the needs of others.
Pray to be responsive to the cries of the downtrodden.
Pray that the children of the righteous will not go hungry.
Pray that God turns sadness and sorrow into joy in Christ.
Pray to be an effective voice and advocate for the less fortunate.
Pray to be obedient to God's calling on our lives and how we can best help others.
Pray that God brings your friends through the storm and they are strengthened by the struggle.

1. _____
2. _____
3. _____
4. _____
5. _____
6. _____
7. _____
8. _____
9. _____
10. _____
11. _____
12. _____
13. _____
14. _____
15. _____
16. _____
17. _____
18. _____
19. _____
20. _____
21. _____
22. _____
23. _____
24. _____
25. _____
26. _____
27. _____
28. _____
29. _____
30. _____
31. _____

Pray for
the poor, oppressed
and the downtrodden.

# 1 March

### Defending Christ will put you at odds with the world.

And why would we be risking our lives every day? My brothers and sisters, I continually face death. This is as sure as my boasting of you and our co-union together in the life of our Lord Jesus Christ, who gives me confidence to share my experiences with you. Tell me, why did I fight "wild beasts" in Ephesus if my hope is in this life only? What was the point of that? If the dead do not rise, then let's party all night, for tomorrow we die! So stop fooling yourselves! Evil companions will corrupt good morals and character.  1 Corinthians 15:33, TPT

Person or situation you are praying for:
Praises and promises:
Prayer:

# 2 March

### Help those in need.

When someone comes to beg from you, give to that person what you have. When things are wrongly taken from you, do not demand they be given back. However you wish to be treated by others is how you should treat everyone else. Are you really showing true love by only loving those who love you back? Even those who don't know God will do that. Are you really showing compassion when you do good deeds only to those who do good deeds to you? Even those who don't know God will do that. If you lend money only to those you know will repay you, what credit is that to your character? Even those who don't know God do that. But love your enemies and continue to treat them well. When you lend money, don't despair if you are never paid back, for it is not lost. You will receive a rich reward and you will be known as true children of the Most High God, having his same nature. For your Father is famous for his kindness to heal even the thankless and cruel. Luke 6:30–35, TPT

Person or situation you are praying for:
Praises and promises:
Prayer:

# 3 March

### When it comes to family and friends, always err on the side of mercy and love.

He that taketh away mercy from his friend, forsaketh the dread of the Lord. (He who taketh away love from his friend, forgetteth the fear of the Lord/abandoneth reverence for the Lord.) Job 6:14, WYC

Person or situation you are praying for:
Praises and promises:
Prayer:

# 4 March

## Sometimes opposites in temperament attract.

Elijah and Elisha were leaving Gilgal when the Eternal One planned to snatch Elijah up into the heavens by the power of a fierce dancing wind. Elijah (to Elisha): I ask you to remain here. The Eternal has commanded me to go all the way to Bethel. Elisha: As certain as your own life and the life of the Eternal, I refuse to abandon you.

So the two men traveled down to Bethel together, where Elisha was approached by the prophets' disciples who lived there. Prophets' Disciples: Are you aware that the Eternal One is going to snatch Elijah, your mentor, away from you today? Elisha: Yes, I am aware of this. I want you to keep quiet about it. Elijah (to Elisha): I beg you to remain here. The Eternal has commanded me to travel to Jericho. Elisha: As certain as your own life and the life of the Eternal, I refuse to abandon you. The two men then traveled to Jericho together, where the prophets' disciples living in Jericho approached Elisha. Prophets' Disciples: Are you aware that the Eternal One is going to snatch your mentor away from you today? Elisha: Yes, I am aware of this. I want you to keep quiet about it. Elijah: I beg you to remain here. The Eternal One has commanded me to travel to the Jordan River. Elisha: As certain as your own life and the life of the Eternal, I refuse to abandon you.

So the two men then traveled to the Jordan River together. While Elijah and Elisha were standing near the Jordan River, 50 of the prophets' disciples from that area stood at a distance from them on the other side. Elijah removed his cloak and rolled it up; then he struck the water with it, and the water divided. Elijah and Elisha then walked across on dry land. After the two had made it to the other side of the Jordan, Elijah spoke to Elisha. Elijah: Tell me what it is you would like me to do for you before I am taken away from you. Elisha: Please, I wish to receive a double portion of your spirit. As your successor, I want to have twice the portion of your power. Elijah: What you have requested of me is challenging, but it will be done if you witness my departure. But if you do not watch, then you will not have your double portion.

Now as the two continued walking along and talking as they normally did, something incredible happened. A blazing chariot pulled by blazing horses stormed down from the heavens and came between Elijah and Elisha. Then Elijah was swept up into heaven by the fiery storm. Elisha witnessed this amazing spectacle. Elisha: My father, O my father! The chariots and riders of Israel! Elisha never saw Elijah again. Elisha grabbed the clothes he was wearing, and he ripped them in half. He picked up Elijah's cloak, which had dropped to the ground when he was taken up into heaven, and then he went back to the Jordan riverbank and stood. He struck the water with the cloak. Elisha: Where is the Eternal One? Where is Elijah's True God? After Elisha struck the water, the Jordan River divided, just as when Elijah had struck the waters. Elisha then walked across on dry land. 2 Kings 2:1–14, VOICE

Person or situation you are praying for:
Praises and promises:
Prayer:

## 5 March

*Sometimes being there for your friends is more important than what you have to say.*

Now Job had three friends: Eliphaz from Teman, Bildad from Shuah, and Zophar from Naamath. When these three received word of the horror that had befallen Job, they left their homes, and agreed to meet together to mourn with and comfort their friend. They approached the town ash heap, but they were still far off when they caught sight of Job. His sores were so severe and his appearance so changed by his condition that they almost didn't recognize him. Upon seeing him and apprehending the extent of his suffering, they cried out, burst into tears, tore their robes, reached down into the dust and ashes at their feet, and threw ash into the air and onto their heads. Then, they sat with him on the ground and stayed there with him for seven days and seven nights, mourning as if he were already dead. All the while no one spoke a single word because they saw his profound agony and grief. Job 2:10–13, VOICE

Person or situation you are praying for:
Praises and promises:
Prayer:

## 6 March

*Anonymously share your increase.*

When you harvest the crops of your land, do not gather the grain all the way to the edges of your fields or pick up what was overlooked during the first round of harvesting. Likewise, do not strip the vines bare in your vineyard or gather the fallen grapes. Leave the fallen fruit and some grapes on the vine for the poor and strangers living among you; for I am the Eternal your God. Leviticus 19:9, 10, VOICE

Person or situation you are praying for:
Praises and promises:
Prayer:

## 7 March

*Help those who work alone or have no one to help them.*

Two people are better than one. When two people work together, they get more work done. If one person falls, the other person can reach out to help. But those who are alone when they fall have no one to help them. Ecclesiastes 4:9, 10, ERV

Person or situation you are praying for:
Praises and promises:
Prayer:

## 8 March
### God is the Judge of all.

Oh, how his pleasant voice is smoother than butter, while his heart is enchanted by war. Oh, how his words are smoother than oil, and yet each is a sword drawn in his hand. Cast your troubles upon the Eternal; His care is unceasing! He will not allow His righteous to be shaken. But You, O God, You will drive them into the lowest pit—Violent, lying people won't live beyond their middle years. But I place my trust in You. Psalm 55:20–23, VOICE

Person or situation you are praying for:
Praises and promises:
Prayer:


## 9 March
### God is my Rock.

The LORD is my light and my salvation; whom shall I fear? The LORD is the stronghold of my life; of whom shall I be afraid? When evildoers assail me, uttering slanders against me, my adversaries and foes, they shall stumble and fall. Though a host encamp against me, my heart shall not fear; though war arise against me, yet I will be confident. One thing have I asked of the LORD, that will I seek after; that I may dwell in the house of the LORD all the days of my life, to behold the beauty of the LORD, and to inquire in his temple. For he will hide me in his shelter in the day of trouble; he will conceal me under the cover of his tent, he will set me high upon a rock. And now my head shall be lifted up above my enemies round about me; and I will offer in his tent sacrifices with shouts of joy; I will sing and make melody to the LORD. Hear, O LORD, when I cry aloud, be gracious to me and answer me! Thou hast said, "Seek ye my face." My heart says to thee, "Thy face, LORD, do I seek." Hide not thy face from me. Turn not thy servant away in anger, thou who hast been my help. Cast me not off, forsake me not, O God of my salvation! For my father and my mother have forsaken me, but the LORD will take me up. Teach me thy way, O LORD; and lead me on a level path because of my enemies. Give me not up to the will of my adversaries; for false witnesses have risen against me, and they breathe out violence. I believe that I shall see the goodness of the LORD in the land of the living! Wait for the Lord; be strong, and let your heart take courage; yea, wait for the LORD! Psalm 27:1–15, RSV

Person or situation you are praying for:
Praises and promises:
Prayer:

## 10 March

*Remember how I carried you through the exodus, liberated you from oppression, destroyed the armies which would have destroyed you?*

Don't revel only in the past, or spend all your time recounting the victories of days gone by. Watch closely: I am preparing something new; it's happening now, even as I speak, and you're about to see it. I am preparing a way through the desert; Waters will flow where there had been none. Wild animals in the fields will honor Me; the wild dogs and surly birds will join in. There will be water enough for My chosen people, trickling springs and clear streams running through the desert. My people, the ones whom I chose and created for My own, will sing My praise. Isaiah 43:18–21, VOICE

Person or situation you are praying for:
Praises and promises:
Prayer:

## 11 March

*Love those who are less fortunate.*

My loved ones, let us devote ourselves to loving one another. Love comes straight from God, and everyone who loves is born of God and truly knows God. Anyone who does not love does not know God, because God is love. 1 John 4:7, 8, VOICE

Person or situation you are praying for:
Praises and promises:
Prayer:

## 12 March

*Always do what is good in God's eyes.*

He hath shewed thee, O man, what is good; and what doth the LORD require of thee, but to do justly, and to love mercy, and to walk humbly with thy God? Micah 6:8, KJV

Person or situation you are praying for:
Praises and promises:
Prayer:

## 13 March

### There is safety in the shadow of the Almighty.

He that dwelleth in the secret place of the most High shall abide under the shadow of the Almighty. I will say of the LORD, He is my refuge and my fortress: my God; in him will I trust. Surely, he shall deliver thee from the snare of the fowler, and from the noisome pestilence. He shall cover thee with his feathers, and under his wings shalt thou trust: his truth shall be thy shield and buckler. Thou shalt not be afraid for the terror by night; nor for the arrow that flieth by day; nor for the pestilence that walketh in darkness; nor for the destruction that wasteth at noonday. A thousand shall fall at thy side, and ten thousand at thy right hand; but it shall not come nigh thee. Only with thine eyes shalt thou behold and see the reward of the wicked. Because thou hast made the LORD, which is my refuge, even the most High, thy habitation; there shall no evil befall thee, neither shall any plague come nigh thy dwelling. For he shall give his angels charge over thee, to keep thee in all thy ways. They shall bear thee up in their hands, lest thou dash thy foot against a stone. Thou shalt tread upon the lion and adder: the young lion and the dragon shalt thou trample under feet. Because he hath set his love upon me, therefore will I deliver him: I will set him on high, because he hath known my name. He shall call upon me, and I will answer him: I will be with him in trouble; I will deliver him, and honour him. With long life will I satisfy him, and shew him my salvation.
Psalm 91

Person or situation you are praying for:
Praises and promises:
Prayer:


## 14 March

### Pray for those who promote and live in unity and harmony.

How truly wonderful and delightful to see brothers and sisters living together in sweet unity! It's as precious as the sacred scented oil flowing from the head of the high priest Aaron, dripping down upon his beard and running all the way down to the hem of his priestly robes. This heavenly harmony can be compared to the dew dripping down from the skies upon Mount Hermon, refreshing the mountain slopes of Israel. For from this realm of sweet harmony God will release his eternal blessing, the promise of life forever! Psalm 133:1–3, TPT

Person or situation you are praying for:
Praises and promises:
Prayer:

## 15 March
### Avoid taking delight in the plight of others.

Better to gnaw on a bit of dry crust in peace than to feast in a house full of stress… Anyone who makes fun of the poor disparages his Maker, and those who celebrate another's misfortune will not escape certain punishment… Those who repay good with evil bring unrelenting trouble on their families. Proverbs 17:1, 5, 13, VOICE

Person or situation you are praying for:
Praises and promises:
Prayer:

## 16 March
### Pray for the friend who is willing to bear your burdens.

Love empowers us to fulfill the law of the Anointed One as we carry each other's troubles. Galatians 6:2, TPT

Person or situation you are praying for:
Praises and promises:
Prayer:

## 17 March
### Pray for, but limit your association with people who have a negative influence on you.

Do not befriend someone given to anger or hang around with a hothead. Odds are, you'll learn his ways, become angry as well, and get caught in a trap. Proverbs 22:24, 25, VOICE

Person or situation you are praying for:
Praises and promises:
Prayer:

## 18 March
### Wisdom comes with age.

Heed counsel, act on instruction, and you will become wise later in life. Proverbs 19:20, VOICE

Person or situation you are praying for:
Praises and promises:
Prayer:

## 19 March
### Pray for those who practice love and kindness.

Discover creative ways to encourage others and to motivate them toward acts of compassion, doing beautiful works as expressions of love. This is not the time to pull away and neglect meeting together, as some have formed the habit of doing, because we need each other! In fact, we should come together even more frequently, eager to encourage and urge each other onward as we anticipate that day dawning. Hebrews 10:24, 25, TPT

Person or situation you are praying for:
Praises and promises:
Prayer:

## 20 March
### Pray for someone struggling at the end of their life.

I have fought the good fight, I have finished the race, I have kept the faith. Henceforth there is laid up for me the crown of righteousness, which the Lord, the righteous judge, will award to me on that Day, and not only to me but also to all who have loved his appearing. 2 Timothy 4:7, 8, RSV

Person or situation you are praying for:
Praises and promises:
Prayer:

## 21 March
### God is always with us.

Be free from the love of money, content with such things as you have, for he has said, "I will in no way leave you, neither will I in any way forsake you." So that with good courage we say, "The Lord is my helper. I will not fear. What can man do to me?" Hebrews 13:5, 6, WEB

Person or situation you are praying for:
Praises and promises:
Prayer:

## 22 March

### Pray for the person you fiercely love and defend.

By the time David had finished speaking to Saul, Saul's son Jonathan was bound to David in friendship, and Jonathan loved David as he loved himself... And Jonathan made a covenant with David because he loved him as he loved himself. He took off the robe he wore and gave it to David, and also his armor, sword, bow, and belt, symbolically transferring to David his right to ascend the throne. 1 Samuel 18:1–4, VOICE

Person or situation you are praying for:
Praises and promises:
Prayer:

## 23 March

### Pray for your greatest critic!

My brothers and sisters, do not assault each other with criticism. If you decide your job is to accuse and judge another believer, then you are a self-appointed critic and judge of the law; if so, then you are no longer a doer of the law and subject to its rule; you stand over it as a judge. Know this—there is One who stands supreme as Judge and Lawgiver. He alone is able to save and to destroy, so who are you to step in and try to judge another? James 4:11, 12, TPT

Person or situation you are praying for:
Praises and promises:
Prayer:

## 24 March

### Death will be conquered.

Lo! I tell you a mystery. We shall not all sleep, but we shall all be changed, in a moment, in the twinkling of an eye, at the last trumpet. For the trumpet will sound, and the dead will be raised imperishable, and we shall be changed. For this perishable nature must put on the imperishable, and this mortal nature must put on immortality. When the perishable puts on the imperishable, and the mortal puts on immortality, then shall come to pass the saying that is written: "Death is swallowed up in victory. O death, where is thy victory? O death, where is thy sting?" The sting of death is sin, and the power of sin is the law. But thanks be to God, who gives us the victory through our Lord Jesus Christ. Therefore, my beloved brethren, be steadfast, immovable, always abounding in the work of the Lord, knowing that in the Lord your labor is not in vain. 1 Corinthians 15:50–58, RSV

Person or situation you are praying for:
Praises and promises:

Prayer:

## 25 March
### Pray for your wise friend.

Those who love a pure heart and speak with grace will find that the king is their friend. Proverbs 22:11, VOICE

Person or situation you are praying for:
Praises and promises:
Prayer:

## 26 March
### Pray for those who join you in ministry and shepherding.

Timothy, you are constantly in my prayers. Day and night I remember you before God and give thanks to Him whom I serve with a clean conscience, as did my ancestors. I really want to see you, especially when I remember how you cried the last time we were together. Yes, I know it would make me joyful to see you again. 2 Timothy 1:3, 4, VOICE

Person or situation you are praying for:
Praises and promises:
Prayer:

## 27 March
### Pray to be someone's 2 a.m. friend.

Then Jesus gave this illustration: "Imagine what would happen if you were to go to one of your friends in the middle of the night and pound on his door and shout, 'Please! Do you have some food you can spare? A friend just arrived at my house unexpectedly and I have nothing to serve him.' But your friend says, 'Why are you bothering me? The door's locked and my family and I are all in bed. Do you expect me to get up and give you our food?' But listen—because of your shameless impudence, even though it's the middle of the night, your friend will get up out of his bed and give you all that you need. So it is with your prayers. Ask and you'll receive. Seek and you'll discover. Knock on heaven's door, and it will one day open for you. Every persistent person will get what he asks for. Every persistent seeker will discover what he needs. And everyone who knocks persistently will one day find an open door. Luke 11:5–10, TPT

Person or situation you are praying for:
Praises and promises:
Prayer:

## 28 March

### We escape corruption through a knowledge of Christ.

His divine power has granted to us all things that pertain to life and godliness, through the knowledge of him who called us to his own glory and excellence, by which he has granted to us his precious and very great promises, that through these you may escape from the corruption that is in the world because of passion, and become partakers of the divine nature. For this very reason make every effort to supplement your faith with virtue, and virtue with knowledge, and knowledge with self-control, and self-control with steadfastness, and steadfastness with godliness, and godliness with brotherly affection, and brotherly affection with love. 2 Peter 1:3–7, RSV

Person or situation you are praying for:
Praises and promises:
Prayer:

## 29 March

### God wishes spiritual eyesight and discernment for everyone.

I continue to pray for your love to grow and increase beyond measure, bringing you into the rich revelation of spiritual insight in all things. This will enable you to choose the most excellent way of all—becoming pure and without offense until the unveiling of Christ. And you will be filled completely with the fruits of righteousness that are found in Jesus, the Anointed One—bringing great praise and glory to God! Philippians 1:9–11, TPT

Person or situation you are praying for:
Praises and promises:
Prayer:

## 30 March
### Our hope is built on Jesus Christ, not anyone else.

Bind up the testimony, seal the teaching among my disciples. I will wait for the LORD, who is hiding his face from the house of Jacob, and I will hope in him. Behold, I and the children whom the LORD has given me are signs and portents in Israel from the LORD of hosts, who dwells on Mount Zion. And when they say to you, "Consult the mediums and the wizards who chirp and mutter," should not a people consult their God? Should they consult the dead on behalf of the living? To the teaching and to the testimony! Surely for this word which they speak there is no dawn. They will pass through the land, greatly distressed and hungry; and when they are hungry, they will be enraged and will curse their king and their God, and turn their faces upward; and they will look to the earth, but behold, distress and darkness, the gloom of anguish; and they will be thrust into thick darkness. Isaiah 8:16–22, RSV

Person or situation you are praying for:
Praises and promises:
Prayer:

## 31 March
### My grace is sufficient for you.

Because of the extravagance of those revelations, and so I wouldn't get a big head, I was given the gift of a handicap to keep me in constant touch with my limitations. Satan's angel did his best to get me down; what he in fact did was push me to my knees. No danger then of walking around high and mighty! At first I didn't think of it as a gift, and begged God to remove it. Three times I did that, and then he told me, My grace is enough; it's all you need. My strength comes into its own in your weakness. Once I heard that, I was glad to let it happen. I quit focusing on the handicap and began appreciating the gift. It was a case of Christ's strength moving in on my weakness. Now I take limitations in stride, and with good cheer, these limitations that cut me down to size—abuse, accidents, opposition, bad breaks. I just let Christ take over! And so the weaker I get, the stronger I become. 2 Corinthians 12:7–10, MSG

Person or situation you are praying for:
Praises and promises:
Prayer:

# March Epilogue

Your written epilogue, is a way of rounding out a literary work, bringing closure, or summarizing the final scene of a dramatic play. In this case, it is a summary of your prayer life and walk with God during the month of March. This page is for you to record your comments and write a few summary statements as you have prayed for others including the poor and oppressed, those who are prisoners of sin, the downtrodden, those without hope, etc. Use this page to wrap up loose ends, write a satisfying end to the story or at least propose a satisfying ending.

An epilogue also includes what might lie ahead or what happens next in your story. Writing an epilogue requires you understand your purpose in life and how prayer, praise and Bible promises have impacted you and those around you. At this time, you may not understand the impact of your prayers but don't let this stop you from daily bowing before God, arguing, confessing, praying, praising and singing His praises!

# April

## Pray for friends and loved ones with financial issues.

Pray we understand God is the source of every good thing! Wealth is here today and gone tomorrow. Riches and honor are with God and not based on our bank account. Pray for contentment in all things that eternally matter, including your financial condition.

Sometimes the poor show more generosity than the rich. Pray for those who are willing to work hard toward their goals. While it is wise to see all of our possessions as belonging to God, accumulation of wealth is not contrary to the Bible. It is how we handle the blessing of wealth that determines our usefulness to God. Pray that those with more, are generous with their means. When God blesses you with resources, don't sit by and let your hard-working family and friends struggle. Family is who we link ourselves with through prayer, kind acts, time in fellowship and association, and support. Instead of living extravagantly, learn to help others in meaningful ways. It is better to live humbly and generously help others who have less.

My father worked his entire life. He is 88 and still works every single day, almost nonstop. As a teenager, I overheard my mother telling one of her friends that my dad wasn't going to let her get rid of his brown polyester suit because he did not want to be better dressed than the poorest man attending church. This also applied to our cars.

This type of standard is a high standard to reach and one that most people never contemplate, although Jesus left us a template. He never owned a home, never claimed a piece of land, didn't own more than one change of clothes, didn't carry money in his pocket, didn't wear fancy shoes, and He walked almost everywhere He needed to go.

This reminds me of a story about a couple of 14th century monks heavy into asceticism. Several times a day, one monk would take his only possession, his drinking mug, down to the spring to drink fresh water. One day he saw another monk at the spring using only his hands to cup the water and drink. He suddenly realized he had begun to worship his mug. On his way back to the monastery, he took his mug and dashed it against a rock, breaking it into several pieces. Nothing of earthly value should stand between us and our heavenly Father. What is your mug?

# April Ideas

Do not let sinful talk come from your mouth.
Pray for financial restoration just as Job was restored.
Pray that the enemy has no control over your money.
Pray your commitment to God transcends all other life issues.
Pray for your friends' success and a blessed, Christ-centered life.
Pray that our trials never separate us from the awesome love of Christ.
Pray for your friends through their difficult times as you would for yourself.
Pray that we always keep Christ in the right perspective, no matter what happens.
Pray that you never let the judgments of others affect your relationship with God.
Pray that your financial difficulties make you sensitive to the similar plights of others.

1. _____
2. _____
3. _____
4. _____
5. _____
6. _____
7. _____
8. _____
9. _____
10. _____
11. _____
12. _____
13. _____
14. _____
15. _____
16. _____
17. _____
18. _____
19. _____
20. _____
21. _____
22. _____
23. _____
24. _____
25. _____
26. _____
27. _____
28. _____
29. _____
30. _____

Pray for friends and loved ones with financial issues.

# 1 April
## God is the source of every good and amazing thing!

My heart overflows with joy when I think of how you showed your love to me by your financial support of my ministry. For even though you have so little, you still continue to help me at every opportunity. I'm not telling you this because I'm in need, for I have learned to be satisfied in any circumstance. I know what it means to lack, and I know what it means to experience overwhelming abundance. For I'm trained in the secret of overcoming all things, whether in fullness or in hunger. And I find that the strength of Christ's explosive power infuses me to conquer every difficulty.

You've so graciously provided for my essential needs during this season of difficulty. For I want you to know that the Philippian church was the only church that supported me in the beginning as I went out to preach the gospel. You were the only church that sowed into me financially, and when I was in Thessalonica, you supported me for well over a year. I mention this not because I'm requesting a gift, but so that the fruit of your generosity may bring you an abundant reward. I now have all I need, more than enough; I'm abundantly satisfied!

For I've received the gift you sent by Epaphroditus and viewed it as a sweet sacrifice, perfumed with the fragrance of your faithfulness, which is so pleasing to God! I am convinced that my God will fully satisfy every need you have, for I have seen the abundant riches of glory revealed to me through the Anointed One, Jesus Christ! And God our Father will receive all the glory and the honor throughout the eternity of eternities! Amen! Give my warm greetings to all the believers in the Anointed One, Jesus. All the brothers and sisters in Christ that are here with me send their loving greetings, especially the converts from Caesar's household. May every one of you overflow with the grace and favor of our Lord Jesus Christ! Love in Christ, Paul. Philippians 4:10–23, TPT

Person or situation you are praying for:
Praises and promises:
Prayer:

# 2 April
## Pray for God's people to be generous with their means and resources.

Give generously and generous gifts will be given back to you, shaken down to make room for more. Abundant gifts will pour out upon you with such an overflowing measure that it will run over the top! Your measurement of generosity becomes the measurement of your return. Luke 6:38, TPT

Person or situation you are praying for:
Praises and promises:
Prayer:

## 3 April

*Pray for God's people to learn the importance of saving money not foolishly spending it on earthly trinkets and fleeting pleasures.*

Precious treasure and oil are in the house of the wise, but the foolish person will devour them.  Proverbs 21:20, LEB

Person or situation you are praying for:
Praises and promises:
Prayer:


## 4 April

*Buildings of God are not built by men's might or power, but by God's might and power.*

And the angel who talked with me came again, and waked me, like a man that is wakened out of his sleep. And he said to me, "What do you see?" I said, "I see, and behold, a lampstand all of gold, with a bowl on the top of it, and seven lamps on it, with seven lips on each of the lamps which are on the top of it. And there are two olive trees by it, one on the right of the bowl and the other on its left." And I said to the angel who talked with me, "What are these, my lord?" Then the angel who talked with me answered me, "Do you not know what these are?" I said, "No, my lord." Then he said to me, "This is the word of the LORD to Zerub'babel: Not by might, nor by power, but by my Spirit, says the LORD of hosts. What are you, O great mountain? Before Zerub'babel you shall become a plain; and he shall bring forward the top stone amid shouts of "Grace, grace to it!" Moreover, the word of the LORD came to me, saying, "The hands of Zerub'babel have laid the foundation of this house; his hands shall also complete it. Then you will know that the LORD of hosts has sent me to you. For whoever has despised the day of small things shall rejoice, and shall see the plummet in the hand of Zerub'babel. These seven are the eyes of the LORD, which range through the whole earth." Then I said to him, "What are these two olive trees on the right and the left of the lamp stand?" And a second time I said to him, "What are these two branches of the olive trees, which are beside the two golden pipes from which the oil is poured out?" He said to me, "Do you not know what these are?" I said, "No, my lord." Then he said, "These are the two anointed who stand by the Lord of the whole earth." Zechariah 4:1–15, RSV

Person or situation you are praying for:
Praises and promises:
Prayer:

## 5 April
### Children of the righteous will not beg for food.

But immoral ones will find their lives cut short; they'll vanish as quickly as wildflowers in the fields. Yes, enemies of the Eternal will vanish like smoke into the cool night air. Evil people borrow and never repay their debts, while the good give generously from their hearts. For God's blessed children will inherit the land, but those cursed by Him stand to gain nothing. If you are right with God, He strengthens you for the journey; the Eternal will be pleased with your life. And even though you trip up, you will not fall on your face because He holds you by the hand. Through my whole life (young and old), I have never witnessed God forsaking those who do right, nor have I seen their children begging for crumbs, because they are always giving and sharing; truly, their children are a joyful blessing. Psalm 37:20–26, VOICE

Person or situation you are praying for:
Praises and promises:
Prayer:


## 6 April
### Pray for those who are deep in debt or are unable to quickly repay their debts.

A good reputation is preferable to riches, and the approval of others is better than precious silver or gold. Rich and poor have something in common: both are created by the Eternal. Prudent people see trouble coming and hide, but the naive walk right into it and take a beating. A humble person who fears the Eternal can expect to receive wealth, honor, and life. Thorny branches and traps lie ahead for those who follow perverse paths; those who want to preserve themselves will steer clear of them. Teach a child how to follow the right way; even when he is old, he will stay on course. The rich lord it over the poor, and the borrower is the slave to the lender. Those who sow injustice reap disaster, and their methods of oppression will fail. Generous people are genuinely blessed because they share their food with the poor. Expel a mocker, and watch the wrangling go with him; rivalry and rude remarks will also stop. Those who love a pure heart and speak with grace will find that the king is their friend. Proverbs 22:1–11, VOICE

Person or situation you are praying for:
Praises and promises:
Prayer:

## 7 April
### Be content with what you have.

Don't be obsessed with money but live content with what you have, for you always have God's presence. For hasn't he promised you, "I will never leave you alone, never! And I will not loosen my grip on your life!" Hebrews 13:5 TPT

Person or situation you are praying for:
Praises and promises:
Prayer:

## 8 April
### Pray for contentment in all things that relate to our eternity in heaven.

Now, since we are God's coworkers, we beg you not to take God's marvelous grace for granted, allowing it to have no effect on your lives. For he says, I listened to you at the time of my favor. And the day when you needed salvation, I came to your aid. So can't you see? Now is the time to respond to his favor! Now is the day of salvation! We will not place obstacles in anyone's way that hinder them from coming to salvation so that our ministry will not be discredited. Yet, as God's servants, we prove ourselves authentic in every way. For example: We have great endurance in hardships and in persecutions. We don't lose courage in a time of stress and calamity. We've been beaten many times, imprisoned, and found ourselves in the midst of riots. We've endured many troubles, had sleepless nights, and gone hungry. We have proved ourselves by our lifestyles of purity, by our spiritual insights, by our patience, and by showing kindness, by the Spirit of holiness and by our uncritical love for you. We commend ourselves to you by our truthful teachings, by the power of God working through us, and with the mighty weapons of righteousness—a sword in one hand and a shield in the other. Amid honor or dishonor, slander or praise, even when we are treated as deceivers and imposters, we remain steadfast and true. We are unknown nobodies whom everyone knows. We are frequently at death's door, yet here we are, still alive! We have been severely punished yet not executed. We may suffer, yet in every season we are always found rejoicing. We may be poor, yet we bestow great riches on many. We seem to have nothing, yet in reality we possess all things. 2 Corinthians 6:1–10, TPT

Person or situation you are praying for:
Praises and promises:
Prayer:

## 9 April
*Pray to avoid financial troubles and for wisdom to plan for the future.*

Don't envy the wealth of the wicked or crave their company. For they are obsessed with causing trouble and their conversations are corrupt. Wise people are builders; they build families, businesses, communities. And through intelligence and insight their enterprises are established and endure. Because of their skilled leadership the hearts of people are filled with the treasures of wisdom and the pleasures of

Person or situation you are praying for:
Praises and promises:
Prayer:


## 10 April
*Pray for financial wisdom for a friend or loved one.*

Co-sign for one you barely know and you will pay a great price! Anyone stupid enough to guarantee the loan of another deserves to have his property seized in payment. Proverbs 27:13, TPT

Person or situation you are praying for:
Praises and promises:
Prayer:


## 11 April
*Pray for those who are willing to work hard to achieve their goals.*

If you work hard at what you do, great abundance will come to you. But merely talking about getting rich while living to only pursue your pleasures brings you face-to-face with poverty. Proverbs 14:23, TPT

Person or situation you are praying for:
Praises and promises:
Prayer:

## 12 April
### Hard work pays off.

Work hard and you'll have all you desire, but chase a fantasy and you could end up with nothing. Proverbs 28:19, TPT

Person or situation you are praying for:
Praises and promises:
Prayer:


## 13 April
### The first few sentences of the Bible show the Creator, Jesus, as working six days and resting on the seventh.

In the beginning, God created the heavens and the earth. Genesis 1:1, WEB

Person or situation you are praying for:
Praises and promises:
Prayer:


## 14 April
### Stay away from crooks and crooked schemes.

God's blessings follow you and await you at every turn: when you don't follow the advice of those who delight in wicked schemes, when you avoid sin's highway, when judgment and sarcasm beckon you, but you refuse. Psalm 1:1, VOICE

Person or situation you are praying for:
Praises and promises:
Prayer:

## 15 April
### There is value in a multitude of financial counselors.

Without counsel, plans go awry, but in the multitude of counselors they are established. Proverbs 15:22, NKJV

Person or situation you are praying for:
Praises and promises:
Prayer:

## 16 April
### It is a privilege to return a portion of what belongs to the Lord.

"Since, I, the LORD, do not go back on my promises, you, sons of Jacob, have not perished. From the days of your ancestors you have ignored my commandments and have not kept them. Return to me, and I will return to you," says the LORD of Heaven's Armies. "But you say, 'How should we return?' Can a person rob God? You are indeed robbing me, but you say, 'How are we robbing you?' In tithes and contributions! You are bound for judgment because you are robbing me; this whole nation is guilty. Bring the entire tithe into the storehouse so that there may be food in my temple. Test me in this matter," says the LORD of Heaven's Armies, "to see if I will not open for you the windows of heaven and pour out blessing for you until there is no room for it all." Malachi 3:6–10, NET

Person or situation you are praying for:
Praises and promises:
Prayer:

## 17 April
### Bring your gifts to the house of God.

Celebrate for seven days in honor of the Eternal your God, in the place the Eternal will choose. The Eternal your God will bless you with abundant produce; He will bless everything you do, and you'll have a lot to celebrate! Three times each year, every male Israelite must appear before Him in the place He chooses for the Feast of Unleavened Bread (Passover), for the Feast of Weeks (Pentecost), and for the Feast of Shelters (Tabernacles). Don't come empty-handed! Decide what amount you want to contribute voluntarily out of what He has blessed you with, and bring that as a gift. Deuteronomy 16:15–17, VOICE

Person or situation you are praying for:
Praises and promises:
Prayer:

## 18 April
*Sometimes the poor show more generosity than the rich.*

Jesus was in the temple, observing all the wealthy wanting to be noticed as they came with their offerings. He noticed a very poor widow dropping two small copper coins in the offering box. "Listen to me," he said. "This poor widow has given a larger offering than any of the wealthy. For the rich only gave out of their surplus, but she sacrificed out of her poverty and gave to God all that she had to live on." Luke 21:1–4, TPT

Person or situation you are praying for:
Praises and promises:
Prayer:

## 19 April
*Be content with what you have; share your excess with others.*

Speaking to the people, Jesus continued, "Be alert and guard your heart from greed and always wishing for what you don't have. For your life can never be measured by the amount of things you possess." Jesus then gave them this illustration: "A wealthy land owner had a farm that produced bumper crops. In fact, it filled his barns to overflowing! He thought, 'What should I do now that every barn is full and I have nowhere else to store more? I know what I'll do! I'll tear down the barns and build one massive barn that will hold all my grain and goods. Then I can just sit back, surrounded with comfort and ease. I'll enjoy life with no worries at all.' God said to him, 'What a fool you are to trust in your riches and not in me. This very night the messengers of death are demanding to take your life. Then who will get all the wealth you have stored up for yourself?' " Luke 12:15–20, TPT

Person or situation you are praying for:
Praises and promises:
Prayer:

## 20 April
*God's blessings are overwhelming.*

Yes, God is more than ready to overwhelm you with every form of grace, so that you will have more than enough of everything, every moment and in every way. He will make you overflow with abundance in every good thing you do. 2 Corinthians 9:8, TPT

Person or situation you are praying for:
Praises and promises:
Prayer:

## 21 April
### You cannot love God and money.

No one can serve two masters. If you try, you will wind up loving the first master and hating the second, or vice versa. People try to serve both God and money, but you can't. You must choose one or the other. Matthew 6:24, VOICE

Person or situation you are praying for:
Praises and promises:
Prayer:

## 22 April
### Be honest in financial matters.

Wealth gained dishonestly dwindles away, but he who gathers by hand makes it grow. Proverbs 13:11, WEB

Person or situation you are praying for:
Praises and promises:
Prayer:

## 23 April
### Material wealth is not our ultimate goal.

Do not wear yourself out to become rich; be wise enough to restrain yourself. Proverbs 23:4, NET

Person or situation you are praying for:
Praises and promises:
Prayer:

## 24 April
*Integrity is more desirable than financially perverse ways.*

The wicked flee when no one pursues, but the righteous are bold as a lion. When a land transgresses it has many rulers; but with men of understanding and knowledge its stability will long continue. A poor man who oppresses the poor is a beating rain that leaves no food. Those who forsake the law praise the wicked, but those who keep the law strive against them. Evil men do not understand justice, but those who seek the LORD understand it completely. Better is a poor man who walks in his integrity than a rich man who is perverse in his ways. He who keeps the law is a wise son, but a companion of gluttons shames his father. He who augments his wealth by interest and increase gathers it for him who is kind to the poor. If one turns away his ear from hearing the law, even his prayer is an abomination. He who misleads the upright into an evil way will fall into his own pit; but the blameless will have a goodly inheritance.
Proverbs 28:1–10, RSV

Person or situation you are praying for:
Praises and promises:
Prayer:

## 25 April
*God is our gold and silver.*

Agree with God, and be at peace; thereby good will come to you. Receive instruction from his mouth, and lay up his words in your heart. If you return to the Almighty and humble yourself, if you remove unrighteousness far from your tents, if you lay gold in the dust, and gold of Ophir among the stones of the torrent bed, and if the Almighty is your gold, and your precious silver; then you will delight yourself in the Almighty, and lift up your face to God. Job 22:20–26, RSV

Person or situation you are praying for:
Praises and promises:
Prayer:

## 26 April
### Help those in need.

This is how we've come to understand and experience love: Christ sacrificed his life for us. This is why we ought to live sacrificially for our fellow believers, and not just be out for ourselves. If you see some brother or sister in need and have the means to do something about it but turn a cold shoulder and do nothing, what happens to God's love? It disappears. And you made it disappear. 1 John 3:17, MSG

Person or situation you are praying for:
Praises and promises:
Prayer:


## 27 April
### Wealth is here today and gone tomorrow.

Tell those rich in this world's wealth to quit being so full of themselves and so obsessed with money, which is here today and gone tomorrow. Tell them to go after God, who piles on all the riches we could ever manage, to do good, to be rich in helping others, to be extravagantly generous. If they do that, they'll build a treasury that will last, gaining life that is truly life. 1 Timothy 6:17, MSG

Person or situation you are praying for:
Praises and promises:
Prayer:


## 28 April
### Riches and honor are with God.

I pray with great faith for you, because I'm fully convinced that the One who began this glorious work in you will faithfully continue the process of maturing you and will put his finishing touches to it until the unveiling of our Lord Jesus Christ! Philippians 1:6, TPT

Person or situation you are praying for:
Praises and promises:
Prayer:

## 29 April
### We are blessed when we give.

I showed you in all such matters that this is how we should work to help the weak, remembering the words of the Lord Jesus, as he put it, "It is more blessed to give than to receive." Acts 20:35, NTE

Person or situation you are praying for:
Praises and promises:
Prayer:

## 30 April
### Spiritual values are more desirable than greed and earthly pleasures.

But those who crave the wealth of this world slip into spiritual snares. They become trapped by the troubles that come through their foolish and harmful desires, driven by greed and drowning in their own sinful pleasures. And they take others down with them into their corruption and eventual destruction. Loving money is the first step toward all kinds of trouble. Some people run after it so much that they have given up their faith. Craving more money pushes them away from the faith into error, compounding misery in their lives! 1 Timothy 6:9, 10, TPT

Person or situation you are praying for:
Praises and promises:
Prayer:

# April Epilogue

Your written epilogue, is a way of rounding out a literary work, bringing closure, or summarizing the final scene of a dramatic play. In this case, it is a summary of your prayer life and walk with God during the month of April. This page is for you to record your comments and write a few summary statements as you have prayed for others including those with major financial concerns, business and / or personal debt, lack of funds, etc. Use this page to wrap up loose ends, write a satisfying end to the story or at least propose a satisfying ending. While we may or may not always follow God's will for our lives, we pray for wisdom and virtue to do our best with financial and other blessings from God.

For those living in the USA, April is the month of reckoning what each citizen owes the government. As Mary and Joseph traveled to Bethlehem to be 'taxed,' they lived under the oppressive governments of Caesar Augustus and his political appointee, Herod the Great, who controlled Jerusalem and the land of Israel. Paying their newly declared taxes in person was also tied to undertaking a massive census. Luke records this event, "And it came to pass in those days, that there went out a decree from Caesar Augustus, that all the world should be taxed. And all went to be taxed, every one into his own city. And Joseph also went up from Galilee, out of the city of Nazareth, into Judaea, unto the city of David, which is called Bethlehem: (because he was of the house and lineage of David) to be taxed with Mary his espoused wife, being great with child." This event likely occurred in the fall, probably toward the end of September or beginning of October; definitely not during the month of December.

The young Caesar Augustus saw the census and the act of giving an oath of allegiance to the Empire and paying odious taxes as a way to suppress the Jews and remain in power. Because both Mary and Joseph were descendants of David, and could be perceived as having legitimate claims to the throne of Israel, they were both required to make the trip to Bethlehem. In addition to burdensome taxes, loyalty oaths and monitoring and tracking (the census) of his citizens, King Herod, in the face of the many Old Testament prophecies of a coming Saviour who would come as a baby boy, decreed all baby boys under the age of two should be murdered. In this context and under pretext of a soon-to-be-born Saviour, Joseph, Mary and Jesus escaped the murderous reign of King Herod and traveled into Egypt where they remained until Herod no longer posed a threat.

As modern-day citizens, we too, pay taxes, participate in commerce and experience government-based monitoring and tracking. Will we swear loyalty to 'Caesar' or to God with our finances? When we dedicate our first fruits including our finances to the Lord's work, he will open up the windows of heaven and pour out for you a blessing until it overflows (Malachi 3:10). Pray for these blessings to be poured out on those with financial concerns and watch and see what God does for them!

An epilogue also includes what might lie ahead or what happens next in your story. Writing an epilogue requires you understand your purpose in life and how prayer, praise and Bible promises have impacted you and those around you. At this time, you may not understand the impact of your prayers but don't let this stop you from daily bowing before God, arguing, confessing, praying, praising and singing His praises!

# May

## Pray for non-politician public figures.

God's wisdom is not man's wisdom. God blesses those who cooperate with His ways. Don't be boastful. Don't dwell on the negative. Have a modest opinion of yourself. Don't follow what unbelievers do. What does the darkness have to do with the light? Do not take a bribe. Don't elevate yourself in the presence of others. Pray for those making moral missteps. Listen and help. Form the habit of justice. Commit your work to the Lord and your plans will be established. Never tire of doing good. Righteously and fairly dispense justice. Don't wait to accept Jesus as your personal Savior, do it right now! Press toward the goal with your fellow life travelers.

There are souls to be plucked from destruction. Some follow a false gospel while others openly reject the gospel. Take this month to pray for public figures such as musicians, actors, well-known business people, authors, radio and TV personalities, etc.

When God is for us, who can be against us?

# May Ideas

Pray for courage and wisdom.
Pray that public figures embrace truth and justice.
Pray for grace to love those who are different from us.
Pray against violence, ideologies of hate, and systems of injustice.
Pray we can walk together, sing together and live together in perfect peace.
Pray for color-blindness, class-blindness, political-blindness when speaking of others.

1. _____
2. _____
3. _____
4. _____
5. _____
6. _____
7. _____
8. _____
9. _____
10. _____
11. _____
12. _____
13. _____
14. _____
15. _____
16. _____
17. _____
18. _____
19. _____
20. _____
21. _____
22. _____
23. _____
24. _____
25. _____
26. _____
27. _____
28. _____
29. _____
30. _____
31. _____

Pray for non-politician public figures.

# 1 May
## Form the habit of justice.

Hallelujah! Thank GOD! And why? Because he's good, because his love lasts. But who on earth can do it—declaim GOD's mighty acts, broadcast all his praises? You're one happy man when you do what's right, one happy woman when you form the habit of justice. Psalm 106:1–3, MSG

Person or situation you are praying for:
Praises and promises:
Prayer:


# 2 May
## Commit your work to the Lord and your plans will be established.

The plans of the mind belong to man, the answer of the tongue is from the LORD. All the ways of a man are pure in his own eyes, but the LORD weighs the spirit. Commit your work to the LORD, and your plans will be established. Proverbs 16:1–3, RSV

Person or situation you are praying for:
Praises and promises:
Prayer:


# 3 May
## What does the darkness have to do with the light?

Do you not know that you are God's temple and that God's Spirit dwells in you? If anyone destroys God's temple, God will destroy him. For God's temple is holy, and that temple you are. Let no one deceive himself. If anyone among you thinks that he is wise in this age, let him become a fool that he may become wise. For the wisdom of this world is folly with God. For it is written, "He catches the wise in their craftiness," and again, "The Lord knows that the thoughts of the wise are futile." 1 Corinthians 3:16–20, RSV

Person or situation you are praying for:
Praises and promises:
Prayer:

## 4 May
### Don't dwell on the negative.

Love overlooks the mistakes of others, but dwelling on the failures of others devastates friendships. Proverbs 17:9, TPT

Person or situation you are praying for:
Praises and promises:
Prayer:

## 5 May
### Pressing toward the goal with our fellow travelers...

I admit that I haven't yet acquired the absolute fullness that I'm pursuing, but I run with passion into his abundance so that I may reach the purpose that Jesus Christ has called me to fulfill and wants me to discover. I don't depend on my own strength to accomplish this; however, I do have one compelling focus: I forget all of the past as I fasten my heart to the future instead. I run straight for the divine invitation of reaching the heavenly goal and gaining the victory-prize through the anointing of Jesus. So let all who are fully mature have this same passion, and if anyone is not yet gripped by these desires, God will reveal it to them. And let us all advance together to reach this victory-prize, following one path with one passion. My beloved friends, imitate my walk with God and follow all those who walk according to the way of life we modeled before you. For there are many who live by different standards. As I've warned you many times (I weep as I write these words), they are enemies of the cross of the Anointed One and doom awaits them. Their god has possessed them and made them mute. Their boast is in their shameful lifestyles and their minds are in the dirt. But we are a colony of heaven on earth as we cling tightly to our life-giver, the Lord Jesus Christ, who will transform our humble bodies and transfigure us into the identical likeness of his glorified body. And using his matchless power, he continually subdues everything to himself. Philippians 3:12–21, TPT

Person or situation you are praying for:
Praises and promises:
Prayer:

## 6 May
### Listen and help.

But be doers of the word, and not hearers only, deceiving yourselves. For if anyone is a hearer of the word and not a doer, he is like a man who observes his natural face in a mirror; for he observes himself and goes away and at once forgets what he was like. But he who looks into the perfect law, the law of liberty, and perseveres, being no hearer that forgets but a doer that acts, he shall be blessed in his doing. James 1:22–25, RSV

Person or situation you are praying for:
Praises and promises:
Prayer:

## 7 May
### Do not be boastful.

Examine your motives to make sure you're not showing off when you do your good deeds, only to be admired by others; otherwise, you will lose the reward of your heavenly Father. So when you give to the poor, don't announce it and make a show of it just to be seen by people, like the hypocrites in the streets and in the marketplace. They've already received their reward! But when you demonstrate generosity, do it with pure motives and without drawing attention to yourself. Give secretly and your Father, who sees all you do, will reward you openly. Matthew 6:1–4, TPT

Person or situation you are praying for:
Praises and promises:
Prayer:

## 8 May
### Never tire of doing good.

For even when we were with you, we gave you this rule: "The one who is unwilling to work shall not eat." We hear that some among you are idle and disruptive. They are not busy; they are busybodies. Such people we command and urge in the Lord Jesus Christ to settle down and earn the food they eat. And as for you, brothers and sisters, never tire of doing what is good. 2 Thessalonians 3:11, NIV

Person or situation you are praying for:
Praises and promises:
Prayer:

## 9 May
### God prays for us.

As additional proof, we know there were many priests under the old system, for they eventually died and their office had to be filled by another. But Jesus permanently holds his priestly office, since he lives forever and will never have a successor! So he is able to save fully from now throughout eternity, everyone who comes to God through him, because he lives to pray continually for them. Hebrews 7:23–25, TPT

Person or situation you are praying for:
Praises and promises:
Prayer:

## 10 May
### Do not commit Balaam's error of financial greed.

In the same way, these sensual "dreamers" corrupt and pollute the natural realm, while on the other hand they reject the spiritual realms of governmental power and repeatedly scoff at heavenly glories. Even the archangel Michael, when he was disputing with the devil over the body of Moses, dared not insult or slander him, but simply said, "The Lord Yahweh rebuke you!" These people insult anything they don't understand. They behave like irrational beasts by doing whatever they feel like doing. Because they live by their animal instincts, they corrupt themselves and bring about their own destruction. How terrible it is for them! For they have followed in the steps of Cain. They have abandoned themselves to Balaam's error because of their greedy pursuit of financial gain. And since they have rebelled like Korah rebelled, they will experience the same fate of Korah and likewise perish. Jude 1:8–11, TPT

Person or situation you are praying for:
Praises and promises:
Prayer:

## 11 May
### Peace and life are gifts from God.

Those who are motivated by the flesh only pursue what benefits themselves. But those who live by the impulses of the Holy Spirit are motivated to pursue spiritual realities. For the mind-set of the flesh is death, but the mind-set controlled by the Spirit finds life and peace. In fact, the mind-set focused on the flesh fights God's plan and refuses to submit to his direction, because it cannot! For no matter how hard they try, God finds no pleasure with those who are controlled by the flesh. Romans 8:5–8, TPT

Person or situation you are praying for:
Praises and promises:
Prayer:

## 12 May
### Do not elevate yourself in the presence of others.

When you are invited to a wedding feast, don't sit in the seat of honor. What if someone who is more distinguished than you has also been invited? Luke 14:8, NLT

Person or situation you are praying for:
Praises and promises:
Prayer:

## 13 May
### Righteously and fairly dispense justice.

The queen of Sheba was fascinated when she heard about the famous Solomon and his devotion to the name of the Eternal One. She traveled a long way to meet him and to challenge him with her difficult questions. She arrived in Jerusalem accompanied by many advisors, assistants, and camels carrying spices and a lot of gold and rare jewels. When she met Solomon, she asked him about everything she could think of. Solomon gave her an answer to every question. The king knew all the answers, and he explained all she asked.

When the queen recognized Solomon's wisdom and observed the palace he had envisioned and constructed, the food on his table, the orderly arrangement of his servants, the attentive service and fine dress of his waiters, his wine servers, and the beautiful stairway that led up to the Eternal's temple, she was in complete awe. So it is true, everything I've heard about you in my land. Your words and wisdom are beyond extraordinary. I confess that when I first heard of your renown, I did not believe such a man could really be alive on the earth. But I have witnessed your greatness with my own eyes, and I believe. You are twice as wise and wealthy as is reported in faraway lands. Your people have been blessed as a result of living under your reign. Those who serve you continually are richly blessed to hear your wisdom day in and day out. Praise the Eternal One your God, who believed in you enough to give you Israel's throne. He is devoted to Israel forever; that is why He has made such a great man as you king. He knows you will dispense righteousness and justice fairly and wisely. The queen then presented Solomon with 9,000 pounds of gold and a large gift of spices and rare jewels. No other gift of spices given to the king ever compared to the gift the queen of Sheba gave to King Solomon. 1 Kings 10:1–10, VOICE

Person or situation you are praying for:
Praises and promises:
Prayer:

## 14 May
### God blesses those who cooperate with his ways.

But Joshua spared the life of Rahab the prostitute, all her family, and all she had because she was faithful to the spies he had sent, and she lived among the Israelites from that day on. When the city lay in smoke and ashes, Joshua pronounced a curse. May the Eternal curse anyone who ever rebuilds this city, this Jericho! If he lays new foundations, it will be over the grave of his firstborn; if he raises new gates, it will be to contain the corpse of his youngest! The Eternal One had helped Joshua, and his fame spread throughout the land. Joshua 6:25–27, VOICE

Person or situation you are praying for:
Praises and promises:
Prayer:

## 15 May
### When God is for you, who can be against you?

When the Philistines heard about David's ascension to the throne of all Israel, they prepared to attack him. But David heard about their movement and sent his troops to attack them. As the Philistines raided the valley of Rephaim, David asked for God's guidance. Shall I fight the Philistines? Will You assure me a victory? Fight them, and I will ensure a victory. David defeated the Philistines at Baal-perazim, so named because "God broke the enemies with my hand as rushing waters break through barriers." The Philistines abandoned their gods there, so David ordered the idols to be burned. The Philistines raided the valley again. Again David asked for God's counsel. This time do not attack them directly. Circle behind their forces and attack from their rear coming out from the balsam trees. When you hear marching in the tops of the balsam trees, then go out to fight. I will have already attacked the Philistine army before you arrive. David obeyed God's command, and he defeated the army of the Philistines from Gibeon to Gezer. David was famous among his neighboring nations, and the Eternal made all other nations afraid of him. 1 Chronicles 14:8–17, VOICE

Person or situation you are praying for:
Praises and promises:
Prayer:

## 16 May
### Pray for those making moral missteps.

And if we have no doubt that He hears our voices, we can be assured that He moves in response to our call. In this regard, if you notice a brother or sister in faith making moral missteps and blunders, disregarding and disobeying God even to the point of God removing this one from the body by death, then pray for that person; and God will grant him life on this journey. But to be clear, there is a sin that is ultimately fatal and leads to death. I am not talking about praying for that fatal sin, but I am talking about all those wrongs and sins that plague God's family that don't lead to death. We all know that everyone fathered by God will not make sin a way of life because God protects His children from the evil one, and the evil one can't touch them. Have confidence in the fact that we belong to God, but also know that the world around us is in the grips of the evil one. We also can be sure of the fact that the Son of God has come and given us a mind so that we may know Him as the embodiment of all that is true. We live in this truth, in His Son Jesus, the Anointed One. He is the True God and eternal life. So, little children, guard yourselves from worshipping anything but him. 1 John 5:16–21, VOICE

Person or situation you are praying for:
Praises and promises:
Prayer:

# 17 May

## Stop judging based on the superficial; embrace standards of mercy and truth.

A controversy was brewing among the people, with so many differing opinions about Jesus. Some were saying, "He's a good man!" While others weren't convinced and insisted, saying, "He's just a demagogue." Yet no one was bold enough to speak out publicly on Jesus's behalf for fear of the Jewish leaders. Not until the feast was half over did Jesus finally appear in the temple courts and begin to teach. The Jewish leaders were astonished by what he taught and said, "How did this man acquire such knowledge? He wasn't trained in our schools—who taught him?"

So Jesus responded, "I don't teach my own ideas, but the truth revealed to me by the One who sent me. If you want to test my teachings and discover where I received them, first be passionate to do God's will, and then you will be able to discern if my teachings are from the heart of God or from my own opinions. Charlatans praise themselves and seek honor from men, but my Father sent me to speak truth on his behalf. And I have no false motive, because I seek only the glory of God. Moses has given you the law, but not one of you is faithful to keep it. So if you are all law-breakers, why then would you seek to kill me?"

Then some in the crowd shouted out, "You must be out of your mind! Who's trying to kill you?" Jesus replied, "I only had to do one miracle, and all of you marvel! Yet isn't it true that Moses and your forefathers ordered you to circumcise your sons even if the eighth day fell on a Sabbath? So if you cut away part of a man on the Sabbath and that doesn't break the Jewish law, why then would you be indignant with me for making a man completely healed on the Sabbath? Stop judging based on the superficial. First you must embrace the standards of mercy and truth."

Then some of the residents of Jerusalem spoke up and said, "Isn't this the one they're trying to kill? So why is he here speaking publicly and not one of the Jewish leaders is doing anything about it? Are they starting to think that he's the Anointed One? But how could he be, since we know this man is from Galilee, but no one will know where the true Messiah comes from, he'll just appear out of nowhere."

Knowing all of this, Jesus one day preached boldly in the temple courts, "So, you think you know me and where I come from? But you don't know the One who sent me—the Father who is always faithful. I have not come simply on my own initiative. The Father has sent me here, and I know all about him, for I have come from his presence." John 7:12–29, TPT

Person or situation you are praying for:
Praises and promises:
Prayer:

## 18 May
### Have a modest opinion of yourself.

Then Jesus addressed both the crowds and his disciples and said, "The religious scholars and the Pharisees sit on Moses' throne as the authorized interpreters of the Law. So, listen and follow what they teach, but don't do what they do, for they tell you one thing and do another. They tie on your backs an oppressive burden of religious obligations and insist that you carry it, but will never lift a finger to help ease your load. Everything they do is done for show and to be noticed by others. They want to be seen as holy, so they wear oversized prayer boxes on their arms and foreheads with Scriptures inside, and wear extra-long tassels on their outer garments. They crave the seats of highest honor at banquets and in their meeting places. And how they love to be admired by men with their titles of respect, aspiring to be recognized in public and have others call them 'Reverend.'

But you are to be different from that. You are not to be called 'master,' for you have only one Master, and you are all brothers and sisters. And you are not to be addressed as 'father,' for you have one Father, who is in heaven. Nor are you to be addressed as 'teacher,' for you have one Teacher, the Anointed One. The greatest among you will be the one who always serves others from the heart. Remember this: If you have a lofty opinion of yourself and seek to be honored, you will be humbled. But if you have a modest opinion of yourself and choose to humble yourself, you will be honored." Matthew 23:1–12, TPT

Person or situation you are praying for:
Praises and promises:
Prayer:

## 19 May
### Don't follow what unbelievers do.

For you have already spent enough time doing what unbelievers love to do—living in debauchery, sensuality, partying, drunkenness, wild drinking parties, and the worship of demons. They marvel that you no longer rush to join them in the excesses of their corrupt lifestyles, and so they vilify you. But one day they will have to give an account to the one who is destined to judge the living and the dead. This is the reason the gospel was preached to the martyrs before they gave their lives. Even though they were judged by human standards, now they live in spirit by God's standards. 1 Peter 4:3–6, TPT

Person or situation you are praying for:
Praises and promises:
Prayer:

# 20 May
## God's wisdom is not man's wisdom.

So where is the wise philosopher who understands? Where is the expert scholar who comprehends? And where is the skilled debater of our time who could win a debate with God? Hasn't God demonstrated that the wisdom of this world system is utter foolishness? For in his wisdom, God designed that all the world's wisdom would be insufficient to lead people to the discovery of himself. He took great delight in baffling the wisdom of the world by using the simplicity of preaching the story of the cross in order to save those who believe it. For the Jews constantly demand to see miraculous signs, while those who are not Jews constantly cling to the world's wisdom, but we preach the crucified Messiah. The Jews stumble over him and the rest of the world sees him as foolishness. But for those who have been chosen to follow him, both Jews and Greeks, he is God's mighty power, God's true wisdom, and our Messiah. For the "foolish" things of God have proven to be wiser than human wisdom. And the "feeble" things of God have proven to be far more powerful than any human ability.

Brothers and sisters, consider who you were when God called you to salvation. Not many of you were wise scholars by human standards, nor were many of you in positions of power. Not many of you were considered the elite when you answered God's call. But God chose those whom the world considers foolish to shame those who think they are wise, and God chose the puny and powerless to shame the high and mighty. He chose the lowly, the laughable in the world's eyes—nobodies—so that he would shame the somebodies. For he chose what is regarded as insignificant in order to supersede what is regarded as prominent, so that there would be no place for prideful boasting in God's presence. For it is not from man that we draw our life but from God as we are being joined to Jesus, the Anointed One. And now he is our God-given wisdom, our virtue, our holiness, and our redemption. 1 Corinthians 1:20–30, TPT

Person or situation you are praying for:
Praises and promises:
Prayer:

## 21 May
### Live as if Jesus will return tomorrow.

Beloved friends, this is now the second letter I have written to you in which I've attempted to stir you up and awaken you to a proper mind-set. So never forget both the prophecies spoken by the holy prophets of old and the teaching of our Lord and Savior spoken by your apostles. Above all, you must understand that in the last days mockers will multiply, chasing after their evil desires. They will say, "So what about this promise of his coming? Our ancestors are dead and buried, yet everything is still the same as it was since from the beginning of time until now." But they conveniently overlook that from the beginning, the heavens and earth were created by God's word. He spoke and the dry ground separated from the waters.  Peter 3:1–5, TPT

Person or situation you are praying for:
Praises and promises:
Prayer:


## 22 May
### You have not because you ask not.

What is the cause of your conflicts and quarrels with each other? Doesn't the battle begin inside of you as you fight to have your own way and fulfill your own desires? You jealously want what others have so you begin to see yourself as better than others. You scheme with envy and harm others to selfishly obtain what you crave, that's why you quarrel and fight. And all the time you don't obtain what you want because you won't ask God for it! And if you ask, you won't receive it for you're asking with corrupt motives, seeking only to fulfill your own selfish desires. You have become spiritual adulterers who are having an affair, an unholy relationship with the world. Don't you know that flirting with the world's values places you at odds with God? Whoever chooses to be the world's friend makes himself God's enemy! James 4:1–4, TPT

Person or situation you are praying for:
Praises and promises:
Prayer:

# 23 May
### Father God, please help me to grow!

Brothers and sisters, I could not address you as people who live by the Spirit but as people who are still worldly, mere infants in Christ. I gave you milk, not solid food, for you were not yet ready for it. Indeed, you are still not ready. You are still worldly. For since there is jealousy and quarreling among you, are you not worldly? Are you not acting like mere humans? For when one says, "I follow Paul," and another, "I follow Apollos," are you not mere human beings? What, after all, is Apollos? And what is Paul? Only servants, through whom you came to believe—as the Lord has assigned to each his task. I planted the seed, Apollos watered it, but God has been making it grow. So neither the one who plants nor the one who waters is anything, but only God, who makes things grow. 1 Corinthians 3:1–7, NIV

Person or situation you are praying for:
Praises and promises:
Prayer:

# 24 May
### Don't let your possessions and wealth blind your decision to follow Christ.

Then a *young* man came up to Jesus. **Young Man:** Teacher, what good deed can I do to assure myself eternal life? **Jesus:** *Strange that you should ask Me what is good. There is only One who is good.* If you want to participate in His *divine* life, obey the Commandments. **Young Man:** Which Commandments *in particular*? **Jesus:** *Well, to begin with,* do not murder, do not commit adultery, do not steal, do not give false testimony, honor your father and mother, and love your neighbor as yourself. **Young Man:** I've kept those Commandments faithfully. What else do I need to do? **Jesus:** If you want to be perfect, go and sell all your possessions and give all your money to the poor; then you will have treasure in heaven. And then come, follow Me. The young man went away sad because he was very wealthy indeed. **Jesus:** This is the truth: it is hard for a rich man to enter the kingdom of heaven. Yes, it is easier for a camel to go through the eye of a needle than for a rich man to enter the kingdom of God. The disciples, hearing this, were stunned. **Disciples:** Who then can be saved? **Jesus:** People cannot save themselves. But with God, all things are possible. **Peter:** *You just told that man to leave everything and follow You.* Well, all of us have done just that. So what should we be expecting? **Jesus:** I tell you this. When *creation is consummated and* all things are renewed, when the Son of Man sits on His throne in glory, you who have followed Me will also sit on thrones. There will be twelve thrones, and you will sit and judge the twelve tribes of Israel. You who have left your house and your fields, or your brothers and sisters, or your father and mother, or even your children in order to follow Me, *at that time when all is renewed, you will receive so much more*: you will receive 100 times what you gave up. You will inherit eternal life. Many of those who are the first will be last, and those who are the last will be first. Matthew 19:16-30 (VOICE)

Person or situation you are praying for:
Praises and promises:
Prayer:

## 25 May
### Greed leads to sacrilegious acts.

Enoch, the seventh after Adam, prophesied of them: "Look! The Master comes with thousands of holy angels to bring judgment against them all, convicting each person of every defiling act of shameless sacrilege, of every dirty word they have spewed of their pious filth." These are the "grumpers," the bellyachers, grabbing for the biggest piece of the pie, talking big, saying anything they think will get them ahead.  Jude 1:14–16, TPT

Person or situation you are praying for:
Praises and promises:
Prayer:

## 26 May
### Don't wait to accept Jesus as your personal Savior. Do it right now!

The sixth Angel poured his bowl on the great Euphrates River: It dried up to nothing. The dry riverbed became a fine roadbed for the kings from the East. From the mouths of the Dragon, the Beast, and the False Prophet I saw three foul demons crawl out—they looked like frogs. These are demon spirits performing signs. They are after the kings of the whole world to get them gathered for battle on the Great Day of God, the Sovereign-Strong. "Keep watch! I come unannounced, like a thief. You are blessed if, awake and dressed, you are ready for me. Too bad if you're found running through the streets, naked and ashamed." Revelation 16:13–15, MSG

Person or situation you are praying for:
Praises and promises:
Prayer:

## 27 May
### Never take a bribe.

You shall appoint judges and officers in all your towns which the LORD your God gives you, according to your tribes; and they shall judge the people with righteous judgment. You shall not pervert justice; you shall not show partiality; and you shall not take a bribe, for a bribe blinds the eyes of the wise and subverts the cause of the righteous. Justice, and only justice, you shall follow, that you may live and inherit the land which the LORD your God gives you. Deuteronomy 16:18–20, RSV

Person or situation you are praying for:
Praises and promises:
Prayer:

## 28 May
### Have no association with blasphemers.

This is especially true of those who follow the corrupt desire of the flesh and despise authority. Bold and arrogant, they are not afraid to heap abuse on celestial beings; yet even angels, although they are stronger and more powerful, do not heap abuse on such beings when bringing judgment on them from the Lord. But these people blaspheme in matters they do not understand. They are like unreasoning animals, creatures of instinct, born only to be caught and destroyed, and like animals they too will perish. They will be paid back with harm for the harm they have done. Their idea of pleasure is to carouse in broad daylight. They are blots and blemishes, reveling in their pleasures while they feast with you. With eyes full of adultery, they never stop sinning; they seduce the unstable; they are experts in greed—an accursed brood! They have left the straight way and wandered off to follow the way of Balaam son of Bezer, who loved the wages of wickedness. But he was rebuked for his wrong doing by a donkey, an animal without speech, who spoke with a human voice and restrained the prophet's madness. These people are springs without water and mists driven by a storm. Blackest darkness is reserved for them. 2 Peter 2:10–17, NIV

Person or situation you are praying for:
Praises and promises:
Prayer:


## 29 May
### Avoid teaching and preaching that sounds pompous and academic and uses fancy words and phrases.

Repeat these basic essentials over and over to God's people. Warn them before God against pious nitpicking, which chips away at the faith. It just wears everyone out. Concentrate on doing your best for God, work you won't be ashamed of, laying out the truth plain and simple. Stay clear of pious talk that is only talk. Words are not mere words, you know. If they're not backed by a godly life, they accumulate as poison in the soul. Hymenaeus and Philetus are examples, throwing believers off stride and missing the truth by a mile by saying the resurrection is over and done with. 2 Timothy 2:14 – 18, MSG

Person or situation you are praying for:
Praises and promises:
Prayer:

## 30 May
### Only God can exact justice in this world.

Everyone tries to get help from the leader, but only GOD will give us justice. Proverbs 29:26,

Person or situation you are praying for:
Praises and promises:
Prayer:

## 31 May
### Jesus understands timing and readiness.

After this Jesus traveled extensively throughout the province of Galilee, but he avoided the province of Judea, for he knew the Jewish leaders in Jerusalem were plotting to have him killed. Now the annual Feast of Tabernacles was approaching. So Jesus's brothers came to advise him, saying, "Why don't you leave the countryside villages and go to Judea where the crowds are, so that your followers can see your miracles? No one can see what you're doing here in the backwoods of Galilee. How do you expect to be successful and famous if you do all these things in secret? Now is your time, go to Jerusalem, come out of hiding, and show the world who you are!" His brothers were pushing him, even though they didn't yet believe in him as the Savior.

Jesus responded, "My time of being unveiled has not yet come, but any time is a suitable opportunity for you to gain man's approval. The world can't hate you, but it does me, for I am exposing their evil deeds. You can go ahead and celebrate the feast without me, my appointed time has not yet come." Jesus lingered in Galilee until his brothers had left for the feast in Jerusalem. Then later, Jesus took a back road and went into Jerusalem in secret. During the feast, the Jewish leaders kept looking for Jesus and asking around, "Where is he? Have you seen him?" John 7:1–11, TPT

Person or situation you are praying for:
Praises and promises:
Prayer:

# May Epilogue

Your written epilogue, is a way of rounding out a literary work, bringing closure, or summarizing the final scene of a dramatic play. In this case, it is a summary of your prayer life and walk with God during the month of May. This page is for you to record your comments and write one or two summary statements as you have prayed for non-politician public figures, etc. While most of us don't know many public figures and praying for them seems like a stretch at best, most public figures need our prayers. Praying for strangers who are also public figures provides us the opportunity to positively impact their personal lives as well as their influence in the public square.

An epilogue also includes what might lie ahead or what happens next in your story. Writing an epilogue requires you understand your purpose in life and how prayer, praise and Bible promises have impacted you and those around you. At this time, you may not understand the impact of your prayers but don't let this stop you from daily bowing before God, arguing, confessing, praying, praising and singing His praises!

# June

## Pray for your prayer partners and spiritual leaders.

Pray for other Christians, especially those in leadership roles. This includes your local church deacons, elders, pastors, board members, and volunteers, etc. Pray for the person or people who hold you accountable. Pray for your prayer partners, your Bible study group, the people who have joined you on your spiritual journey. We are all one in Christ. No one is better than another. No person is inferior by virtue of their gender, race, skin color, etc.

Religious and spiritual leaders bear an extra responsibility to walk in integrity and light. Be trustworthy, a person above reproach. Live in unity with one another and set aside anything that divides. Fellowship with other believers builds faith. Going alone in this experience called life, is not an option. Find fellowship and acceptance with a group of like-minded believers who uphold Biblical standards and live a holy life, pleasing and acceptable unto the Lord.

Be passionate about doing the right thing. Do not expect justice in this life. Those who passionately pursue the Lord will lack no good thing. Do not mock God or his holy ones. Forgive 490 times. Do not lose your bold, courageous faith, for you are destined for a great reward!

# June Ideas

Pray for those who do not have a voice.
Pray for those who have been hurt by church members.
Pray to move the hearts and minds of those in leadership roles.
Pray that we willingly submit to God's sovereignty over our lives.
Pray that our words to God and others never stand to condemn us.
Pray for a church leadership team that is inclusive, and seeks true Christ followers.
Pray for a pastor that does not belittle other pastors who think or believe differently.
Pray for everyone involved in church life, including volunteers and those working behind the scenes.

1. _____
2. _____
3. _____
4. _____
5. _____
6. _____
7. _____
8. _____
9. _____
10. _____

19.
20.
21.
22.
23.
24.
25.

Pray for your prayer partners and spiritual leaders.

28.

# 1 June
## God calls us His children.

If you call "Father" the one who judges everyone impartially according to what they have done, you must live in reverent fear as long as you are strangers in a strange land. For you know that it was not with perishable things like silver or gold that you have been ransomed from the worthless way of life handed down to you by your ancestors, but with the precious blood of the Messiah, like that of a lamb without blemish or defect. On the one hand, he was foreknown before the creation of the world, but on the other hand, he was revealed at the end of time for your sake. 1 Peter 1:17–20, ISV

Person or situation you are praying for:
Praises and promises:
Prayer:

# 2 June
## Take hold of the wonderful mysteries of the gospel!

This salvation was the focus of the prophets who prophesied of this outpouring of grace that was destined for you. They made a careful search and investigation of the meaning of their God-given prophecies as they probed into the mysteries of who would fulfill them and the time period when it would all take place. The Spirit of the Anointed One was in them and was pointing prophetically to the sufferings that Christ was destined to suffer and the glories that would be released afterward. God revealed to the prophets that their ministry was not for their own benefit but for yours. And now, you have heard these things from the evangelists who preached the gospel to you through the power of the Holy Spirit sent from heaven—the gospel containing wonderful mysteries that even the angels long to get a glimpse of. 1 Peter 1:10–12, TPT

Person or situation you are praying for:
Praises and promises:
Prayer:

## 3 June

*Do not lose your bold, courageous faith, for you are destined for a great reward!*

For if we continue to persist in deliberate sin after we have known and received the truth, there is not another sacrifice for sin to be made for us. But this would qualify one for the certain, terrifying expectation of judgment and the raging fire ready to burn up his enemies! Anyone who disobeyed Moses' law died without mercy on the simple evidence of two or three witnesses. How much more severely do you suppose a person deserves to be judged who has contempt for God's Son, and who scorns the blood of the new covenant that made him holy, and who mocks the Spirit who gives him grace? For we know him who said, "I have the right to take revenge and pay them back for their evil!" And also, "The Lord God will judge his own people!"

It is the most terrifying thing of all to come under the judgment of the Living God! Don't you remember those days right after the Light shined in your hearts? You endured a great marathon season of suffering hardships, yet you stood your ground. And at times you were publicly and shamefully mistreated, being persecuted for your faith; then at others times you stood side by side with those who preach the message of hope. You sympathized with those in prison and when all your belongings were confiscated you accepted that violation with joy; convinced that you possess a treasure growing in heaven that could never be taken from you. So don't lose your bold, courageous faith, for you are destined for a great reward! Hebrews 10:26–35, TPT

Person or situation you are praying for:
Praises and promises:
Prayer:

## 4 June

*Each person builds on Christ, the foundation of our faith.*

By the grace God has given me, I laid a foundation as a wise builder, and someone else is building on it. But each one should build with care. For no one can lay any foundation other than the one already laid, which is Jesus Christ. If anyone builds on this foundation using gold, silver, costly stones, wood, hay or straw, their work will be shown for what it is, because the Day will bring it to light. It will be revealed with fire, and the fire will test the quality of each person's work. If what has been built survives, the builder will receive a reward. If it is burned up, the builder will suffer loss but yet will be saved—even though only as one escaping through the flames. 1 Corinthians 3:10–15, NIV

Person or situation you are praying for:
Praises and promises:
Prayer:

## 5 June

### Fellowship with believers builds faith.

I yearn to come and be face-to-face with you and get to know you. For I long to impart to you the gift of the Spirit that will empower you to stand strong in your faith. Now, this means that when we come together and are side by side, something wonderful will be released. We can expect to be co-encouraged and co-comforted by each other's faith! Romans 1:11, 12, TPT

Person or situation you are praying for:
Praises and promises:
Prayer:

## 6 June

### Forgive 490 times.

Later Peter approached Jesus and said, "How many times do I have to forgive my fellow believer who keeps offending me? Seven times?" Jesus answered, "Not seven times, Peter, but seventy times seven times!" Matthew 18:18–20, TPT

Person or situation you are praying for:
Praises and promises:
Prayer:

## 7 June

### Be passionate about doing the right thing.

We have cause to celebrate because the grace of God has appeared, offering the gift of salvation to all people. Grace arrives with its own instruction: run away from anything that leads us away from God; abandon the lusts and passions of this world; live life now in this age with awareness and self-control, doing the right thing and keeping yourselves holy. Watch for His return; expect the blessed hope we all will share when our great God and Savior, Jesus the Anointed, appears again. He gave His body for our sakes and will not only break us free from the chains of wickedness, but He will also prepare a community uncorrupted by the world that He would call His own—people who are passionate about doing the right thing. Titus 2:11–15, VOICE

Person or situation you are praying for:
Praises and promises:
Prayer:

## 8 June
### Do not be a Pharisee.

You guys don't get it. Did the potter make the outside but not the inside too? If you were full of goodness within, you could overflow with generosity from within, and if you did that, everything would be clean for you. Woe to you, Pharisees! Judgment will come on you! You are fastidious about tithing, keeping account of every little leaf of mint and herb, but you neglect what really matters: justice and the love of God! If you'd get straight on what really matters, then your fastidiousness about little things would be worth something. Woe to you, Pharisees! Judgment will come on you! What you really love is having people fawn over you when you take the seat of honor in the synagogue or when you are greeted in the public market. Wake up! See what you've become! Woe to you; you're like a field full of unmarked graves. People walk on the field and have no idea of the corruption that's a few inches beneath their feet. Luke 11:40–44, VOICE

Person or situation you are praying for:
Praises and promises:
Prayer:

## 9 June
### When we confess our sins, He is faithful and just to forgive our sins.

If we boast that we have no sin, we're only fooling ourselves and are strangers to the truth. But if we freely admit our sins when his light uncovers them, he will be faithful to forgive us every time. God is just to forgive us our sins because of Christ, and he will continue to cleanse us from all unrighteousness. If we claim that we're not guilty of sin when God uncovers it with his light, we make him a liar and his word is not in us. 1 John 1:8–10, TPT

Person or situation you are praying for:
Praises and promises:
Prayer:

## 10 June
### Pray to willingly submit to God's sovereignty over our lives.

For the eyes of the Lord Yahweh rest upon the godly, and his heart responds to their prayers. But he turns his back on those who practice evil. 1 Peter 3:12, TPT

Person or situation you are praying for:
Praises and promises:
Prayer:

## 11 June

### Those who passionately pursue the Lord will lack no good thing.

Even the strong and the wealthy grow weak and hungry, but those who passionately pursue the Lord will never lack any good thing. Come, children of God, and listen to me. I'll share the lesson I've learned of fearing the Lord. Do you want to live a long, good life, enjoying the beauty that fills each day? Then never speak a lie or allow wicked words to come from your mouth. Keep turning your back on every sin, and make "peace" your life motto. Practice being at peace with everyone. The Lord sees all we do; he watches over his friends, day and night. His godly ones receive the answers they seek whenever they cry out to him. But the Lord has made up his mind to oppose evildoers and to wipe out even the memory of them from the face of the earth. Yet when holy lovers of God cry out to him with all their hearts, the Lord will hear them and come to rescue them from all their troubles.

The Lord is close to all whose hearts are crushed by pain, and he is always ready to restore the repentant one. Even when bad things happen to the good and godly ones, the Lord will save them and not let them be defeated by what they face. God will be your bodyguard to protect you when trouble is near. Not one bone will be broken. But the wicked commit slow suicide. For they hate and persecute the lovers of God. Make no mistake about it, God will hold them guilty and punish them; they will pay the penalty! Psalm 34:15–21, TPT

Person or situation you are praying for:
Praises and promises:
Prayer:

## 12 June

### Do not mock God nor his holy ones.

Enoch, the seventh direct descendant from Adam, prophesied of their doom when he said, "Look! Here comes the Lord Yahweh with his countless myriads of holy ones. He comes to execute judgment against them all and to convict each one of them for their ungodly deeds and for all the terrible words that ungodly sinners have spoken against him." These people are always complaining and never satisfied—finding fault with everyone. They follow their own evil desires and their mouths speak scandalous things. They enjoy using seductive flattery to manipulate others. Jude 1:14–16, TPT

Person or situation you are praying for:
Praises and promises:
Prayer:

# 13 June
## Our only reply: "The Lord Yahweh rebuke you!"

Dearly loved friend, I was fully intending to write to you about our amazing salvation we all participate in, but felt the need instead to challenge you to vigorously defend and contend for the beliefs that we cherish. For God, through the apostles, has once for all entrusted these truths to his holy believers. There have been some who have sneaked in among you unnoticed. They are depraved people whose judgment was prophesied in Scripture a long time ago. They have perverted the message of God's grace into a license to commit immorality and turn against our only absolute Master, our Lord Jesus Christ.

I need to remind you, even though you are familiar with it all, that the Lord Jesus saved his people out of Egypt but subsequently destroyed those who were guilty of unbelief. In the same way, there were heavenly messengers in rebellion who went outside their rightful domain of authority and abandoned their appointed realms. God bound them in everlasting chains and is keeping them in the dark abyss of the netherworld until the judgment of the great day. In a similar way, the cities of Sodom and Gomorrah and nearby towns gave themselves to sexual immorality and the unnatural desire of different flesh. Now they all serve as examples of those who experience the punishment of eternal fire. In the same way, these sensual "dreamers" corrupt and pollute the natural realm, while on the other hand they reject the spiritual realms of governmental power and repeatedly scoff at heavenly glories. Even the archangel Michael, when he was disputing with the devil over the body of Moses, dared not insult or slander him, but simply said, "The Lord Yahweh rebuke you!" These people insult anything they don't understand. They behave like irrational beasts by doing whatever they feel like doing. Because they live by their animal instincts, they corrupt themselves and bring about their own destruction. How terrible it is for them! For they have followed in the steps of Cain. They have abandoned themselves to Balaam's error because of their greedy pursuit of financial gain. And since they have rebelled like Korah rebelled, they will experience the same fate of Korah and likewise perish.

These false teachers are like dangerous hidden reefs at your love feasts, lying in wait to shipwreck the immature. They feast among you without reverence, having no shepherd but themselves. They are clouds with no rain, swept along by the winds. Like fruitless late-autumn trees—twice dead, barren, and plucked up by the roots! They are wild waves of the sea, flinging out the foam of their shame and disgrace. They are misleading like wandering stars, for whom the complete darkness of eternal gloom has been reserved. Jude 1:3–13, TPT

Person or situation you are praying for:
Praises and promises:
Prayer:

## 14 June
### Do not be self-centered, prideful, arrogant; be slow to anger.

A person who quickly gets angry causes trouble. But a person who controls his temper stops a quarrel. Proverbs 15:18, ICB

Person or situation you are praying for:
Praises and promises:
Prayer:

## 15 June
### Love letters from the One who loves us . . .

From John to the seven churches in western Turkey: May the kindness of God's grace and peace overflow to you from him who is, and who was, and who is to come, and from the seven spirits who are in front of his throne, and from Jesus Christ the Faithful Witness, the Firstborn from among the dead and the ruling King, who rules over the kings of the earth! Now to the one who constantly loves us and has loosed us from our sins by his own blood, and to the one who has made us to rule as a kingly priesthood to serve his God and Father—to him be glory and dominion throughout the eternity of eternities! Amen! Rev 1:4–6, TPT

Person or situation you are praying for:
Praises and promises:
Prayer:

## 16 June
### Letter to Ephesus

I know all that you've done for me—you have worked hard and persevered. I know that you don't tolerate evil. You have tested those who claimed to be apostles and proved they are not, for they were imposters. I also know how you have bravely endured trials and persecutions because of my name, yet you have not become discouraged. But I have this against you: you have abandoned the passionate love you had for me at the beginning. Think about how far you have fallen! Repent and do the works of love you did at first. I will come to you and remove your lampstand from its place of influence if you do not repent. Although, to your credit, you despise the practices of the Nicolaitans, which I also despise. The one whose heart is open let him listen carefully to what the Spirit is saying now to all the churches. To the one who overcomes I will give access to feast on the fruit of the Tree of Life that is found in the paradise of God. Revelation 2:2–7, TPT

Person or situation you are praying for:
Praises and promises:
Prayer:

## 17 June
### Letter to Smyrna

I am aware of all the painful difficulties you have passed through and your financial hardships, even though, in fact, you possess rich treasure. And I am fully aware of the slander that has come against you from those who claim to be Jews but are really not, for they are a satanic congregation. Do not yield to fear in the face of the suffering to come, but be aware of this: the devil is about to have some of you thrown into prison to test your faith. For ten days you will have distress, but remain faithful to the day you die and I will give you the victor's crown of life. The one whose heart is open let him listen carefully to what the Spirit is presently saying to all the churches. The one who conquers will not be harmed by the second death. Revelation 2:9–11, TPT

Person or situation you are praying for:
Praises and promises:
Prayer:


## 18 June
### Letter to Pergamum

I know where you live—where Satan sits enthroned, yet you still cling faithfully to the power of my name. You did not deny your faith in me even in the days of my faithful martyr Antipas, who was executed in your city, where Satan lives. Nevertheless, I have a few things against you. There are some among you who hold to the teachings of Balaam, who taught Balak to entice the Israelites to eat things that were sacrificed to idols and to commit sexual immorality. Furthermore, you have some who hold to the doctrines of the Nicolaitans. So repent, then, or I will come quickly to war against them with the sword of my mouth. But the one whose heart is open let him listen carefully to what the Spirit is presently saying to all the churches. To everyone who is victorious I will let him feast on the hidden manna and give him a shining white stone. And written upon the white stone is inscribed his new name, known only to the one who receives it. Revelation 2:13–17, TPT

Person or situation you are praying for:
Praises and promises:
Prayer:

## 19 June
### Letter to Thyatira

I know all that you've done for me—your love and faith, your ministry and steadfast perseverance. In fact, you now excel in these virtues even more than at the first. But I have this against you: you tolerate that woman Jezebel, who calls herself a prophetess and is seducing my loving servants. She is teaching that it is permissible to indulge in sexual immorality and to eat food sacrificed to idols. I have waited for her to repent from her vile immorality, but she refuses to do so. Now I will lay her low with terrible distress along with all her adulterous partners if they do not repent. And I will strike down her followers with a deadly plague. Then all the congregations will realize that I am the one who thoroughly searches the most secret thought and the innermost being. I will give to each one what their works deserve. But to the rest of you in Thyatira who don't adhere to the teachings of Jezebel and have not been initiated into deep satanic secrets, I say to you (without laying upon you any other burden): Cling tightly to all that you have until I appear. To everyone who is victorious and continues to do my works to the very end I will give you authority over the nations to shepherd them with a royal scepter. And the rebellious will be shattered as clay pots—even as I also received authority from the presence of my Father. I will give the morning star to the one who experiences victory. So, the one whose heart is open let him listen carefully to what the Spirit is presently saying to all the churches. Revelation 2:19–29, TPT

Person or situation you are praying for:
Praises and promises:
Prayer:

## 20 June
### Letter to Sardis.

I know all that you do and I know that you have a reputation for being really "alive," but you're actually dead! Wake up and strengthen all that remains before it dies, for I haven't found your works to be perfect in the sight of my God. So, remember all the things you've received and heard, then turn back to God and obey them. For if you continue to slumber, I will come to you like a thief, and you'll have no idea at what hour I will come. Yet there are still a few in Sardis who have remained pure, and they will walk in fellowship with me in brilliant light, for they are worthy. And the one who experiences victory will be dressed in white robes and I will never, no never erase your name from the Book of Life. I will acknowledge your name before my Father and his angels. So, the one whose heart is open let him listen carefully to what the Spirit is now saying to all the churches. Revelation 3:2–6, TPT

Person or situation you are praying for:
Praises and promises:
Prayer:

## 21 June
### Letter to Philadelphia

I know all that you've done. Now I have set before you a wide-open door that none can shut. For I know that you possess only a little power, yet you've kept my word and haven't denied my name. Watch how I deal with those of the synagogue of Satan who say that they are Jews but are not, for they're lying. I will make them come and bow down at your feet and acknowledge how much I've loved you. Because you've passionately kept my message of perseverance, I will also keep you from the hour of proving that is coming to test every person on earth. But I come swiftly, so cling tightly to what you have, so that no one may seize your crown of victory. For the one who is victorious, I will make you to be a pillar in the sanctuary of my God, permanently secure. I will write on you the name of my God and the name of the city of my God—the New Jerusalem, descending from my God out of heaven. And I'll write my own name on you. So the one whose heart is open let him listen carefully to what the Spirit is now saying to all the churches. Revelation 3:8–13, TPT

Person or situation you are praying for:
Praises and promises:
Prayer:

## 22 June
### Letter to Laodicea.

Write the following to the messenger of the congregation in Laodicea, for these are the words of the Amen, the faithful and true witness, the ruler of God's creation: I know all that you do, and I know that you are neither frozen in apathy nor fervent with passion. How I wish you were either one or the other! But because you are neither cold nor hot, but lukewarm, I am about to spit you from my mouth. For you claim, "I'm rich and getting richer—I don't need a thing." Yet you are clueless that you're miserable, poor, blind, barren, and naked! So I counsel you to purchase gold perfected by fire, so that you can be truly rich. Purchase a white garment to cover and clothe your shameful Adam-nakedness. Purchase eye salve to be placed over your eyes so that you can truly see. All those I dearly love I unmask and train. So repent and be eager *to pursue what is right*. Behold, I'm standing at the door, knocking. If your heart is open to hear my voice and you open the door *within*, I will come in to you and feast with you, and you will feast with me. And to the one who conquers I will give the privilege of sitting with me on my throne, just as I conquered and sat down with my Father on his throne. The one whose heart is open let him listen carefully to what the Spirit is saying now to the churches. Revelation 3:14-22

Person or situation you are praying for:
Praises and promises:
Prayer:

## 23 June

*God will soon wipe away all of our tears.*

For the Lamb at the center of the throne continuously shepherds them unto life—guiding them to the everlasting fountains of the water of life. And God will wipe from their eyes every last tear! Revelation 7:17, TPT

Person or situation you are praying for:
Praises and promises:
Prayer:

## 24 June

*We are all one in Christ, no one is better than another.*

When Peter came in, Cornelius went to meet him. He fell down at his feet and worshipped him. "Get up!" said Peter, lifting him up. "I'm just a man, too." Acts 10:25, 26, NTE

Person or situation you are praying for:
Praises and promises:
Prayer:

## 25 June

*Be trustworthy, a person above reproach.*

"Whoever can be trusted with very little can also be trusted with much, and whoever is dishonest with very little will also be dishonest with much. So, if you have not been trustworthy in handling worldly wealth, who will trust you with true riches? And if you have not been trustworthy with someone else's property, who will give you property of your own? No one can serve two masters. Either you will hate the one and love the other, or you will be devoted to the one and despise the other. You cannot serve both God and money." The Pharisees, who loved money, heard all this and were sneering at Jesus. He said to them, "You are the ones who justify yourselves in the eyes of others, but God knows your hearts. What people value highly is detestable in God's sight." Luke 16:10–15, NIV

Person or situation you are praying for:
Praises and promises:
Prayer:

## 26 June
### Many hands make light work.

Pray for unity in purpose to join together the diverse parts of God's team. All are essential and none are greater than the other. The whole is greater than the individual parts. The carver encourages the goldsmith, and the molder helps at the anvil. "Good," they say. "It's coming along fine." Carefully they join the parts together, then fasten the thing in place so it won't fall over. Isaiah 41:7–13, NLT

Person or situation you are praying for:
Praises and promises:
Prayer:


## 27 June
### Live in unity with one another and set aside anything that divides.

I urge you, my brothers and sisters, for the sake of the name of our Lord Jesus Christ, to agree to live in unity with one another and put to rest any division that attempts to tear you apart. Be restored as one united body living in perfect harmony. Form a consistent choreography among yourselves, having a common perspective with shared values.

My dear brothers and sisters, I have a serious concern I need to bring up with you, for I have been informed by those of Chloe's house church that you have been destructively arguing among yourselves. And I need to bring this up because each of you is claiming loyalty to different preachers. Some are saying, "I am a disciple of Paul," or, "I follow Apollos," or, "I am a disciple of Peter the Rock," and some, "I belong only to Christ." But let me ask you, is Christ divided up into groups? Did I die on the cross for you? At your baptism did you pledge yourselves to follow Paul? Thank God I only baptized two from Corinth— Crispus and Gaius! So now no one can say that in my name I baptized others. (Yes, I also baptized Stephanus and his family. Other than that, I don't remember baptizing anyone else.) For the Anointed One has sent me on a mission, not to see how many I could baptize, but to proclaim the good news. And I declare this message stripped of all philosophical arguments that empty the cross of its true power. For I trust in the all-sufficient cross of Christ alone. 1 Corinthians 1:10–17, TPT

Person or situation you are praying for:
Praises and promises:
Prayer:

## 28 June
### Do not expect justice in this life.

Wanting to release Jesus, Pilate appealed to them again. But they kept shouting, "Crucify him! Crucify him!" For the third time he spoke to them: "Why? What crime has this man committed? I have found in him no grounds for the death penalty. Therefore, I will have him punished and then release him." But with loud shouts they insistently demanded that he be crucified, and their shouts prevailed. So, Pilate decided to grant their demand. He released the man who had been thrown into prison for insurrection and murder, the one they asked for, and surrendered Jesus to their will. Luke 23:20–25, NIV

Person or situation you are praying for:
Praises and promises:
Prayer:

## 29 June
### Your new life is hidden in God.

It comes down to this: since you have been raised with the Anointed One, the Liberating King, set your mind on heaven above. The Anointed is there, seated at God's right hand. Stay focused on what's above, not on earthly things, because your old life is dead and gone. Your new life is now hidden, enmeshed with the Anointed who is in God. On that day when the Anointed One—who is our very life—is revealed, you will be revealed with Him in glory!

So, kill your earthly impulses: loose sex, impure actions, unbridled sensuality, wicked thoughts, and greed (which is essentially idolatry). It's because of these, that God's wrath is coming [upon the sons and daughters of disobedience], so avoid them at all costs. These are the same things you once pursued, and together you spawned a life of evil. But now make sure you shed such things: anger, rage, spite, slander, and abusive language. And don't go on lying to each other since you have sloughed away your old skin along with its evil practices for a fresh new you, which is continually renewed in knowledge according to the image of the One who created you. In this re-creation there is no distinction between Greek and Jew, circumcised and uncircumcised, barbarian and conqueror, or slave and free because the Anointed is the whole and dwells in us all. Since you are all set apart by God, made holy and dearly loved, clothe your-selves with a holy way of life: compassion, kindness, humility, gentleness, and patience. Put up with one another. Forgive. Pardon any offenses against one another, as the Lord has pardoned you, because you should act in kind. Col 3:1–13, VOICE

Person or situation you are praying for:
Praises and promises:
Prayer:

## 30 June
### Fasten your hearts to the love of God.

But you, my delightfully loved friends, remember the prophecies of the apostles of our Lord Jesus, the Anointed One. They taught you, "In the last days there will always be mockers, motivated by their own ungodly desires." These people cause divisions and are followers of their own natural instincts, devoid of the life of the Spirit. But you, my delightfully loved friends, constantly and progressively build yourselves up on the foundation of your most holy faith by praying every moment in the Spirit. Fasten your hearts to the love of God and receive the mercy of our Lord Jesus Christ, who gives us eternal life. Keep being compassionate to those who still have doubts, and snatch others out of the fire to save them. Be merciful over and over to them, but always couple your mercy with the fear of God. Be extremely careful to keep yourselves free from the pollutions of the flesh.

Now, to the one with enough power to prevent you from stumbling into sin and bring you faultless before his glorious presence to stand before him with ecstatic delight, to the only God our Savior, through our Lord Jesus Christ, be endless glory and majesty, great power and authority—from before he created time, now, and throughout all the ages of eternity. Amen.
Jude 1:17–25, TPT

Person or situation you are praying for:
Praises and promises:
Prayer:

# June Epilogue

A written epilogue, is a way of rounding out a literary work, bringing closure, or summarizing the final scene of a dramatic play. In this case, it is a summary of your prayer life and walk with God during the month of June. This page is for you to record your comments and write one or two summary statements as you have prayed for your prayer partners and spiritual leaders in your realm as well as outside of your sphere, etc. While most of us don't know many public figures and praying for them seems like a stretch at best, most public figures need our prayers. Praying for strangers who are also public figures provides us the opportunity to positively impact their personal lives as well as their influences in the public arena. Many spiritual leaders are discouraged and feel their contributions are not valued. I have found that over time, the value of most spiritual leaders is revealed by their fruits. Either their personal life is vibrant and aligns with their outward values or they are living a double life which cannot withstand outside scrutiny forever. No one is perfect, but most spiritual leaders as well as their families need our prayers.

If you are reading this book, you probably have one or more prayer partners. They too need prayer outside of your mutual interactions. In fact, sometimes prayer partners, while they may reveal some of their deepest desires and hopes, oftentimes are unable to fully verbalize their needs and deepest desires. These are the unspoken prayers that always exist even between spouses, siblings, best friends, etc. The spoken and unspoken prayers are the ones we need to verbalize for our prayer partners.

An epilogue also includes what might lie ahead or what happens next in your story. Writing an epilogue requires you understand your purpose in life and how prayer, praise and Bible promises have impacted you and those around you. At this time, you may not understand the impact of your prayers but don't let this stop you from daily bowing before God, arguing, confessing, praying, praising and singing His praises!

_____
_____
_____
_____
_____

# July

## Pray for couples and families in distress.

Values such as hard work, family orientation, love, tenderness, equality, devotion, respect, and a good reputation, never go out of style. Take care of your family. When you marry and have children, your time is now enjoined with them. This does not preclude taking personal time for prayer, devotions, reading, and an occasional play date with your friends, etc. Your family is always your mission field. This does not end when your children become adults, or when they do stupid things. It does not end when your 17-year old daughter gets pregnant and doesn't want to marry the father. It doesn't end when she chooses an abortion. It doesn't end when your son runs away from home or wrecks your car or truck. It doesn't end when your spouse is so self-centered they believe the world revolves around them. It doesn't end when your spouse loses their job and then refuses to work. It doesn't end when you arrive at the "poor house." It doesn't end when your spouse gets a debilitating disease. It doesn't end when your spouse is unfaithful. It doesn't end when your family tells you to divorce your spouse and move on (of course precluding abusive situations).

Some resolutions to our problems in life happen within hours and other times resolutions take years, even decades. During this time, demonstrate love to everyone. Protect your reputation, keep your word, make good on your promises. All things work together for good for those who love Him and are called to do His purposes. Trust the Lord completely and do not rely on your own opinions or feelings.

Take this month to pray for a person, couple, or family who is struggling. Reach out to struggling families and walk with them. Through your example, teach others how to live. Be a blessing to others, especially when you are further along in your walk with the Lord. Lift them up in prayer and help them to connect to God's promises.

# July Ideas

Pray for love to be the standard of your life.
Pray for families to draw near in times of distress.
Pray for families to operate in ways which glorify God.
Pray for couples and families to live in peace and joy.
Pray for families to seek God's will in everything they do.
Pray to forgive those who hurt us in the same way God forgives us.
Pray that each family stands against evil forces aligned against them.
Pray for couples to honor the institution of marriage in ways that glorify God.
Prayerfully rebuke every thought of envy, jealousy and hatred toward one another.

1. _____
2. _____
3. _____
4. _____
5. _____
6. _____
7. _____
8. _____
9. _____
10. _____

19.
20.
21.
22.
23.
24.
25.

Pray for couples and families in distress.

# 1 July
## Jealousy tears families apart.

Joseph, being seventeen years old, was shepherding the flock with his brothers; he was a lad with the sons of Bilhah and Zilpah, his father's wives; and Joseph brought an ill report of them to their father. Now Israel loved Joseph more than any other of his children, because he was the son of his old age; and he made him a long robe with sleeves. But when his brothers saw that their father loved him more than all his brothers, they hated him, and could not speak peaceably to him. Now Joseph had a dream, and when he told it to his brothers they only hated him the more. He said to them, "Hear this dream which I have dreamed: behold, we were binding sheaves in the field, and lo, my sheaf arose and stood upright; and behold, your sheaves gathered round it, and bowed down to my sheaf." His brothers said to him, "Are you indeed to reign over us? Or are you indeed to have dominion over us?" So they hated him yet more for his dreams and for his words.

Then he dreamed another dream, and told it to his brothers, and said, "Behold, I have dreamed another dream; and behold, the sun, the moon, and eleven stars were bowing down to me." But when he told it to his father and to his brothers, his father rebuked him, and said to him, "What is this dream that you have dreamed? Shall I and your mother and your brothers indeed come to bow ourselves to the ground before you?" And his brothers were jealous of him, but his father kept the saying in mind. Genesis 37:1–11, NIV

Person or situation you are praying for:
Praises and promises:
Prayer:

# 2 July
## Take care of your family.

For if a believer fails to provide for their own relatives when they are in need, they have compromised their convictions of faith and need to be corrected, for they are living worse than the unbelievers. 1 Timothy 5:8, TPT

Person or situation you are praying for:
Praises and promises:
Prayer:

## 3 July
### Demonstrate love to everyone.

Anyone can say, "I love God," yet have hatred toward another believer. This makes him a phony, because if you don't love a brother or sister, whom you can see, how can you truly love God, whom you can't see? For he has given us this command: whoever loves God must also demonstrate love to others. 1 John 4:20, 21, TPT

Person or situation you are praying for:
Praises and promises:
Prayer:


## 4 July
### All things work together for good for those who love him and are called to do His purposes.

For in hope we were saved. Now hope that is seen is not hope, because who hopes for what he sees? But if we hope for what we do not yet have, we wait for it patiently. In the same way, the Spirit helps us in our weakness. We do not know what we ought to pray for, but the Spirit himself intercedes for us through wordless groans. And he who searches our hearts knows the mind of the Spirit, because the Spirit intercedes for God's people in accordance with the will of God. And we know that in all things God works for the good of those who love him, who have been called according to his purpose. For those God foreknew he also predestined to be conformed to the image of his Son, that he might be the firstborn among many brothers and sisters. And those he predestined, he also called; those he called, he also justified; those he justified, he also glorified. Romans 8:24–30, NIV

Person or situation you are praying for:
Praises and promises:
Prayer:

# 5 July
*Trust the Lord completely, and do not rely on your own opinions.*

My child, if you truly want a long and satisfying life, never forget the things that I've taught you. Follow closely every truth that I've given you. Then you will have a full, rewarding life. Hold on to loyal love and don't let go, and be faithful to all that you've been taught. Let your life be shaped by integrity, with truth written upon your heart. That's how you will find favor and understanding with both God and men— you will gain the reputation of living life well. Trust in the Lord completely, and do not rely on your own opinions. With all your heart rely on him to guide you, and he will lead you in every decision you make. Become intimate with him in whatever you do, and he will lead you wherever you go. Don't think for a moment that you know it all, for wisdom comes when you adore him with undivided devotion and avoid everything that's wrong. Then you will find the healing refreshment your body and spirit long for. Glorify God with all your wealth, honoring him with your very best, with every increase that comes to you. Then every dimension of your life will overflow with blessings from an uncontainable source of inner joy! Proverbs 3:1–10, TPT

Person or situation you are praying for:
**Praises and promises:**
Prayer:

# 6 July
*Treat each other with tender devotion, respect, and love.*

And to the husbands, you are to demonstrate love for your wives with the same tender devotion that Christ demonstrated to us, his bride. For he died for us, sacrificing himself to make us holy and pure, cleansing us through the showering of the pure water of the Word of God. All that he does in us is designed to make us a mature church for his pleasure, until we become a source of praise to him, glorious and radiant, beautiful and holy, without fault or flaw. Husbands have the obligation of loving and caring for their wives the same way they love and care for their own bodies, for to love your wife is to love your own self.

No one abuses his own body, but pampers it—serving and satisfying its needs. That's exactly what Christ does for his church! He serves and satisfies us as members of his body. For this reason, a man is to leave his father and his mother and lovingly hold to his wife, since the two have become joined as one flesh. Marriage is the beautiful design of the Almighty, a great and sacred mystery — meant to be a vivid example of Christ and his church. So every married man should be gracious to his wife just as he is gracious to himself. And every wife should be tenderly devoted to her husband. Ephesians 5:25–33, TPT

Person or situation you are praying for:
**Praises and promises:**
Prayer:

## 7 July
### The Lord is far from the wicked but hears the righteous.

A gentle answer turns away wrath, but a harsh word stirs up anger. The tongue of the wise makes knowledge acceptable, but the mouth of fools spouts folly. The eyes of the LORD are in every place, watching the evil and the good. A soothing tongue is a tree of life, but perversion in it crushes the spirit. A fool rejects his father's discipline, but he who regards reproof is sensible. Great wealth is in the house of the righteous, but trouble is in the income of the wicked. The lips of the wise spread knowledge, but the hearts of fools are not so. The sacrifice of the wicked is an abomination to the LORD, but the prayer of the upright is His delight. The way of the wicked is an abomination to the LORD, but He loves one who pursues righteousness. Grievous punishment is for him who forsakes the way; he who hates reproof will die. Sheol and Abaddon lie open before the LORD, how much more the hearts of men! A scoffer does not love one who reproves him, he will not go to the wise.

A joyful heart makes a cheerful face, but when the heart is sad, the spirit is broken. The mind of the intelligent seeks knowledge, but the mouth of fools feeds on folly. All the days of the afflicted are bad, but a cheerful heart has a continual feast. Better is a little with the fear of the LORD than great treasure and turmoil with it. Better is a dish of vegetables where love is than a fattened ox served with hatred. A hot-tempered man stirs up strife, but the slow to anger calms a dispute. The way of the lazy is as a hedge of thorns, but the path of the upright is a highway. A wise son makes a father glad, but a foolish man despises his mother. Folly is joy to him who lacks sense, but a man of understanding walks straight.

Without consultation, plans are frustrated, but with many counselors they succeed. A man has joy in an apt answer, and how delightful is a timely word! The path of life leads upward for the wise that he may keep away from Sheol below. The LORD will tear down the house of the proud, but He will establish the boundary of the widow. Evil plans are an abomination to the LORD, but pleasant words are pure. He who profits illicitly troubles his own house, but he who hates bribes will live. The heart of the righteous ponders how to answer, but the mouth of the wicked pours out evil things. The LORD is far from the wicked, but He hears the prayer of the righteous. Bright eyes gladden the heart; good news puts fat on the bones. He whose ear listens to the life-giving reproof will dwell among the wise. He who neglects discipline despises himself, but he who listens to reproof acquires understanding. The fear of the LORD is the instruction for wisdom, and before honor comes humility. Proverbs 15, NASB

Person or situation you are praying for:
Praises and promises:
Prayer:

## 8 July
### Honor your parents.

You are to honor your father and mother. If you do, you and your children will live long and well in the land the Eternal your God has promised to give you. Exodus 20:12, VOICE

Person or situation you are praying for:
Praises and promises:
Prayer:

## 9 July
### Cherish each season of life.

Teacher: For everything that happens in life—there is a season, a right time for everything under heaven: A time to be born, a time to die; a time to plant, a time to collect the harvest; A time to kill, a time to heal; a time to tear down, a time to build up; A time to cry, a time to laugh; a time to mourn, a time to dance; A time to scatter stones, a time to pile them up; A time for a warm embrace, a time for keeping your distance; A time to search, a time to give up as lost; a time to keep, a time to throw out; A time to tear apart, a time to bind together; a time to be quiet, a time to speak up; A time to love, a time to hate; a time to go to war, a time to make peace. Ecclesiastes 3:1–8, VOICE

Person or situation you are praying for:
Praises and promises:
Prayer:

## 10 July
### Pray for families who use their great resources to advance the conditions of the poor.

At that time there was a Roman military officer, Cornelius, who was in charge of one hundred men stationed in Caesarea. He was the captain of the Italian regiment, a devout man of extraordinary character who worshiped God and prayed regularly, together with all his family. He also had a heart for the poor and gave generously to help them. One afternoon about three o'clock, he had an open vision and saw the angel of God appear right in front of him, calling out his name, "Cornelius!" Startled, he was overcome with fear by the sight of the angel. He asked, "What do you want, Lord?" The angel said, "All of your prayers and your generosity to the poor have ascended before God as an eternal offering. Now, send some men to Joppa at once. Have them find a man named Simon the Rock, who is staying as a guest in the home of Simon the tanner, whose house is by the sea. Acts 10:1–6, TPT

Person or situation you are praying for:
Praises and promises:
Prayer:

# 11 July

## Do not repay evil with doing evil, but repay evil with doing good.

When Saul returned from following the Philistines, he was told, "Behold, David is in the wilderness of Enge'di." Then Saul took three thousand chosen men out of all Israel, and went to seek David and his men in front of the Wildgoats' Rocks. And he came to the sheepfolds by the way, where there was a cave; and Saul went in to relieve himself. Now David and his men were sitting in the innermost parts of the cave. And the men of David said to him, "Here is the day of which the LORD said to you, 'Behold, I will give your enemy into your hand, and you shall do to him as it shall seem good to you.'" Then David arose and stealthily cut off the skirt of Saul's robe. And afterward David's heart smote him, because he had cut off Saul's skirt.

He said to his men, "The LORD forbid that I should do this thing to my lord, the LORD's anointed, to put forth my hand against him, seeing he is the LORD's anointed." So David persuaded his men with these words, and did not permit them to attack Saul. And Saul rose up and left the cave, and went upon his way. Afterward David also arose, and went out of the cave, and called after Saul, "My lord the king!" And when Saul looked behind him, David bowed with his face to the earth, and did obeisance. And David said to Saul, "Why do you listen to the words of men who say, 'Behold, David seeks your hurt'? Lo, this day your eyes have seen how the LORD gave you today into my hand in the cave; and some bade me kill you, but I spared you. I said, 'I will not put forth my hand against my lord; for he is the LORD's anointed.' See, my father, see the skirt of your robe in my hand; for by the fact that I cut off the skirt of your robe, and did not kill you, you may know and see that there is no wrong or treason in my hands. I have not sinned against you, though you hunt my life to take it. May the LORD judge between me and you, may the LORD avenge me upon you; but my hand shall not be against you. As the proverb of the ancients says, 'Out of the wicked comes forth wickedness'; but my hand shall not be against you. After whom has the king of Israel come out? After whom do you pursue? After a dead dog! After a flea! May the LORD therefore be judge, and give sentence between me and you, and see to it, and plead my cause, and deliver me from your hand."

When David had finished speaking these words to Saul, Saul said, "Is this your voice, my son David?" And Saul lifted up his voice and wept. He said to David, "You are more righteous than I; for you have repaid me good, whereas I have repaid you evil. And you have declared this day how you have dealt well with me, in that you did not kill me when the LORD put me into your hands. For if a man finds his enemy, will he let him go away safe? So may the LORD reward you with good for what you have done to me this day. And now, behold, I know that you shall surely be king, and that the kingdom of Israel shall be established in your hand." 1 Samuel 24:1–21, RSV

Person or situation you are praying for:
Praises and promises:
Prayer:

## 12 July

Pray for fathers to be involved with their children and take intense interest in their social, spiritual, physical, and mental development.

You fathers, don't provoke your children to wrath, but nurture them in the discipline and instruction of the Lord. Ephesians 6:4, WEB

Person or situation you are praying for:
Praises and promises:
Prayer:

## 13 July

God wants your children to be your glory and not a curse.

Train up a child in the way he should go, and when he is old he will not depart from it. Proverbs 22:6, WEB

Person or situation you are praying for:
Praises and promises:
Prayer:

## 14 July

Protect your reputation, keep your word, make good on your promises.

A good name is more desirable than great riches, and loving favor is better than silver and gold. Proverbs 22:1, WEB

Person or situation you are praying for:
Praises and promises:
Prayer:

## 15 July
*Pray for your children and friends to find a good marriage partner.*

A good woman is hard to find, and worth far more than diamonds. Her husband trusts her without reserve, and never has reason to regret it. Never spiteful, she treats him generously all her life long. She shops around for the best yarns and cottons, and enjoys knitting and sewing. She's like a trading ship that sails to faraway places and brings back exotic surprises. She's up before dawn, preparing breakfast for her family and organizing her day. She looks over a field and buys it, then, with money she's put aside, plants a garden.

First thing in the morning, she dresses for work, up her sleeves, eager to get started. She senses the worth of her work, is in no hurry to call it quits for the day. She's skilled in the crafts of home and hearth, diligent in homemaking. She's quick to assist anyone in need, reaches out to help the poor. She doesn't worry about her family when it snows; their winter clothes are all mended and ready to wear. She makes her own clothing, dresses in colorful linens and silks. Her husband is greatly respected when he deliberates with the city fathers. She designs gowns and sells them, brings the sweaters she knits to the dress shops. Her clothes are well-made and elegant, say, and she always says it kindly. She keeps an eye on everyone in her household, and keeps them all busy and productive.

Her children respect and bless her; her husband joins in with words of praise: "Many women have done wonderful things, you've outclassed them all!" Charm can mislead and beauty soon fades. The woman to be admired and praised is the woman who lives in the Fear-of-GOD. Give her everything she deserves! Festoon her life with praises! Proverbs 31:10–31, MSG

Person or situation you are praying for:
Praises and promises:
Prayer:

## 16 July
*Pray for those who may be confused about which God or gods to worship.*

If you decide that it's a bad thing to worship GOD, then choose a god you'd rather serve—and do it today. Choose one of the gods your ancestors worshiped from the country beyond The River, or one of the gods of the Amorites, on whose land you're now living. As for my family and I, we'll worship GOD. Joshua 24:15, MSG

Person or situation you are praying for:
Praises and promises:
Prayer:

## 17 July
### Pray to avoid adultery.

Good friend, follow your father's good advice; don't wander off from your mother's teachings. Wrap yourself in them from head to foot; wear them like a scarf around your neck. Wherever you walk, they'll guide you; whenever you rest, they'll guard you; when you wake up, they'll tell you what's next. For sound advice is a beacon, good teaching is a light, moral discipline is a life path. Proverbs 6:20-23, MSG

Person or situation you are praying for:
Praises and promises:
Prayer:

## 18 July
### Mothers, pray for your children!

Oh, son of mine, what can you be thinking of! Child whom I bore! The son I dedicated to God! Don't dissipate your virility on fortune-hunting women, promiscuous women who shipwreck leaders. Proverbs 31:2, 3, MSG

Person or situation you are praying for:
Praises and promises:
Prayer:

## 19 July
### A house divided cannot stand.

Then Jesus entered a house, and again a crowd gathered, so that he and his disciples were not even able to eat. When his family heard about this, they went to take charge of him, for they said, "He is out of his mind." And the teachers of the law who came down from Jerusalem said, "He is possessed by Beelzebul! By the prince of demons he is driving out demons." So Jesus called them over to him and began to speak to them in parables: "How can Satan drive out Satan? If a kingdom is divided against itself, that kingdom cannot stand. If a house is divided against itself, that house cannot stand. And if Satan opposes himself and is divided, he cannot stand; his end has come. In fact, no one can enter a strong man's house without first tying him up. Then he can plunder the strong man's house. Truly I tell you, people can be forgiven all their sins and every slander they utter, but whoever blasphemes against the Holy Spirit will never be forgiven; they are guilty of an eternal sin." Mark 3:20–29, NIV

Person or situation you are praying for:
Praises and promises:
Prayer:

## 20 July
### Pray for a marriage "on the rocks."

And the Pharisees, having come near, questioned him, if it is lawful for a husband to put away a wife, tempting him, and he answering said to them, "What did Moses command you?" and they said, "Moses suffered to write a bill of divorce, and to put away." And Jesus answering said to them, "For the stiffness of your heart he wrote you this command, but from the beginning of the creation, a male and a female God did make them; on this account shall a man leave his father and mother, and shall cleave unto his wife, and they shall be— the two—for one flesh; so that they are no more two, but one flesh; what therefore God did join together, let not man put asunder." Mark 10:2–9, YLT

Person or situation you are praying for:
Praises and promises:
Prayer:


## 21 July
### Love God and experience the blessings of keeping his righteous statutes and judgments.

Now this is the commandment, and these are the statutes and judgments which the LORD your God has commanded to teach you, that you may observe them in the land which you are crossing over to possess, that you may fear the LORD your God, to keep all His statutes and His commandments which I command you, you and your son and your grandson, all the days of your life, and that your days may be prolonged. Therefore hear, O Israel, and be careful to observe it, that it may be well with you, and that you may multiply greatly as the LORD God of your fathers has promised you — 'a land flowing with milk and honey.' "Hear, O Israel: The LORD our God, the LORD is one! You shall love the Lord your God with all your heart, with all your soul, and with all your strength. And these words which I command you today shall be in your heart. You shall teach them diligently to your children, and shall talk of them when you sit in your house, when you walk by the way, when you lie down, and when you rise up. You shall bind them as a sign on your hand, and they shall be as frontlets between your eyes. You shall write them on the doorposts of your house and on your gates." Deuteronomy 6:1–9, NKJV

Person or situation you are praying for:
Praises and promises:
Prayer:

## 22 July
### Establish wise counsel and listen to them.

And the LORD sent Nathan to David. He came to him, and said to him, "There were two men in a certain city, the one rich and the other poor. The rich man had very many flocks and herds; but the poor man had nothing but one little ewe lamb, which he had bought. And he brought it up, and it grew up with him and with his children; it used to eat of his morsel, and drink from his cup, and lie in his bosom, and it was like a daughter to him. Now there came a traveler to the rich man, and he was unwilling to take one of his own flock or herd to prepare for the wayfarer who had come to him, but he took the poor man's lamb, and prepared it for the man who had come to him."

Then David's anger was greatly kindled against the man; and he said to Nathan, "As the LORD lives, the man who has done this deserves to die; and he shall restore the lamb fourfold, because he did this thing, and because he had no pity."

Nathan said to David, "You are the man. Thus says the LORD, the God of Israel, 'I anointed you king over Israel, and I delivered you out of the hand of Saul; and I gave you your master's house, and your master's wives into your bosom, and gave you the house of Israel and of Judah; and if this were too little, I would add to you as much more. Why have you despised the word of the LORD, to do what is evil in his sight? You have smitten Uri'ah the Hittite with the sword, and have taken his wife to be your wife, and have slain him with the sword of the Ammonites. Now therefore the sword shall never depart from your house, because you have despised me, and have taken the wife of Uri'ah the Hittite to be your wife.' Thus says the LORD, 'Behold, I will raise up evil against you out of your own house; and I will take your wives before your eyes, and give them to your neighbor, and he shall lie with your wives in the sight of this sun. For you did it secretly; but I will do this thing before all Israel, and before the sun.'"

David said to Nathan, "I have sinned against the LORD." And Nathan said to David, "The LORD also has put away your sin; you shall not die. Nevertheless, because by this deed you have utterly scorned the LORD, the child that is born to you shall die." Then Nathan went to his house. 2 Samuel 12:1–15, RSV

Person or situation you are praying for:
Praises and promises:
Prayer:

## 23 July
### God hears our cries for help.

I cry with a loud voice to the Lord. I pray with my voice to the Lord. I talk and complain to Him. I tell Him all my trouble. When my spirit had grown weak within me, You knew my path. They have hidden a trap for me in the way where I walk. Look to the right and see. For there is no one who thinks about me. There is no place for me to go to be safe. No one cares about my soul. I cried out to You, O Lord. I said, "You are my safe place, my share in the land of the living. Listen to my cry, for I am brought down. Save me from those who make it hard for me. For they are too strong for me. Bring my soul out of prison, so that I may give thanks to Your name. Those who are right and good will gather around me. For You will give much to me." Psalm 142, NLV

Person or situation you are praying for:
Praises and promises:
Prayer:

## 24 July
### Christ in us, glory!

For this reason I kneel before the Father, from whom every family in heaven and on earth is named. I pray that according to the wealth of his glory he will grant you to be strengthened with power through his Spirit in the inner person, that Christ will dwell in your hearts through faith, so that, because you have been rooted and grounded in love, you will be able to comprehend with all the saints what is the breadth and length and height and depth, and thus to know the love of Christ that surpasses knowledge, so that you will be filled up to all the fullness of God. Now to him who by the power that is working within us is able to do far beyond all that we ask or think, to him be the glory in the church and in Christ Jesus to all generations, forever and ever. Amen. Ephesians 3:14–21, NET

Person or situation you are praying for:
Praises and promises:
Prayer:

## 25 July
### Keep your life pure and undefiled.

Honor the sanctity of marriage and keep your vows of purity to one another, for God will judge sexual immorality in any form, whether single or married. Hebrews 13:4, TPT

Person or situation you are praying for:
Praises and promises:
Prayer:

## 26 July
### God is not to be mocked.

Hezeki'ah received the letter from the hand of the messengers, and read it; and Hezeki'ah went up to the house of the LORD, and spread it before the LORD. And Hezeki'ah prayed before the LORD, and said: "O LORD the God of Israel, who art enthroned above the cherubim, thou art the God, thou alone, of all the kingdoms of the earth; thou hast made heaven and earth. Incline thy ear, O LORD, and hear; open thy eyes, O LORD, and see; and hear the words of Sennach'erib, which he has sent to mock the living God. Of a truth, O LORD, the kings of Assyria have laid waste the nations and their lands, and have cast their gods into the fire; for they were no gods, but the work of men's hands, wood and stone; therefore, they were destroyed. So now, O LORD our God, save us, I beseech thee, from his hand, that all the kingdoms of the earth may know that thou, O LORD, art God alone." ...And that night the angel of the LORD went forth, and slew a hundred and eighty-five thousand in the camp of the Assyrians; and when men arose early in the morning, behold, these were all dead bodies. 2 Kings 19:14–19, 35, RSV

Person or situation you are praying for:
Praises and promises:
Prayer:

## 27 July
### Pray for those caught up in sibling rivalry.

Then Cain said to his brother Abel, "Let us go out into the field." And when they were in the field, Cain rose up against his brother Abel and killed him. Then Yahweh said to Cain, "Where is Abel your brother?" And he said, "I do not know; am I my brother's keeper?" And he said, "What have you done? The voice of your brother's blood is crying out to me from the ground. Genesis 4:8–10, LEB

Person or situation you are praying for:
Praises and promises:
Prayer:

## 28 July
*We look forward to the day when God's glory will shine forth in everyone.*

And I lifted my eyes and saw, and behold, a man with a measuring line in his hand! Then I said, "Where are you going?" And he said to me, "To measure Jerusalem, to see what is its breadth and what is its length." And behold, the angel who talked with me came forward, and another angel came forward to meet him, and said to him, "Run, say to that young man, 'Jerusalem shall be inhabited as villages without walls, because of the multitude of men and cattle in it. For I will be to her a wall of fire round about, says the LORD, and I will be the glory within her.'" Zechariah 2:1–5, RSV

Person or situation you are praying for:
Praises and promises:
Prayer:

## 29 July
*God restores what is lost.*

Now Eli'sha had said to the woman whose son he had restored to life, "Arise, and depart with your household, and sojourn wherever you can; for the LORD has called for a famine, and it will come upon the land for seven years." So the woman arose, and did according to the word of the man of God; she went with her household and sojourned in the land of the Philistines seven years. And at the end of the seven years, when the woman returned from the land of the Philistines, she went forth to appeal to the king for her house and her land. Now the king was talking with Geha'zi the servant of the man of God, saying, "Tell me all the great things that Eli'sha has done." And while he was telling the king how Eli'sha had restored the dead to life, behold, the woman whose son he had restored to life appealed to the king for her house and her land. And Geha'zi said, "My lord, O king, here is the woman, and here is her son whom Eli'sha restored to life." And when the king asked the woman, she told him. So the king appointed an official for her, saying, "Restore all that was hers, together with all the produce of the fields from the day that she left the land until now." 2 Kings 8:1–6, RSV

Person or situation you are praying for:
Praises and promises:
Prayer:

# 30 July
## By your example, teach others how to live.

This, beloved, is the truth: until heaven and earth disappear, not one letter, not one pen stroke, will disappear from the sacred law—for everything, everything in the sacred law will be fulfilled and accomplished. Anyone who breaks even the smallest, most obscure commandment—not to mention teaches others to do the same—will be called small and obscure in the kingdom of heaven. Those who practice the law and teach others how to live the law will be called great in the kingdom of heaven. For I tell you this: you will not enter the kingdom of heaven unless your righteousness goes deeper than the Pharisees', even more righteous than the most learned learner of the law. Matthew 5:18–20, VOICE

Person or situation you are praying for:
Praises and promises:
Prayer:

# 31 July
## Establish the kind of relationships that cause you to build fond remembrances of each other.

Then Jacob took a stone and set it up as a pillar. Jacob said to his kinsmen, "Gather stones." So they took stones and made a heap, and they ate there by the heap. Now Laban called it Jegar-sahadutha, but Jacob called it Galeed. Laban said, "This heap is a witness between you and me this day." Therefore it was named Galeed, and Mizpah, for he said, "May the LORD watch between you and me when we are absent one from the other." Genesis 31:45–49, NASB

Person or situation you are praying for:
Praises and promises:
Prayer:

# July Epilogue

A written epilogue, is a way of rounding out a literary work, bringing closure, or summarizing the final scene of a dramatic play. In this case, it is a summary of your prayer life and walk with God during the month of July. This page is for you to record your comments and write one or two summary statements as you have prayed for couples and families in distress. Distress takes many forms. Emotional, physical symptoms, financial infidelity, broken relationships, long-term grieving, addictions, etc. Sometimes people are so damaged they primarily inwardly grieve, refusing to ask for help. These people need prayer but will never ask. Others participate in self-harm. Others isolate themselves. Distress may not be obvious but almost everyone experiences it in varying degrees.

Prayer is powerful. There are consequences or maybe more accurately, there are outcomes when you pray for others. For many months a friend and I faithfully prayed for her adult children. In each case, it seemed like an impossible situation that had no good resolution. And then one evening during our prayer time, we realized one of the situations we had been praying for had steadily improved. Not even a year later, the second situation seemed to miraculously improve. Prayer makes a difference, even in the face of dire circumstances. Sometimes ONLY prayer works.

There is never a shortage of people in distress. Couples navigating divorce waters, parents dealing with rebellious children, children caring for their aging parents, medical issues leading to difficult times, everyone has distress so finding people to pray for this past month hasn't been hard. Your prayers have been invaluable. Now watch and see what God does.

An epilogue also includes what might lie ahead or what happens next in your story. Writing an epilogue requires you understand your purpose in life and how prayer, praise and Bible promises have impacted you and those around you. At this time, you may not understand the impact of your prayers but don't let this stop you from daily bowing before God, arguing, confessing, praying, praising and singing His praises!

_____
_____
_____

# August

## Pray for world leaders.

The world is on fire with strife, war, violence, hunger, greed, heartlessness, pride, deceit, pandemics, disease, poverty, starvation, and Godlessness. Pray for areas and countries experiencing natural disasters, pandemics, pestilence, droughts, food shortages, economic collapse, dictatorships, lawlessness, greed, and extreme poverty, etc.

The world operates at the mercy and generosity of God. We read in the Bible that God sets up kings and takes them down; nothing is outside of His power (Romans 13). We may not see the hand of God guiding events, but if we study the Bible, these events should not come as a surprise.

Pray for those without a knowledge of God to fully understand His intentions for us as individuals and communities. Pray to be part of a society that honors God in all its ways. Pray to be part of a community that honors all forms of life at all stages of life. Pray for people and countries who worship idols. Pray against modern materialism. Cooperate with God, and your latter days will be better than your beginnings.

Christ has set us free! Prepare to participate in God's everlasting covenant. Sleep easy tonight—you belong to the Lord. Father, very soon, we "ain't gonna study war no more." The oppression of the poor will be over. Justice and righteousness will be restored. The Stone rejected by men will form the cornerstone of the heavenly kingdom! Christ sets us free!

Get to know God, as He is the greatest and only source of true wisdom and knowledge. Every word and promise in the Bible comes with power. Be doers and not only hearers of the Word. Until Christ returns, be part of His kingdom here on earth and spread good news and do as many random acts of kindness as you can!

# August Ideas

Pray for Godless countries.
Pray for the healing of the nations.
Pray for idol-worshipping countries.
Pray for world leaders to heed God's word.
Pray against deception for our world leaders.
Pray for leaders who steadfastly demonstrate Christian leadership.

1. _____
   _____
2. _____
   _____
3. _____
   _____
4. _____
   _____
5. _____
   _____
6. _____
   _____
7. _____
   _____
8. _____
   _____
9. _____
   _____
10. _____

19.

20.

21.

22.

23.

24.

25.

Pray for world leaders.

## 1 August
### Oppression of the truly poor is a violation of justice and righteousness.

For when dreams increase and words grow many, there is vanity; but God is the one you must fear. If you see in a province the oppression of the poor and the violation of justice and righteousness, do not be amazed at the matter, for the high official is watched by a higher, and there are yet higher ones over them. But this is gain for a land in every way: a king committed to cultivated fields. He who loves money will not be satisfied with money, nor he who loves wealth with his income; this also is vanity. Ecclesiastes 5:7–10, ESV

Person or situation you are praying for:
Praises and promises:
Prayer:

## 2 August
### Every word and promise in the Bible comes with power.

So turn your heart to me, face me now, and be saved wherever you are, even from the ends of the earth, for I alone am God, and there is no other. I make this solemn oath to you in my own name; this word sent from my mouth in righteousness will not return unfulfilled: "Truly every knee will bow before me and every tongue will solemnly swear allegiance to me!" All will say of me, "Yes! Only in Yahweh do I find righteousness and strength!" And all who were angry with me will come before me and regret it! Isaiah 45:22–24, TPT

Person or situation you are praying for:
Praises and promises:
Prayer:

## 3 August
### Prepare to participate in God's everlasting covenant.

For I the LORD love justice, I hate robbery and wrong; I will faithfully give them their recompense, and I will make an everlasting covenant with them. Their descendants shall be known among the nations, and their offspring in the midst of the peoples; all who see them shall acknowledge them, that they are a people whom the LORD has blessed. Isaiah 61:8, 9, RSV

Person or situation you are praying for:
Praises and promises:
Prayer:

## 4 August

*Be doers and not only hearers of the Word.*

Pure and undefiled religion before God and the Father is this: to visit orphans and widows in their trouble, and to keep oneself unspotted from the world. James 1:27, NKJV

Person or situation you are praying for:
Praises and promises:
Prayer:


## 5 August

*For thine is the kingdom and the power and the glory forever. Amen!*

When you pray, there is no need to repeat empty phrases, praying like those who don't know God, for they expect God to hear them because of their many words. There is no need to imitate them, since your Father already knows what you need before you ask him. Pray like this: *"Our Father, dwelling in the heavenly realms, may the glory of your name be the center on which our lives turn. Manifest your kingdom realm, and cause your every purpose to be fulfilled on earth, just as it is fulfilled in heaven. We acknowledge you as our Provider of all we need each day. Forgive us the wrongs we have done as we ourselves release forgiveness to those who have wronged us. Rescue us every time we face tribulation and set us free from evil. For you are the King who rules with power and glory forever. Amen."* And when you pray, make sure you forgive the faults of others so that your Father in heaven will also forgive you. But if you withhold forgiveness from others, your Father withholds forgiveness from you. Matthew 6:7–15, TPT

Person or situation you are praying for:
Praises and promises:
Prayer:


## 6 August

*Righteousness and justice are the foundation of Your throne.*

It's not right to go easy on the guilty, or come down hard on the innocent. Proverbs 18:5, MSG

Person or situation you are praying for:
Praises and promises:
Prayer:

## 7 August
*Say a prayer for a country in distress.*

No more gloom for those who are in distress! Although the Lord greatly humbled the regions of Zebulun and Naphtali, he will one day bestow upon them great honor, from the Mediterranean eastward to the other side of the Jordan and throughout the Galilee of the gentiles. Those who walked in darkness have seen a radiant light shining upon them. They once lived in the shadows of death, but now a glorious light has dawned! Lord, you have multiplied the nation and given them overwhelming joy! They are ecstatic in your presence and rejoice like those who bring in a great harvest and those who divide up the spoils of victory! For you have broken the chains that have bound your people and lifted off the heavy bar across their shoulders, the rod the oppressor used against them. You have shattered all their bondage, just as you did when Midian's armies were defeated. Every boot of marching troops and every uniform caked with blood will be burned as fuel for the fire. Isaiah 9:1–12, TPT

Person or situation you are praying for:
Praises and promises:
Prayer:

## 8 August
*Avoid false asceticism.*

Now the Spirit expressly says that in later times some will depart from the faith by giving heed to deceitful spirits and doctrines of demons, through the pretensions of liars whose consciences are seared, who forbid marriage and enjoin abstinence from foods which God created to be received with thanksgiving by those who believe and know the truth. For everything created by God is good, and nothing is to be rejected if it is received with thanksgiving; for then it is consecrated by the word of God and prayer. 1 Timothy 4:1–5, RSV

Person or situation you are praying for:
Praises and promises:
Prayer:

## 9 August
*Pray for people and countries who worship idols.*

My little children, keep away from idols. 1 John 5:21, VOICE

Person or situation you are praying for:
Praises and promises:
Prayer:

## 10 August
### Pray for people living in prosperous and affluent countries.

To all the rich of this world, I command you not to be wrapped in thoughts of pride over your prosperity, or rely on your wealth, for your riches are unreliable and nothing compared to the living God. Trust instead in the one who has lavished upon us all good things, fulfilling our every need. Remind the wealthy to be rich in good works of extravagant generosity, willing to share with others. This will provide a beautiful foundation for their lives and secure for them a great future, as they lay their hands upon the meaning of true life. So, my son Timothy, don't forget all that has been deposited within you. Escape from the empty echoes of men and the perversion of twisted reasoning. For those who claim to possess this so-called knowledge have already wandered from the true faith. May God's grace empower you always! Love in Christ, Paul. 1 Timothy 6:17–21, TPT

Person or situation you are praying for:
Praises and promises:
Prayer:

## 11 August
### Pray for those who are worldly to reject slavery to evil and accept freedom in Christ.

Now I'm sure of this: the sufferings we endure now are not even worth comparing to the glory that is coming and will be revealed in us. For all of creation is waiting, yearning for the time when the children of God will be revealed. You see, all of creation has collapsed into emptiness, not by its own choosing, but by God's. Still He placed within it a deep and abiding hope that creation would one day be liberated from its slavery to corruption and experience the glorious freedom of the children of God. For we know that all creation groans in unison with birthing pains up until now. Romans 8:18–22, VOICE

Person or situation you are praying for:
Praises and promises:
Prayer:

## 12 August
### Pray the rich and poor will find common ground and get to know the Lord.

Respect everyone. Love the community of believers. Reverence God. Honor your ruler. Proverbs 22:2, RSV

Person or situation you are praying for:
Praises and promises:
Prayer:

## 13 August

*Pray for countries experiencing natural disasters.*

God is our refuge and strength, a very present help in trouble. Therefore we will not fear though the earth gives way, though the mountains be moved into the heart of the sea, though its waters roar and foam, though the mountains tremble at its swelling. Selah. There is a river whose streams make glad the city of God, the holy habitation of the Most High. God is in the midst of her; she shall not be moved; God will help her when morning dawns. The nations rage, the kingdoms totter; he utters his voice, the earth melts. The LORD of hosts is with us; the God of Jacob is our fortress. Selah Come, behold the works of the LORD, how he has brought desolations on the earth. He makes wars cease to the end of the earth; he breaks the bow and shatters the spear; he burns the chariots with fire. "Be still, and know that I am God. I will be exalted among the nations, I will be exalted in the earth!" Psalm 46:1–10, ESV

Person or situation you are praying for:
Praises and promises:
Prayer:


## 14 August

*Pray against modern materialism.*

What good comes to anyone who works so hard, all to gain a few possessions? I have seen the kinds of tasks God has given each of us to do to keep one busy, and I know God has made everything beautiful for its time. God has also placed in our minds a sense of eternity; we look back on the past and ponder over the future, yet we cannot understand the doings of God. I know there is nothing better for us than to be joyful and to do good throughout our lives; to eat and drink and see the good in all of our hard work is a gift from God. I know everything God does endures for all time. Nothing can be added to it; nothing can be taken away from it. We humans can only stand in awe of all God has done. What has been and what is to be, already is. And God holds accountable all the pursuits of humanity. Ecclesiastes 3:9–15, VOICE

Person or situation you are praying for:
Praises and promises:
Prayer:

# 15 August
## Do not squander God's resources He has loaned to you.

And he also said to the disciples, "A certain man was rich, who had a manager. And charges were brought to him that this person was squandering his possessions. And he summoned him and said to him, 'What is this I hear about you? Give the account of your management, because you can no longer manage.' And the manager said to himself, 'What should I do, because my master is taking away the management from me? I am not strong enough to dig; I am ashamed to beg. I know what I should do, so that when I am removed from the management they will welcome me into their homes!'

And he summoned each one of his own master's debtors and said to the first, 'How much do you owe my master?' And he said, 'A hundred measures of olive oil.' So he said to him, 'Take your promissory note and sit down quickly and write fifty.' Then he said to another, 'And how much do you owe?' And he said, 'A hundred measures of wheat.' He said to him, 'Take your promissory note and write eighty.' And the master praised the dishonest manager, because he had acted shrewdly. For the sons of this age are shrewder than the sons of light with regard to their own generation. And I tell you, make friends for yourselves by means of unrighteous wealth, so that when it runs out they will welcome you into the eternal dwellings.

The one who is faithful in very little is also faithful in much, and the one who is dishonest in very little is also dishonest in much. If then you have not been faithful with unrighteous wealth, who will entrust to you the true riches? And if you have not been faithful with what belongs to another, who will give you your own?

No domestic slave is able to serve two masters, for either he will hate the one and love the other, or he will be devoted to one and will despise the other. You are not able to serve God and money." Now the Pharisees, who were lovers of money, heard all these things, and they ridiculed him. And he said to them, "You are the ones who justify themselves in the sight of men, but God knows your hearts! For what is considered exalted among men is an abomination in the sight of God." Luke 16:1–15, LEB

Person or situation you are praying for:
Praises and promises:
Prayer:

## 16 August
### Pray for generational purity and fidelity.

But you were afraid of the fire and wouldn't go up the mountain, so I stood between you and the Eternal and told you what He was saying. Eternal One (speaking to the people of Israel through Moses): I am the Eternal. I am your True God. I led you out of Egypt where you were slaves. You are to worship no other gods before me—My presence is enough. You are not to make idols of anything in the sky above or on the earth below or down in the sea. You are not to bow down in worship of any images of other gods, for I am the Eternal your God. I am jealous for worship, bringing punishment on you and your children to come, even down to your great-grandchildren, to whoever hates Me. Instead, those who obey My commands and truly love Me will receive My loyal love endlessly, even for a thousand generations. Deuteronomy 5:5–10, VOICE

Person or situation you are praying for:
Praises and promises:
Prayer:


## 17 August
### Cooperate with God and your latter days may be better than your beginnings.

Then the LORD answered Job out of the whirlwind, and said: "Where were you when I laid the foundations of the earth? Tell Me, if you have understanding. Who determined its measurements? Surely you know! Or who stretched the line upon it? To what were its foundations fastened? Or who laid its cornerstone, when the morning stars sang together, and all the sons of God shouted for joy? "Shall the one who contends with the Almighty correct Him? He who rebukes God, let him answer it." Then Job answered the LORD and said: "I know that You can do everything, and that no purpose of Yours can be withheld from You. You asked, 'Who is this who hides counsel without knowledge?' Therefore, I have uttered what I did not understand, things too wonderful for me, which I did not know. Listen, please, and let me speak; you said, 'I will question you, and you shall answer Me.' "I have heard of You by the hearing of the ear, but now my eye sees you. Therefore, I abhor myself, and repent in dust and ashes." Now the LORD blessed the latter days of Job more than his beginning. After this Job lived one hundred and forty years, and saw his children and grandchildren for four generations. So Job died, old and full of days. Job 38:1, 4–7; 40:2; 42:1–6; 42:12; 42:16, 17, NKJV

Person or situation you are praying for:
Praises and promises:
Prayer:

## 18 August
### Revenge belongs to the Lord.

Beloved, don't be obsessed with taking revenge, but leave that to God's righteous justice. For the Scriptures say: "If you don't take justice in your own hands, I will release justice for you," says the Lord. Romans 12:19, TPT

Person or situation you are praying for:
Praises and promises:
Prayer:

## 19 August
### Pray to be part of a society that honors God in all its ways.

Solomon completed building The Temple of GOD and the royal palace—the projects he had set his heart on doing. Everything was done—success! Satisfaction!

GOD appeared to Solomon that very night and said, "I accept your prayer; yes, I have chosen this place as a temple for sacrifice, a house of worship. If I ever shut off the supply of rain from the skies or order the locusts to eat the crops or send a plague on my people, and my people, my God-defined people, respond by humbling themselves, praying, seeking my presence, and turning their backs on their wicked lives, I'll be there ready for you: I'll listen from heaven, forgive their sins, and restore their land to health. From now on I'm alert day and night to the prayers offered at this place. Believe me, I've chosen and sanctified this Temple that you have built: My Name is stamped on it forever; my eyes are on it and my heart in it always. As for you, if you live in my presence as your father David lived, pure in heart and action, living the life I've set out for you, attentively obedient to my guidance and judgments, then I'll back your kingly rule over Israel—make it a sure thing on a sure foundation.

"The same covenant guarantee I gave to David your father I'm giving to you, namely, 'You can count on always having a descendant on Israel's throne.' But if you or your sons betray me, ignoring my guidance and judgments, taking up with alien gods by serving and worshipping them, then the guarantee is off: I'll wipe Israel right off the map and repudiate this Temple I've just sanctified to honor my Name. And Israel will be nothing but a bad joke among the peoples of the world. And this Temple, splendid as it now is, will become an object of contempt; tourists will shake their heads, saying, 'What happened here? What's the story behind these ruins?' Then they'll be told, 'The people who used to live here betrayed their GOD, the very God who rescued their ancestors from Egypt; they took up with alien gods, worshipping and serving them. That's what's behind this God visited devastation.' " 2 Chronicles 7:11–22, MSG

Person or situation you are praying for:
Praises and promises:
Prayer:

## 20 August

*Pray for those without a knowledge of God to fully understand His intentions for us as individuals and for this world.*

Good people, cheer GOD! Right-living people sound best when praising. Use guitars to reinforce your Hallelujahs! Play his praise on a grand piano! Invent your own new song to him; give him a trumpet fanfare. For GOD's Word is solid to the core; everything he makes is sound inside and out. He loves it when everything fits, when his world is in plumb-line true. Earth is drenched in GOD's affectionate satisfaction. The skies were made by GOD's command; he breathed the word and the stars popped out. He scooped Sea into his jug, put Ocean in his keg. Earth-creatures, bow before GOD; world-dwellers — down on your knees! Here's why: he spoke and there it was, in place the moment he said so. GOD takes the wind out of Babel pretense, he shoots down the world's power-schemes. GOD's plan for the world stands up, all his designs are made to last. Blessed is the country with GOD for God; blessed are the people he has put in his will. Psalm 33:1–12, MSG

Person or situation you are praying for:
Praises and promises:
Prayer:

## 21 August

*Pray for those living in the world and apart from God to come to know their Savior and Creator.*

The God who made the world and everything in it, this Master of sky and land, doesn't live in custom-made shrines or need the human race to run errands for him, as if he couldn't take care of himself. He makes the creatures; the creatures don't make him. Starting from scratch, he made the entire human race and made the earth hospitable, with plenty of time and space for living so we could seek after God, and not just grope around in the dark but actually find him. He doesn't play hide-and-seek with us. He's not remote; he's near. We live and move in him, can't get away from him! One of your poets said it well: "We're the God-created." Well, if we are the God-created, it doesn't make a lot of sense to think we could hire a sculptor to chisel a god out of stone for us, does it? Acts 17:24–29, MSG

Person or situation you are praying for:
Praises and promises:
Prayer:

## 22 August
### Very soon, we "ain't gonna study war no more."

The Message Isaiah got regarding Judah and Jerusalem: There's a day coming when the mountain of GOD's House Will be The Mountain—solid, towering over all mountains. All nations will river toward it, people from all over set out for it. They'll say, "Come, let's climb GOD's Mountain, go to the House of the God of Jacob. He'll show us the way he works so we can live the way we're made." Zion's the source of the revelation. GOD's Message comes from Jerusalem. He'll settle things fairly between nations. He'll make things right between many peoples. They'll turn their swords into shovels, their spears into hoes. No more will nation fight nation; they won't play war anymore. Come, family of Jacob, let's live in the light of GOD. Isaiah 2:1–5, MSG

Person or situation you are praying for:
Praises and promises:
Prayer:

## 23 August
### Healing of the nations occurs in heaven.

Then the Angel showed me Water-of-Life River, crystal bright. It flowed from the Throne of God and the Lamb, right down the middle of the street. The Tree of Life was planted on each side of the River, producing twelve kinds of fruit, a ripe fruit each month. The leaves of the Tree are for healing the nations. Never again will anything be cursed. The Throne of God and of the Lamb is at the center. His servants will offer God service—worshipping, they'll look on his face, their foreheads mirroring God. Never again will there be any night. No one will need lamplight or sunlight. The shining of God, the Master, is all the light anyone needs. And they will rule with him age after age after age. Revelation 22:1–5, MSG

Person or situation you are praying for:
Praises and promises:
Prayer:

## 24 August
### God knows our heart and motives.

It's as easy for God to steer a king's heart for his purposes as it is for him to direct the course of a stream. You may think you're right all the time, but God thoroughly examines our motives. It pleases God more when we demonstrate godliness and justice than when we merely offer him a sacrifice. Arrogance, superiority, and pride are the fruits of wickedness and the true definition of sin. Brilliant ideas pay off and bring you prosperity, but making hasty, impatient decisions will only lead to financial loss. You can make a fortune dishonestly, but your crime will hold you in the snares of death! Violent rebels don't have a chance, for their rejection of truth and their love of evil will drag them deeper into darkness. You can discern that a person is guilty by his devious actions and the innocence of a person by his honest, sincere ways.  Proverbs 21:1–8, TPT

Person or situation you are praying for:
Praises and promises:
Prayer:

## 25 August
### The world operates at the mercy and generosity of God.
### God is not the author of evil but He allows Satan free reign over the earth to fully demonstrate the extent of Satan's evil works.
### God allows this to occur to fully illustrate the great controversy that will one day be resolved when Christ returns and Satan is vanquished.

To God belong wisdom and power; counsel and understanding are his. What he tears down cannot be rebuilt; those he imprisons cannot be released. If he holds back the waters, there is drought; if he lets them loose, they devastate the land. To him belong strength and insight; both deceived and deceiver are his. He leads rulers away stripped and makes fools of judges. He takes off the shackles put on by kings and ties a loincloth around their waist. He leads priests away stripped and overthrows officials long established. He silences the lips of trusted advisers and takes away the discernment of elders. He pours contempt on nobles and disarms the mighty. He reveals the deep things of darkness and brings utter darkness into the light. He makes nations great, and destroys them; he enlarges nations, and disperses them. He deprives the leaders of the earth of their reason; he makes them wander in a trackless waste. They grope in darkness with no light; he makes them stagger like drunkards. Job 12:13–25, NIV

Person or situation you are praying for:
Praises and promises:
Prayer:

## 26 August
### Christ has set us free!

But if you bite each other and devour each other, watch out! You may end up being destroyed by each other. Let me say this to you: live by the spirit, and you won't do what the flesh wants you to. For the flesh wants to go against the spirit, and the spirit against the flesh. They are opposed to each other, so that you can't do what you want. But if you are led by the spirit, you are not under the law. Now the works of the flesh are obvious. They are such things as fornication, uncleanness, licentiousness, idolatry, sorcery, hostilities, strife, jealousy, bursts of rage, selfish ambition, factiousness, divisions, moods of envy, drunkenness, wild partying, and similar things. I told you before, and I tell you again: people who do such things will not inherit God's kingdom. Fruit of the Spirit but the fruit of the spirit is love, joy, peace, great-heartedness, kindness, generosity, faithfulness, gentleness, self-control. There is no law that opposes things like that! Galatians 5:15–23, NTE

Person or situation you are praying for:
Praises and promises:
Prayer:

## 27 August
### Demanding and self-righteous behaviors are not compatible with being part of Christ's kingdom.

Your attitude should be the kind that was shown us by Jesus Christ, who, though he was God, did not demand and cling to his rights as God, but laid aside his mighty power and glory, taking the disguise of a slave and becoming like men. And he humbled himself even further, going so far as actually to die a criminal's death on a cross. Yet it was because of this that God raised him up to the heights of heaven and gave him a name which is above every other name, that at the name of Jesus every knee shall bow in heaven and on earth and under the earth, and every tongue shall confess that Jesus Christ is Lord, to the glory of God the Father. Philippians 2:5–11, TLB

Person or situation you are praying for:
Praises and promises:
Prayer:

## 28 August
### Sleep easy tonight—you belong to the Lord.

But now the Lord who created you, O Israel, says: Don't be afraid, for I have ransomed you; I have called you by name; you are mine. When you go through deep waters and great trouble, I will be with you. When you go through rivers of difficulty, you will not drown! When you walk through the fire of oppression, you will not be burned up—the flames will not consume you. For I am the Lord your God, your Savior, the Holy One of Israel. I gave Egypt and Ethiopia and Seba to Cyrus in exchange for your freedom, as your ransom. Others died that you might live; I traded their lives for yours because you are precious to me and honored, and I love you. Don't be afraid, for I am with you. I will gather you from east and west, from north and south. I will bring my sons and daughters back to Israel from the farthest corners of the earth. All who claim me as their God will come, for I have made them for my glory; I created them. Bring them back to me—blind as they are and deaf when I call (although they see and hear!). Gather the nations together! Which of all their idols ever has foretold such things? Which can predict a single day ahead? Where are the witnesses of anything they said? If there are no witnesses, then they must confess that only God can prophesy. But I have witnesses, O Israel, says the Lord! You are my witnesses and my servants, chosen to know and to believe me and to understand that I alone am God. There is no other God; there never was and never will be. I am the Lord, and there is no other Savior. Whenever you have thrown away your idols, I have shown you my power. With one word I have saved you. You have seen me do it; you are my witnesses that it is true. From eternity to eternity I am God. No one can oppose what I do.
Isaiah 43:1–13, TLB

Person or situation you are praying for:
Praises and promises:
Prayer:

## 29 August
### Wisdom is to know God.

The starting point for acquiring wisdom is to be consumed with awe as you worship Jehovah-God. To receive the revelation of the Holy One, you must come to the one who has living-understanding. Proverbs 9:10, TPT

Person or situation you are praying for:
Praises and promises:
Prayer:

## 30 August
### The Stone rejected by men has redeemed man!

So keep coming to him who is the Living Stone—though he was rejected and discarded by men but chosen by God and is priceless in God's sight. Come and be his "living stones" who are continually being assembled into a sanctuary for God. For now you serve as holy priests, offering up spiritual sacrifices that he readily accepts through Jesus Christ. For it says in Scripture: Look! I lay a cornerstone in Zion, a chosen and priceless stone! And whoever believes in him will certainly not be disappointed. As believers you know his great worth—indeed, his preciousness is imparted to you. But for those who do not believe: The stone that the builders rejected and discarded has now become the cornerstone and a stone that makes them stumble and a rock to trip over. They keep stumbling over the message because they refuse to believe it. And this they were destined to do. 1 Peter 2:4–8, TPT

Person or situation you are praying for:
Praises and promises:
Prayer:


## 31 August
### The greatest conspiracy theory ever – the history of the world in one dream, interpreted by one man who served under four kings!

Then Daniel went to his house and told his friends, Hananiah, Mishael and Azariah, what had happened. He told them to ask for loving-pity from the God of heaven about this secret, so that Daniel and his friends might not be killed with the other wise men of Babylon. Then the secret was made known to Daniel in a special dream during the night. He gave honor and thanks to the God of heaven. Daniel said, "Let the name of God be honored forever and ever, for wisdom and power belong to Him. He changes the times and the years. He takes kings away, and puts kings in power. He gives wisdom to wise men and much learning to men of understanding. He makes known secret and hidden things. He knows what is in the darkness. Light is with Him. I give thanks and praise to You, O God of my fathers. For You have given me wisdom and power. Even now You have made known what we asked of You. You have made the king's dream known to us." Daniel 2:17–23, NLV

Person or situation you are praying for:
Praises and promises:
Prayer:

# August Epilogue

A written epilogue, is a way of rounding out a literary work, bringing closure, or summarizing the final scene of a dramatic play. In this case, it is a summary of your prayer life and walk with God during the month of August. This page is for you to record your comments and write one or two summary statements as you have prayed for world leaders.

Praying for someone you will most likely never meet or personally know can be a cold and seemingly thankless task. However, we may never understand how our prayers have impacted strangers until we get to heaven. As of 2024, there are 195 countries in the world. This means there are 195 heads of state and thousands of others in support of these world leaders. Many are corrupt. Most are complicit in wars for profit. However, if we understand what we read in the Bible, specifically in the book of Daniel, we see it is God who... *'changes times and seasons; he deposes kings and raises up others. He gives wisdom to the wise and knowledge to the discerning.'* Daniel 2:21.

So, it seems if God is setting up our political leaders, the least we can do is to pray for them. While it may seem like an exercise in futility, prayer potentially changes the vessel praying as much as it changes the subject of the praying person. Praying for world leaders means you will spend time learning about them, their families, their issues, etc. It means you may learn about a 'wild tinpot president' in Africa who is fighting to preserve Christian values and has lost 9 members of his family defending the faith. If you do a search using the term, 'political leaders who need prayer' you will come up with some very interesting web pages.

If you have prayed for world leaders for the past month, you have broadened your perspective. You have learned about brave men and women who are in power only because God has placed them in their powerful positions. They lead for a time and then someone else rises. This is much like what is described in the Old Testament. This leader was a good king or this king did bad in the sight of God. So, there is nothing new under the sun except that you are a praying person who has decided to participate with God in deposing and raising up political leaders. Never underestimate your sincere prayers on the behalf of strangers and especially on behalf of the world's political leaders.

_____

_____

# September

## Pray for missionaries.

Care for the most helpless and vulnerable in society and you will be ministering to Christ. No one can match the wisdom of a spirit-led disciple of Christ. Actions and faith are connected. Young age is not an exemption from doing God's work. Hold nothing back in proclaiming God's Word.

Never fear when you are on a mission from God. Pray for missionaries to stay connected to the Source. Go ye into the world, baptize the people and set them free. Keep the faith, pray together, believe only in God. Don't be afraid to share your faith with a stranger. Fearlessly preach the word of God. It is God who ordains your work, not men. Live a holy life. In quietness, confidence, and faithfulness—wait upon the Lord.

# September Ideas

Pray for the fruitfulness of missionary work.
Pray each missionary is daily encouraged and uplifted.
Pray each missionary remains pure and steadfast in their faith.
Pray each missionary is protected from the weapons of the evil one.
Pray each missionary finds meaning in their daily trials and tribulations.
Pray the missionaries will be gifted with endurance and strength while in God's service.

1. _____
2. _____
3. _____
4. _____
5. _____
6. _____
7. _____
8. _____
9. _____
10. _____

19.
20.
21.
22.
23.
24.
25.

Pray for missionaries.

28.

## 1 September
*In quietness, confidence, and faithfulness—wait upon the Lord.*

For thus saith the Lord GOD, the Holy One of Israel; In returning and rest shall ye be saved; in quietness and in confidence shall be your strength: and ye would not. But ye said, No; for we will flee upon horses; therefore shall ye flee: and, We will ride upon the swift; therefore shall they that pursue you be swift. One thousand shall flee at the rebuke of one; at the rebuke of five shall ye flee: till ye be left as a beacon upon the top of a mountain, and as an ensign on an hill. And therefore will the LORD wait, that he may be gracious unto you, and therefore will he be exalted, that he may have mercy upon you: for the LORD is a God of judgment: blessed are all they that wait for him. Isaiah 30:15–18, KJV

Person or situation you are praying for:
Praises and promises:
Prayer:

## 2 September
*Live a holy life.*

Therefore, prepare your minds for action, keep a clear head, and set your hope completely on the grace to be given you when Jesus, the Messiah, is revealed. As obedient children, do not be shaped by the desires that used to influence you when you were ignorant. Instead, be holy in every aspect of your life, just as the one who called you is holy. For it is written, "You must be holy, because I am holy." 1 Peter 1:13–16, ISV

Person or situation you are praying for:
Praises and promises:
Prayer:

## 3 September
*Christ, not me.*

We don't preach ourselves, but rather the lordship of Jesus Christ, for we are your servants for Jesus's sake. For God, who said, "Let brilliant light shine out of darkness," is the one who has cascaded his light into us—the brilliant dawning light of the glorious knowledge of God as we gaze into the face of Jesus Christ. 2 Corinthians 4:5, 6, TPT

Person or situation you are praying for:
Praises and promises:
Prayer:

# 4 September
## Never fear when you are on a mission for God.

When the king of Aram was at war with Israel, he would confer with his officers and say, "We will mobilize our forces at such and such a place." But immediately Elisha, the man of God, would warn the king of Israel, "Do not go near that place, for the Arameans are planning to mobilize their troops there." So the king of Israel would send word to the place indicated by the man of God. Time and again Elisha warned the king, so that he would be on the alert there.

The king of Aram became very upset over this. He called his officers together and demanded, "Which of you is the traitor? Who has been informing the king of Israel of my plans?" "It's not us, my lord the king," one of the officers replied. "Elisha, the prophet in Israel, tells the king of Israel even the words you speak in the privacy of your bedroom!"

"Go and find out where he is," the king commanded, "so I can send troops to seize him." And the report came back: "Elisha is at Dothan." So one night the king of Aram sent a great army with many chariots and horses to surround the city. When the servant of the man of God got up early the next morning and went outside, there were troops, horses, and chariots everywhere. "Oh, sir, what will we do now?" the young man cried to Elisha. "Don't be afraid!" Elisha told him. "For there are more on our side than on theirs!" Then Elisha prayed, "O LORD, open his eyes and let him see!" The LORD opened the young man's eyes, and when he looked up, he saw that the hillside around Elisha was filled with horses and chariots of fire. As the Aramean army advanced toward him, Elisha prayed, "O LORD, please make them blind." So the LORD struck them with blindness as Elisha had asked. Then Elisha went out and told them, "You have come the wrong way! This isn't the right city! Follow me, and I will take you to the man you are looking for." And he led them to the city of Samaria.

As soon as they had entered Samaria, Elisha prayed, "O LORD, now open their eyes and let them see." So the LORD opened their eyes, and they discovered that they were in the middle of Samaria. When the king of Israel saw them, he shouted to Elisha, "My father, should I kill them? Should I kill them?" "Of course not!" Elisha replied. "Do we kill prisoners of war? Give them food and drink and send them home again to their master." So the king made a great feast for them and then sent them home to their master. After that, the Aramean raiders stayed away from the land of Israel. 2 Kings 6:8–23, NLT

Person or situation you are praying for:
Praises and promises:
Prayer:

## 5 September
### Be as shrewd as a snake and as harmless as a dove.

Jesus commissioned these twelve to go out into the ripened harvest fields with these instructions: "Don't go into any non-Jewish or Samaritan territory. Go instead and find the lost sheep among the people of Israel. And as you go, preach this message: 'Heaven's kingdom realm is accessible, close enough to touch.' You must continually bring healing to lepers and to those who are sick, and make it your habit to break off the demonic presence from people, and raise the dead back to life. Freely you have received the power of the kingdom, so freely release it to others. You won't need a lot of money. Travel light, and don't even pack an extra change of clothes in your backpack. Trust God for everything, because the one who works for him deserves to be provided for.

"Whatever village or town you enter, search for a godly man who will let you into his home until you leave for the next town. Once you enter a house, speak to the family there and say, 'God's blessing of peace be upon this house!' And if those living there welcome you, let your peace come upon the house. But if you are rejected, that blessing of peace will come back upon you. And if anyone doesn't listen to you and rejects your message, when you leave that house or town, shake the dust off your feet as a prophetic act that you will not take their defilement with you. Mark my words, on the day of judgment the wicked people who lived in the land of Sodom and Gomorrah will have a lesser degree of judgment than the city that rejects you, for the people of Sodom and Gomorrah did not have the opportunity that was given to them! Now, remember, it is I who sends you out, even though you feel vulnerable as lambs going into a pack of wolves. So be as shrewd as snakes yet as harmless as doves."
Matthew 10:5–16, TPT

Person or situation you are praying for:
Praises and promises:
Prayer:

## 6 September
### Leave behind your old self for a new self in Christ.

So abandon every form of evil, deceit, hypocrisy, feelings of jealousy and slander. 1 Peter 2:1, TPT

Person or situation you are praying for:
Praises and promises:
Prayer:

## 7 September

*Young age is not an exemption from doing God's work.*

Now the word of the LORD came to me saying, "Before I formed you in the womb I knew you, and before you were born I consecrated you; I appointed you a prophet to the nations." Then I said, "Ah, Lord GOD! Behold, I do not know how to speak, for I am only a youth." But the LORD said to me, "Do not say, 'I am only a youth'; for to all to whom I send you you shall go, and whatever I command you you shall speak. Be not afraid of them, for I am with you to deliver you, says the LORD." Then the LORD put forth his hand and touched my mouth; and the LORD said to me, "Behold, I have put my words in your mouth. See, I have set you this day over nations and over kingdoms, to pluck up and to break down, to destroy and to overthrow, to build and to plant." And the word of the LORD came to me, saying, "Jeremiah, what do you see?" And I said, "I see a rod of almond." Then the LORD said to me, "You have seen well, for I am watching over my word to perform it." The word of the Lord came to me a second time, saying, "What do you see?" And I said, "I see a boiling pot, facing away from the north." Then the LORD said to me, "Out of the north evil shall break forth upon all the inhabitants of the land. For lo, I am calling all the tribes of the kingdoms of the north, says the LORD; and they shall come and every one shall set his throne at the entrance of the gates of Jerusalem, against all its walls round about, and against all the cities of Judah. And I will utter my judgments against them, for all their wickedness in forsaking me; they have burned incense to other gods, and worshiped the works of their own hands. But you, gird up your loins; arise, and say to them everything that I command you. Do not be dismayed by them, lest I dismay you before them. And I, behold, I make you this day a fortified city, an iron pillar, and bronze walls, against the whole land, against the kings of Judah, its princes, its priests, and the people of the land. They will fight against you; but they shall not prevail against you, for I am with you, says the LORD, to deliver you." Jeremiah 1:4–19, RSV

Person or situation you are praying for:
Praises and promises:
Prayer:

## 8 September

*Actions and faith are connected.*

But how are men to call upon him in whom they have not believed? And how are they to believe in him of whom they have never heard? And how are they to hear without a preacher? And how can men preach unless they are sent? As it is written, "How beautiful are the feet of those who preach good news!" But they have not all obeyed the gospel; for Isaiah says, "Lord, who has believed what he has heard from us?" So faith comes from what is heard, and what is heard comes by the preaching of Christ. Romans 10:14–17, RSV

Person or situation you are praying for:
Praises and promises:

Prayer:

## 9 September
*Preach the gospel in Christ and not what is convenient.*

Timothy, in the presence of our great God and our Lord Jesus Christ, the One who is destined to judge both the living and the dead by the revelation of his kingdom—I solemnly instruct you to proclaim the Word of God and stand upon it no matter what! Rise to the occasion and preach when it is convenient and when it is not. Preach in the full expression of the Holy Spirit—with wisdom and patience as you instruct and teach the people. For the time is coming when they will no longer listen and respond to the healing words of truth because they will become selfish and proud. They will seek out teachers with soothing words that line up with their desires, saying just what they want to hear. They will close their ears to the truth and believe nothing but fables and myths. So be alert to all these things and overcome every form of evil. Carry in your heart the passion of your calling as a church planter and evangelist, and fulfill your ministry calling. 2 Timothy 4:1–5, TPT

Person or situation you are praying for:
Praises and promises:
Prayer:

## 10 September
*Care for the helpless and vulnerable in society and you will be ministering to Christ.*

" 'For when you saw me hungry, you fed me. When you found me thirsty, you gave me something to drink. When I had no place to stay, you invited me in, and when I was poorly clothed, you covered me. When I was sick, you tenderly cared for me, and when I was in prison you visited me.' Then the godly will answer him, 'Lord, when did we see you hungry or thirsty and give you food and something to drink? When did we see you with no place to stay and invite you in? When did we see you poorly clothed and cover you? When did we see you sick and tenderly care for you, or in prison and visit you?' And the King will answer them, 'Don't you know? When you cared for one of the least important of these my little ones, my true brothers and sisters, you demonstrated love for me.' " Matthew 25:35–40, TPT

Person or situation you are praying for:
Praises and promises:
Prayer:

## 11 September
### Hold nothing back in proclaiming God's Word.

I've been a part of your lives and shared with you many times the message of God's kingdom realm. But now I leave you, and you will not see my face again. If any of you should be lost, I will not be blamed, for my conscience is clean, because I've taught you everything I could about God's eternal plan and I've held nothing back. So guard your hearts. Be true shepherds over all the flock and feed them well. Remember, it was the Holy Spirit who appointed you to guard and oversee the churches that belong to Jesus, the Anointed One, which he purchased and established by his own blood. Acts 28:25–28, TPT

Person or situation you are praying for:
Praises and promises:
Prayer:

## 12 September
### God comes to our rescue!

When we suffer for Jesus, it works out for your healing and salvation. If we are treated well, given a helping hand and encouraging word, that also works to your benefit, spurring you on, face forward, unflinching. Your hard times are also our hard times. When we see that you're just as willing to endure the hard times as to enjoy the good times, we know you're going to make it, no doubt about it. We don't want you in the dark, friends, about how hard it was when all this came down on us in Asia province. It was so bad we didn't think we were going to make it. We felt like we'd been sent to death row, that it was all over for us. As it turned out, it was the best thing that could have happened. Instead of trusting in our own strength or wits to get out of it, we were forced to trust God totally—not a bad idea since he's the God who raises the dead! And he did it, rescued us from certain doom. And he'll do it again, rescuing us as many times as we need rescuing. You and your prayers are part of the rescue operation—I don't want you in the dark about that either. I can see your faces even now, lifted in praise for God's deliverance of us, a rescue in which your prayers played such a crucial part. Now that the worst is over, we're pleased we can report that we've come out of this with conscience and faith intact, and can face the world—and even more importantly, face you with our heads held high. But it wasn't by any fancy footwork on our part. It was God who kept us focused on him, uncompromised. Don't try to read between the lines or look for hidden meanings in this letter. We're writing plain, unembellished truth, hoping that you'll now see the whole picture as well as you've seen some of the details. We want you to be as proud of us as we are of you when we stand together before our Master Jesus. 2 Corinthians 1:6–14, MSG

Person or situation you are praying for:
Praises and promises:
Prayer:

## 13 September
*God is not the author of confusion, illusion, murkiness, and tumult.*

The Anarchist's coming is all Satan's work. All his power and signs and miracles are fake, evil sleight of hand that plays to the gallery of those who hate the truth that could save them. And since they're so obsessed with evil, God rubs their noses in it—gives them what they want. Since they refuse to trust truth, they're banished to their chosen world of lies and illusions. Meanwhile, we've got our hands full continually thanking God for you, our good friends—so loved by God! God picked you out as his from the very start. Think of it: included in God's original plan of salvation by the bond of faith in the living truth. This is the life of the Spirit he invited you to through the Message we delivered, in which you get in on the glory of our Master, Jesus Christ. So, friends, take a firm stand, feet on the ground and head high. Keep a tight grip on what you were taught, whether in personal conversation or by our letter. May Jesus himself and God our Father, who reached out in love and surprised you with gifts of unending help and confidence, put a fresh heart in you, invigorate your work, enliven your speech. 2 Thessalonians 2:9–17, MSG

Person or situation you are praying for:
Praises and promises:
Prayer:

## 14 September
*Do what pleases God and not your friends and family.*

Brothers and sisters, you yourselves know that our coming to you was not a waste of time. You remember how we had just suffered through brutal and insulting attacks in Philippi; but because of God, we boldly stepped into the open to tell you His good news, even though it would likely mean more conflict for us. For we haven't approached you—or anyone else for that matter—with some error or impure motives or deceitful agenda; but as we have been approved by God and entrusted with the good news, that's how we are telling the world. We aren't trying to please everybody, but God, the only One who can truly examine our motives. As you know, we didn't sandwich the truth between cunning compliments—we told it straight— and before the eye of God, we never conspired to make a single cent off of you. We didn't come seeking respect from people—not from you or anyone else—although we could have leveraged our position as emissaries[a] of the Anointed One, the Liberating King. Instead, we proved to be gentle among you, like a nursing mother caring for her own children. We were so taken by you that we not only eagerly shared with you God's good news, but we also shared with you our own lives. That's how much you've come to mean to us. 1 Thessalonians 2:1–8, VOICE

Person or situation you are praying for:
Praises and promises:
Prayer:

# 15 September

*There has never been anyone like Jesus Christ, the Conqueror, Counselor, Prince of Peace, Mighty God, Everlasting Father, Holy One, etc.*

John's disciples reported back to him the news of all these events taking place. He sent two of them to the Master to ask the question, "Are you the One we've been expecting, or are we still waiting?" The men showed up before Jesus and said, "John the Baptizer sent us to ask you, 'Are you the One we've been expecting, or are we still waiting?' "

In the next two or three hours, Jesus healed many from diseases, distress, and evil spirits. To many of the blind he gave the gift of sight. Then he gave his answer: "Go back and tell John what you have just seen and heard: The blind see, the lame walk, lepers are cleansed, the deaf hear, the dead are raised, the wretched of the earth have God's salvation hospitality extended to them. "Is this what you were expecting? Then count yourselves fortunate!"

After John's messengers left to make their report, Jesus said more about John to the crowd of people. "What did you expect when you went out to see him in the wild? A weekend camper? Hardly. What then? A sheik in silk pajamas? Not in the wilderness, not by a long shot. What then? A messenger from God? That's right, a messenger! Probably the greatest messenger you'll ever hear. He is the messenger Malachi announced when he wrote, I'm sending my messenger on ahead to make the road smooth for you. "Let me lay it out for you as plainly as I can: No one in history surpasses John the Baptizer, but in the kingdom he prepared you for, the lowliest person is ahead of him. The ordinary and disreputable people who heard John, by being baptized by him into the kingdom, are the clearest evidence; the Pharisees and religious officials would have nothing to do with such a baptism, wouldn't think of giving up their place in line to their inferiors. Luke 7:19–30, MSG

Person or situation you are praying for:
Praises and promises:
Prayer:

## 16 September
*No one can match the wisdom of a spirit-led disciple of Christ.*

Stephen, brimming with God's grace and energy, was doing wonderful things among the people, unmistakable signs that God was among them. But then some men from the meeting place whose membership was made up of freed slaves, Cyrenians, Alexandrians, and some others from Cilicia and Asia, went up against him trying to argue him down. But they were no match for his wisdom and spirit when he spoke. So in secret they bribed men to lie: "We heard him cursing Moses and God." That stirred up the people, the religious leaders, and religion scholars. They grabbed Stephen and took him before the High Council. They put forward their bribed witnesses to testify: "This man talks nonstop against this Holy Place and God's Law. We even heard him say that Jesus of Nazareth would tear this place down and throw out all the customs Moses gave us." As all those who sat on the High Council looked at Stephen, they found they couldn't take their eyes off him—his face was like the face of an angel! Acts 6:8–15, MSG

Person or situation you are praying for:
Praises and promises:
Prayer:

## 17 September
*No one is beyond the reach of Christ's saving grace.*

Young Saul went on a rampage—hunting the church, house after house, dragging both men and women to prison. All those who had been scattered by the persecution moved from place to place; and wherever they went, they weren't afraid or silent. Instead, they spread the message of Jesus. Philip, for example, headed north to the city of Samaria, and he told them the news of the Anointed One. The crowds were united in their desire to understand Philip's message. They not only listened with their ears, but they witnessed miraculous signs with their eyes. Unclean spirits cried out with loud screams as they were exorcised from people. Paralyzed people and lame people moved and walked in plain view. So the city was swept with joy. Acts 8:3–8, VOICE

Person or situation you are praying for:
Praises and promises:
Prayer:

# 18 September

*Men and women in Christ, baptize the repentant and welcome them into fellowship with Christ.*

After Peter and John had testified and taught the word of God in that city, they returned to Jerusalem, stopping at many Samaritan villages along the way to preach the hope of the gospel. Then the Lord's angel said to Philip, "Now go south from Jerusalem on the desert road to Gaza." He left immediately on his assignment.

Along the way he encountered an Ethiopian who believed in the God of the Jews, who was the minister of finance for Candace, queen of Ethiopia. He was on his way home from worshipping God in Jerusalem. As he rode along in his chariot, he was reading from the scroll of Isaiah. The Holy Spirit said to Philip, "Go and walk alongside the chariot." So Philip ran to catch up. As he drew closer he overheard the man reading from the scroll of Isaiah the prophet. Philip asked him, "Sir, do you understand what you're reading?" The man answered, "How can I possibly make sense of this without someone explaining it to me?" So he invited Philip up into his chariot to sit with him.

The portion from Isaiah he was reading was this: He was led away to the slaughter like a lamb to be offered. He was like a lamb that is silent before those who sheared him—he never even opened his mouth. In his lowliness justice was stripped away from him. And who could fully express his struggles? For his life was taken from the earth. The Ethiopian asked Philip, "Please, can you tell me who the prophet is speaking of? Is it himself or another man?" Philip started with this passage and shared with him the wonderful message of Jesus. As they were traveling down the road, the man said, "Look, here's a pool of water. Why don't I get baptized right now?" Philip replied, "If you believe with all your heart, I'll baptize you." The man answered, "I believe that Jesus is the Anointed One, the Son of God." The Ethiopian stopped his chariot, and they went down into the water and Philip baptized him. When they came up out of the water, Philip was suddenly snatched up by the Spirit of the Lord and instantly carried away to the city of Ashdod, where he reappeared, preaching the gospel in that city. The man never saw Philip again. He returned to Ethiopia full of great joy. Philip, however, traveled on to all of the towns of that region, bringing them the good news, until he arrived at Caesarea. Acts 8:25–40, TPT

Person or situation you are praying for:
Praises and promises:
Prayer:

## 19 September

*Avoid all forms of spiritual blindness, instead choosing life and light.*

So Saul and Barnabas, and their assistant Mark (known as John), were directed by the Holy Spirit to go to Seleucia, and from there they sailed to Cyprus. When they arrived at Salamis, they went to the synagogues and preached the manifestation of our Lord. From there they crossed the island as far as Paphos, where they encountered a Jewish false prophet, a sorcerer named Elymas, who also went by the name of "son of Jesus." He had gained influence as the spiritual advisor to the regional governor, Sergius Paulus, considered by many to be a wise and intelligent leader.

The governor requested a meeting with Barnabas and Saul because he wanted to hear the message of God's word. But Elymas, whose name means "sorcerer," stood up against them and tried to prevent the governor from believing their message. Saul, also known as Paul, stared into his eyes and rebuked him. Filled with the Holy Spirit, he said, "You son of the devil! You are full of every form of fraud and deceit and an enemy of all that is right. When will you stop perverting the truth of God into lies? At this very moment the hand of God's judgment comes down upon you and you will be blind — so blind you won't even be able to see the light of the sun." As Paul spoke these words, a shadowy mist and darkness came over the sorcerer, leaving him blind and groping about, begging someone to lead him around by the hand. When the governor witnessed this, he believed and was awestruck by the power of the message of the Lord. Acts 13:4–12, TPT

Person or situation you are praying for:
Praises and promises:
Prayer:

## 20 September

*Pray for missionaries, that they hear the guidance of the Lord and that He always guides their steps.*

The Holy Spirit had forbidden Paul and his partners to preach the word in the southwestern provinces of Turkey, so they ministered throughout the region of central and west-central Turkey. When they got as far west as the borders of Mysia, they repeatedly attempted to go north into the province of Bithynia, but again the Spirit of Jesus would not allow them to enter. So instead they went right on through the province of Mysia to the seaport of Troas. Acts 6:6–8, TPT

Person or situation you are praying for:
Praises and promises:
Prayer:

## 21 September
### Never take any glory for yourself.

In Lystra, Paul and Barnabas encountered a man who from birth had never walked, for he was crippled in his feet. He listened carefully to Paul as he preached. All of a sudden, Paul discerned that this man had faith in his heart to be healed. So he shouted, "You! In the name of our Lord Jesus, stand up on your feet!" The man instantly jumped to his feet, stood for the first time in his life, and walked! When the crowds saw the miracle Paul had done, they shouted in their own language, "The gods have come down to us as men!" They addressed Barnabas as "Zeus" and Paul as "Hermes," because he was the spokesman.

Now, outside of the city stood the temple of Zeus. The priest of the temple, in order to honor Paul and Barnabas, brought bulls with wreaths of flowers draped on them to the gates of the courtyard where they were staying. The crowds clamored to offer them as sacrifices to the apostles. He even brought flower wreaths as crowns to place on their heads. When the apostles understood what was happening, they were mortified and tore their clothes as a sign of dismay. They rushed into the crowd and shouted, "People, what are you doing? We're only weak human beings like everyone else. This is why we've come to tell you the good news, so that you would turn away from these worthless myths and turn to the living God. He is the Creator of all things: the earth, the heavens, the sea, and everything they contain. In previous generations he allowed the nations to pursue their own ways, yet he has never left himself without clear evidence of his goodness. For he blesses us with rain from heaven and seasons of fruitful harvests, and he nourishes us with food to meet our needs. He satisfies our lives, and euphoria fills our hearts." Even after saying these things, they were barely able to restrain the people from offering sacrifices to them. Acts 14:8–18, TPT

Person or situation you are praying for:
Praises and promises:
Prayer:

## 22 September
### Don't be afraid to share your faith with a stranger.

When the Sabbath day came, we went outside the gates of the city to the nearby river, for there appeared to be a house of prayer and worship there. Sitting on the riverbank we struck up a conversation with some of the women who had gathered there. One of them was Lydia, a business woman from the city of Thyatira who was a dealer of exquisite purple cloth and a Jewish convert. While Paul shared the good news with her, God opened her heart to receive Paul's message. She devoted herself to the Lord, and we baptized her and her entire family. Afterward she urged us to stay in her home, saying, "Since I am now a believer in the Lord, come and stay in my house." So we were persuaded to stay there. Acts 16:13–15, TPT

Person or situation you are praying for:
Praises and promises:
Prayer:

## 23 September
### Fearlessly preach the word of God.

For three months Paul taught openly and fearlessly in the synagogue, arguing persuasively for them to enter into God's kingdom realm. But some of them hardened their hearts and stubbornly refused to believe. When they spoke evil of the Way in front of the congregation, Paul withdrew from them and took the believers with him. Every day for over two years, he taught them in the lecture hall of Tyrannus, which resulted in everyone living in the province of Asia, Jews and non-Jews, hearing the prophetic word of the Lord. Acts 19:8–10, TPT

Person or situation you are praying for:
Praises and promises:
Prayer:

## 24 September
### Go ye into the world, baptize the people, and set them free.
### Keep the faith, pray together, believe only in God.

Meanwhile, the eleven disciples heard the wonderful news from the women and left for Galilee, to the mountain where Jesus had arranged to meet them. The moment they saw him, they worshiped him, but some still had lingering doubts. Then Jesus came close to them and said, "All the authority of the universe has been given to me. Now go in my authority and make disciples of all nations, baptizing them in the name of the Father, the Son, and the Holy Spirit. And teach them to faithfully follow all that I have commanded you. And never forget that I am with you every day, even to the completion of this age." Matthew 28:16–20, TPT

Person or situation you are praying for:
Praises and promises:
Prayer:

## 25 September
### God is for everyone.

After all, is God the God of the Jews only, or is he equally the God for all of humanity? Of course, he's the God of all people! Since there is only one God, he will treat us all the same—he eliminates our guilt and makes us right with him by faith no matter who we are. Does emphasizing our faith invalidate the law? Absolutely not. Instead, our faith establishes the role the law should rightfully have. Psalm 143:8, TPT

Person or situation you are praying for:
Praises and promises:
Prayer:

# 26 September

*In your mission work, be calm and don't cause undue commotion.*

At that time a major disturbance erupted in Ephesus over the people following God's way. It began with a wealthy man named Demetrius, who had built a large business and enriched many craftsmen by manufacturing silver shrines for the Greek goddess Artemis. Demetrius called a meeting of his employees, along with all the various tradespeople of Ephesus, and said, "You know that our prosperous livelihood is being threatened by this Paul, who is persuading crowds of people to turn away from our gods. We make a good living by doing what we do, but everywhere Paul goes, not only here in Ephesus but throughout western Turkey, he convinces people that there's no such thing as a god made with hands. Our businesses are in danger of being discredited. And not only that, but the temple of our great goddess Artemis is being dishonored and seen as worthless. She is the goddess of all of western Turkey and is worshiped in all the world. But if this outrage continues, everyone everywhere will suffer the loss of her magnificent greatness." When the people heard this, they were filled with boiling rage. They shouted over and over, "Artemis, the great goddess of the Ephesians!" The entire city was thrown into chaos as everyone rushed into the stadium together, dragging with them Gaius and Aristarchus, Paul's traveling companions from Macedonia. When Paul attempted to go in and speak to the massive crowd, the disciples wouldn't let him. Some of the high-ranking governmental officials of the region, because they loved him, sent Paul an urgent message, saying, "Whatever you do, don't step foot into that stadium!" The frenzied crowd shouted out one thing, and others shouted something else, until they were all in mass confusion, with many not even knowing why they were there! Some of the Jews pushed forward a Jewish man named Alexander to be their spokesman, and different factions of the crowd shouted instructions at him. He stood before the people and motioned for everyone to be quiet so he could be heard. But when he began to speak, they realized that he was a Jew, so they shouted him down. For nearly two hours they shouted over and over, "Great is Artemis, the goddess of the Ephesians!" Eventually the mayor of the city was able to quiet them down. He said, "Fellow citizens! Who in the world doesn't know that we are devoted to the great temple of Artemis and to her image that fell from Zeus out of heaven? Since no one can deny it, you should all just be quiet. Calm down and don't do anything hasty. For you have brought these men before us who aren't guilty of any crime. They are neither temple robbers nor blasphemers of our goddess. So if Demetrius and the men of his trade have a case against someone, the courts are open. They can appear before the judge and press charges. But if you're looking for anything further to bring up, it must be argued before the court and settled there, not here. Don't you realize we're putting our city in danger of being accused of a riot by the Roman authorities? There's no good explanation we can give them for all this commotion!" After he had said this, he dispersed the crowds and sent them away. Acts 19:21–41, TPT

Person or situation you are praying for:
Praises and promises:
Prayer:

## 27 September
### It is God who ordains your work, not men.

However, from Miletus, Paul had sent a message to the elders of the church in Ephesus and asked them to come meet with him. When they arrived, he said to them, "All of you know how I've lived and conducted myself while I was with you. From the first day I set foot in western Turkey I've operated in God's miracle power with great humility and served you with many tears. I've endured numerous ordeals because of the plots of the Jews. You know how I've taught you in public meetings and in your homes, and that I've not held anything back from you that would help you grow. I urged both Jews and non-Jews to turn from sin to God and to have faith in our Lord Jesus.

"And now I am being compelled by the Holy Spirit to go to Jerusalem, without really knowing what will happen to me there. Yet I know that the Holy Spirit warns me in town after town, saying, 'Chains and afflictions are prepared for you.' But whether I live or die is not important, for I don't esteem my life as indispensable. It's more important for me to fulfill my destiny and to finish the ministry my Lord Jesus has assigned to me, which is to faithfully preach the wonderful news of God's grace. I've been a part of your lives and shared with you many times the message of God's kingdom realm. But now I leave you, and you will not see my face again. If any of you should be lost, I will not be blamed, for my conscience is clean, because I've taught you everything I could about God's eternal plan and I've held nothing back. So guard your hearts. Be true shepherds over all the flock and feed them well. Remember, it was the Holy Spirit who appointed you to guard and oversee the churches that belong to Jesus, the Anointed One, which he purchased and established by his own blood. "I know that after I leave, imposters who have no loyalty to the flock will come among you like savage wolves. Even some from among your very own ranks will rise up, twisting the truth to seduce people into following them instead of Jesus. So be alert and discerning. Remember that for three years, night and day, I've never stopped warning each of you, pouring out my heart to you with tears.

"And so now, I entrust you into God's hands and the message of his grace, which is all that you need to become strong. All of God's blessings are imparted through the message of his grace, which he provides as the spiritual inheritance given to all of his holy ones. I haven't been after your money or any of your possessions. You all know that I've worked with my hands to meet my own needs and the needs of those who've served with me. I've left you an example of how you should serve and take care of those who are weak. For we must always cherish the words of our Lord Jesus, who taught, 'Giving brings a far greater blessing than receiving.' "

After Paul finished speaking, he knelt down and prayed with them. Then they all cried with great weeping as one after another hugged Paul and kissed him. What broke their hearts the most were his words "You will not see my face again." Then they tearfully accompanied Paul back to the ship. Acts 20:17–38, TPT

Person or situation you are praying for:
Praises and promises:
Prayer:

## 28 September
*Do not judge others or you may condemn yourself.*

No matter who you are, before you judge the wickedness of others, you had better remember this: you are also without excuse, for you too are guilty of the same kind of things! When you judge others, and then do the same things they do, you condemn yourself. We know that God's judgment falls upon those who practice these things. God is always right, because he has all the facts. And no matter who you think you are, when you judge others who do these things and then do the same things yourself, what makes you think that you will escape God's judgment? Romans 2:1–3, TPT

Person or situation you are praying for:
Praises and promises:
Prayer:

## 29 September
*The gospel is for every participant in God's creation!*
*Pray for all living things to believe on the Lord our Savior.*

Afterward he appeared to the eleven themselves as they sat at table; and he upbraided them for their unbelief and hardness of heart, because they had not believed those who saw him after he had risen. And he said to them, "Go into all the world and preach the gospel to the whole creation. He who believes and is baptized will be saved; but he who does not believe will be condemned." Mark 16:14–16, RSV

Person or situation you are praying for:
Praises and promises:
Prayer:

## 30 September

*God has many things beyond our ability to imagine, in store for His people.*

My brothers and sisters, when I first came to proclaim to you the secrets of God, I refused to come as an expert, trying to impress you with my eloquent speech and lofty wisdom. For while I was with you I was determined to be consumed with one topic—Jesus, the crucified Messiah. I stood before you feeling inadequate, filled with reverence for God, and trembling under the sense of the importance of my words. The message I preached and how I preached it was not an attempt to sway you with persuasive arguments but to prove to you the almighty power of God's Holy Spirit. For God intended that your faith not be established on man's wisdom but by trusting in his almighty power.

However, there is a wisdom that we continually speak of when we are among the spiritually mature. It's wisdom that didn't originate in this present age, nor did it come from the rulers of this age who are in the process of being dethroned. Instead, we continually speak of this wonderful wisdom that comes from God, hidden before now in a mystery. It is his secret plan, destined before the ages, to bring us into glory. None of the rulers of this present world order understood it, for if they had, they never would have crucified the Lord of shining glory. This is why the Scriptures say: Things never discovered or heard of before, things beyond our ability to imagine—these are the many things God has in store for all his lovers.

But God now unveils these profound realities to us by the Spirit. Yes, he has revealed to us his inmost heart and deepest mysteries through the Holy Spirit, who constantly explores all things. After all, who can really see into a person's heart and know his hidden impulses except for that person's spirit? So it is with God.

His thoughts and secrets are only fully understood by his Spirit, the Spirit of God. For we did not receive the spirit of this world system but the Spirit of God, so that we might come to understand and experience all that grace has lavished upon us. And we articulate these realities with the words imparted to us by the Spirit and not with the words taught by human wisdom. We join together Spirit-revealed truths with Spirit-revealed words. Someone living on an entirely human level rejects the revelations of God's Spirit, for they make no sense to him. He can't understand the revelations of the Spirit because they are only discovered by the illumination of the Spirit. Those who live in the Spirit are able to carefully evaluate all things, and they are subject to the scrutiny of no one but God. For Who has ever intimately known the mind of the Lord Yahweh well enough to become his counselor? Christ has, and we possess Christ's perceptions. 1 Corinthians 2, TPT

Person or situation you are praying for:
Praises and promises:
Prayer:

# September Epilogue

    A written epilogue, is a way of rounding out a literary work, bringing closure, or summarizing the final scene of a dramatic play. In this case, it is a summary of your prayer life and walk with God during the month of September. This page is for you to record your comments and write one or two summary statements as you have prayed for missionaries around the world and possibly even in your own community.

    It seems like everyone is on a mission to be a missionary these days. Churches arrange for elaborate trips to exotic locations so their members can experience immersion in a different culture and come home with compelling stories of persuasion and possibly even conversion. People spend a lot of money and time for these experiences but what about those who are more than 'hit-and-run' missionaries. Those who stay where God has placed them against all odds – when it doesn't make sense to most of us. What about the orthopedic surgeon who lives in Chad and repairs bones without an enormous paycheck and without all the glitz and glamour of being a socialite, driving the latest fast car, snagging a new trophy wife or husband every few years, vacationing on exclusive, private islands. What about the surgeon couple who had all three of their children, each born in different country and they work their entire lives as missionary surgeons and when they retire, the only living arrangement they can afford is a trailer on the coast of Oregon? What about the pastor who upon arriving at their destination loses his wife to a local disease and yet he stays on and dedicates the rest of his life to helping the locals? Praying for missionaries is never a null proposition. Something is going to happen. They are living their lives in accordance with God's will for them, so our prayers for missionaries are amplified in ways that can truly be miraculous. Your prayers for missionaries this past month have truly been a blessing of which you may only understand someday when you get to heaven. You have not passed up experiencing a great blessing for yourself and your family by your prayers for missionaries this past month.

_____
_____
_____
_____

# October

## Pray for the sick and for those who need healing.

Jesus atoned not only for our sin but for our infirmities and sickness. We praise God He is willing and able to bear all our infirmities and strengthen and heal all our disease. Through prayer, the soul is brought into a sacred nearness to God. It is renewed with knowledge.

Prayer fortifies the soul against the assaults of the enemy. Our prayers never burden or weary God. When you wake in the morning, kneel at your bedside and ask God for strength adequate for the day. In prayer, ask the Lord to pervade your life with sweetness of character.

He heals the wounds of every shattered heart. He healed the sick, raised the dead, made the blind man to see—He was the man from Galilee.

Pray and sing your praises! Prayer is an exalted privilege we should attain throughout the day with the God of the universe. Jesus invites us to pray. Jesus desires the closest and most intimate communion with you through prayer and meditation. Prayer enables us to live in the sunshine of His presence.

God keeps His promises. God rescues the righteous. We may be knocked down but not out. Break off every yoke of bondage! In all your ways, acknowledge the Lord and lean not unto your own understanding.

# October Ideas

Pray to be forgiven of your sins.
Pray to be healed by the Great Physician.
Pray to be kept from the pit of destruction.
Pray that love for God transcends physical ailments.
Thank Jesus Christ he has atoned not only for our sins but our infirmities.
Pray that through the stripes Christ endured, we have access to complete healing.

1. _____
2. _____
3. _____
4. _____
5. _____
6. _____
7. _____
8. _____
9. _____
10. _____

19.
20.
21.
22.
23.
24.
25.

Pray for the sick and for those who need healing.

# 1 October

### Jesus atoned not only for our sin but for our infirmities and sickness.

When the even was come, they brought unto him many that were possessed with devils: and he cast out the spirits with his word, and healed all that were sick: that it might be fulfilled which was spoken by Esaias the prophet, saying, Himself took our infirmities, and bare our sicknesses. Matthew 8:16, 17, KJV

Person or situation you are praying for:
Praises and promises:
Prayer:

# 2 October

### Pray and sing your praises!

Are there any believers in your fellowship suffering great hardship and distress? Encourage them to pray! Are there happy, cheerful ones among you? Encourage them to sing out their praises! Are there any sick among you? Then ask the elders of the church to come and pray over the sick and anoint them with oil in the name of our Lord. And the prayer of faith will heal the sick and the Lord will raise them up, and if they have committed sins they will be forgiven. James 5:13–15, TPT

Person or situation you are praying for:
Praises and promises:
Prayer:

# 3 October

### Jesus invites us to pray.

Most of all, friends, always rejoice in the Lord! I never tire of saying it: Rejoice! Keep your gentle nature so that all people will know what it looks like to walk in His footsteps. The Lord is ever present with us. Don't be anxious about things; instead, pray. Pray about everything. He longs to hear your requests, so talk to God about your needs and be thankful for what has come. And know that the peace of God (a peace that is beyond any and all of our human understanding) will stand watch over your hearts and minds in Jesus, the Anointed One. Finally, brothers and sisters, fill your minds with beauty and truth. Meditate on whatever is honorable, whatever is right, whatever is pure, whatever is lovely, whatever is good, whatever is virtuous and praiseworthy. Philippians 4:4–8, TPT

Person or situation you are praying for:
Praises and promises:
Prayer:

## 4 October

*Prayer with the God of the universe, is an exalted privilege we should use throughout the day.*

When Jesus entered the village of Capernaum, a captain in the Roman army approached him, asking for a miracle. "Lord," he said, "I have a son who is lying in my home, paralyzed and suffering terribly." Jesus responded, "I will go with you and heal him." But the Roman officer interjected, "Lord, who am I to have you come into my house? I understand your authority, for I too am a man who walks under authority and have authority over soldiers who serve under me. I can tell one to go and he'll go, and another to come and he'll come. I order my servants and they'll do whatever I ask. So I know that all you need to do is to stand here and command healing over my son and he will be instantly healed." Jesus was astonished when he heard this and said to those who were following him, "He has greater faith than anyone I've encountered in Israel! Listen to what I am about to tell you. Multitudes of non-Jewish people will stream from the east and the west, to enter into the banqueting feast with Abraham, Isaac, and Jacob in the heavenly kingdom. But many Israelites, born to be heirs of the kingdom, will be turned away and banished into the darkness where there will be bitter weeping and unbearable anguish." Then Jesus turned to the Roman officer and said, "Go home. All that you have believed for will be done for you!" And his son was healed at that very moment. Matthew 8:5–13, TPT

Person or situation you are praying for:
Praises and promises:
Prayer:

## 5 October

*We praise God that Jesus was willing and able to bear all our infirmities on the cross. He is able to strengthen and heal all our disease if it will be for our good and His glory.*

Yet he was the one who carried our sicknesses and endured the torment of our sufferings. We viewed him as one who was being punished for something he himself had done, as one who was struck down by God and brought low. But it was because of our rebellious deeds that he was pierced and because of our sins that he was crushed. He endured the punishment that made us completely whole, and in his wounding we found our healing. Like wayward sheep, we have all wandered astray. Each of us has turned from God's paths and chosen our own way; even so, Yahweh laid the guilt of our every sin upon him. [Note: A nuanced translation of Isaiah 53:5 could be, "In the fellowship of being one with him is our healing."] Isaiah 53:4–6, TPT

Person or situation you are praying for:
Praises and promises:
Prayer:

# 6 October

*Jesus desires the closest and most intimate communion with us through our prayer and meditation.*

He himself carried our sins in his body on the cross so that we would be dead to sin and live for righteousness. Our instant healing flowed from his wounding. 1 Peter 2:24, TPT

Person or situation you are praying for:
Praises and promises:
Prayer:


# 7 October

*God keeps His promises.*

GOD wasn't attracted to you and didn't choose you because you were big and important—the fact is, there was almost nothing to you. He did it out of sheer love, keeping the promise he made to your ancestors. GOD stepped in and mightily bought you back out of that world of slavery, freed you from the iron grip of Pharaoh, king of Egypt. Know this: GOD, your God, is God indeed, a God you can depend upon. He keeps his covenant of loyal love with those who love him and observe his commandments for a thousand generations. But he also pays back those who hate him, pays them the wages of death; he isn't slow to pay them off—those who hate him, he pays right on time. So keep the command and the rules and regulations that I command you today. Do them. And this is what will happen: When you, on your part, will obey these directives, keeping and following them, GOD, on his part, will keep the covenant of loyal love that he made with your ancestors: He will love you, he will bless you, he will increase you. He will bless the babies from your womb and the harvest of grain, new wine, and oil from your fields; he'll bless the calves from your herds and lambs from your flocks in the country he promised your ancestors that he'd give you. You'll be blessed beyond all other peoples: no sterility or barrenness in you or your animals. GOD will get rid of all sickness. And all the evil afflictions you experienced in Egypt he'll put not on you but on those who hate you. Deuteronomy 7:7–15, MSG

Person or situation you are praying for:
Praises and promises:
Prayer:

## 8 October

*Worship and praise the true God for your healing and not man and his gods.*

Now at Lystra there was a man sitting, who could not use his feet; he was a cripple from birth, who had never walked. He listened to Paul speaking; and Paul, looking intently at him and seeing that he had faith to be made well, said in a loud voice, "Stand upright on your feet." And he sprang up and walked. And when the crowds saw what Paul had done, they lifted up their voices, saying in Lycao'nian, "The gods have come down to us in the likeness of men!" Barnabas they called Zeus, and Paul, because he was the chief speaker, they called Hermes. And the priest of Zeus, whose temple was in front of the city, brought oxen and garlands to the gates and wanted to offer sacrifice with the people. But when the apostles Barnabas and Paul heard of it, they tore their garments and rushed out among the multitude, crying, "Men, why are you doing this? We also are men, of like nature with you, and bring you good news, that you should turn from these vain things to a living God who made the heaven and the earth and the sea and all that is in them. Acts 14:8–15, RSV

Person or situation you are praying for:
Praises and promises:
Prayer:

## 9 October

*Through prayer, the soul is brought into a sacred nearness to God,*
*and is renewed with knowledge, and grasps the meaning of true holiness.*

I'm alive for a reason—I can't worship You if I'm dead. If I'm six feet under, how can I thank You? I'm exhausted. I cannot even speak, my voice fading as sighs. Every day ends in the same place—lying in bed, covered in tears, my pillow wet with sorrow. My eyes burn, devoured with grief; they grow weak as I constantly watch for my enemies. All who are evil, stay away from me because the Eternal hears my voice, listens as I cry. The Eternal God hears my simple prayers; He receives my request. All who seek to destroy me will be humiliated; they will turn away and suddenly crumble in shame. Psalm 6:5–10, VOICE

Person or situation you are praying for:
Praises and promises:
Prayer:

# 10 October

*Prayer enables us to live in the sunshine of His presence.*

Naaman was general of the army under the king of Aram. He was important to his master, who held him in the highest esteem because it was by him that GOD had given victory to Aram: a truly great man, but afflicted with a grievous skin disease. It so happened that Aram, on one of its raiding expeditions against Israel, captured a young girl who became a maid to Naaman's wife. One day she said to her mistress, "Oh, if only my master could meet the prophet of Samaria, he would be healed of his skin disease." Naaman went straight to his master and reported what the girl from Israel had said. "Well then, go," said the king of Aram. "And I'll send a letter of introduction to the king of Israel." So he went off, taking with him about 750 pounds of silver, 150 pounds of gold, and ten sets of clothes. Naaman delivered the letter to the king of Israel. The letter read, "When you get this letter, you'll know that I've personally sent my servant Naaman to you; heal him of his skin disease." When the king of Israel read the letter, he was terribly upset, ripping his robe to pieces. He said, "Am I a god with the power to bring death or life that I get orders to heal this man from his disease? What's going on here? That king's trying to pick a fight, that's what!"

Elisha the man of God heard what had happened, that the king of Israel was so distressed that he'd ripped his robe to shreds. He sent word to the king, "Why are you so upset, ripping your robe like this? Send him to me so he'll learn that there's a prophet in Israel." So Naaman with his horses and chariots arrived in style and stopped at Elisha's door. Elisha sent out a servant to meet him with this message: "Go to the River Jordan and immerse yourself seven times. Your skin will be healed and you'll be as good as new." Naaman lost his temper. He turned on his heel saying, "I thought he'd personally come out and meet me, call on the name of GOD, wave his hand over the diseased spot, and get rid of the disease. The Damascus rivers, Abana and Pharpar, are cleaner by far than any of the rivers in Israel. Why not bathe in them? I'd at least get clean." He stomped off, mad as a hornet.

But his servants caught up with him and said, "Father, if the prophet had asked you to do something hard and heroic, wouldn't you have done it? So why not this simple 'wash and be clean'?" So he did it. He went down and immersed himself in the Jordan seven times, following the orders of the Holy Man. His skin was healed; it was like the skin of a little baby. He was as good as new. He then went back to the Holy Man, he and his entourage, stood before him, and said, "I now know beyond a shadow of a doubt that there is no God anywhere on earth other than the God of Israel. In gratitude let me give you a gift." "As GOD lives," Elisha replied, "the God whom I serve, I'll take nothing from you." Naaman tried his best to get him to take something, but he wouldn't do it. "If you won't take anything," said Naaman, "let me ask you for something: Give me a load of dirt, as much as a team of donkeys can carry, because I'm never again going to worship any god other than GOD." 2 Kings 5:1–17, MSG

Person or situation you are praying for:
Praises and promises:
Prayer:

## 11 October

*Prayer fortifies the soul against the assaults of the enemy.*

Large crowds followed Jesus when He came down from the mountain. And as Jesus was going along, a leper approached Him and knelt down before Him. Lord, if You wish to, please heal me and make me clean! Jesus (stretching out His hand): Of course, I wish to. Be clean. Immediately the man was healed. Jesus: Don't tell anyone what just happened. Rather, go to the priest, show yourself to him, and give a wave offering as Moses commanded. Your actions will tell the story of what happened here today. Matthew 8:1–4, VOICE

Person or situation you are praying for:
Praises and promises:
Prayer:

## 12 October

*Our prayers never burden or weary God.*

Jesus the Anointed One is always the same: yesterday, today, and forever. Do not be carried away by diverse and strange ways of believing or worshipping. It is good for the heart to be strengthened by grace, not by regulations about what you can eat (which do no good even for those who observe them). Hebrews 13:8, 9, VOICE

Person or situation you are praying for:
Praises and promises:
Prayer:

## 13 October

*In prayer, ask the Lord to pervade your life with Christ's sweetness of character.*

Moses led Israel from the Red Sea on to the Wilderness of Shur. They traveled for three days through the wilderness without finding any water. They got to Marah, but they couldn't drink the water at Marah; it was bitter. That's why they called the place Marah (Bitter). And the people complained to Moses, "So what are we supposed to drink?" So, Moses cried out in prayer to GOD. GOD pointed him to a stick of wood. Moses threw it into the water and the water turned sweet. That's the place where GOD set up rules and procedures; that's where he started testing them. GOD said, "If you listen, listen obediently to how GOD tells you to live in his presence, obeying his commandments and keeping all his laws, then I won't strike you with all the diseases that I inflicted on the Egyptians; I am GOD your healer." They came to Elim where there were twelve springs of water and seventy palm trees. They set up camp there by the water. Exodus 15:22–27, MSG

Person or situation you are praying for:
Praises and promises:
Prayer:

## 14 October

### God rescues the righteous.

For the Eternal watches over the righteous, and His ears are attuned to their prayers. He is always listening. But He will punish evildoers, and nothing they do will last. They will soon be forgotten. When the upright need help and cry to the Eternal, He hears their cries and rescues them from all of their troubles. When someone is hurting or brokenhearted, the Eternal moves in close and revives him in his pain. Hard times may well be the plight of the righteous—they may often seem overwhelmed—but the Eternal rescues the righteous from what oppresses them. He will protect all of their bones; not even one bone will be broken. Evil moves in and ultimately murders the wicked; the enemies of the righteous will be condemned. The Eternal will liberate His servants; those who seek refuge in Him will never be condemned. Psalm 34:15–22, VOICE

Person or situation you are praying for:
Praises and promises:
Prayer:

## 15 October

### We may be knocked down but not out.

We are like common clay jars that carry this glorious treasure within, so that the extraordinary overflow of power will be seen as God's, not ours. Though we experience every kind of pressure, we're not crushed. At times we don't know what to do, but quitting is not an option. We are persecuted by others, but God has not forsaken us. We may be knocked down, but not out. We continually share in the death of Jesus in our own bodies so that the resurrection life of Jesus will be revealed through our humanity. 2 Corinthians 4:7–10, TPT

Person or situation you are praying for:
Praises and promises:
Prayer:

## 16 October
### Break off every yoke of bondage!

This is the kind of fast that I desire: Remove the heavy chains of oppression! Stop exploiting your workers! Set free the crushed and mistreated! Break off every yoke of bondage! Share your food with the hungry! Provide for the homeless and bring them into your home! Clothe the naked! Don't turn your back on your own flesh and blood! Then my favor will bathe you in sunlight until you are like the dawn bursting through a dark night. And then suddenly your healing will manifest. You will see your righteousness march out before you, and the glory of Yahweh will protect you from all harm! Then Yahweh will answer you when you pray. When you cry out for help, he will say, "I am here." If you banish every form of oppression, the scornful accusations, and vicious slander, and if you offer yourselves in compassion for the hungry and relieve those in misery, then your dawning light will rise in the darkness and your gloom will turn into noonday splendor! Isaiah 58:6–10, TPT

Person or situation you are praying for:
Praises and promises:
Prayer:

## 17 October
### In all your ways, acknowledge the Lord and lean not unto your own understanding.

My son, do not forget my teaching, but let your heart keep my commandments, for length of days and years of life and peace they will add to you. Let not steadfast love and faithfulness forsake you; bind them around your neck; write them on the tablet of your heart. So you will find favor and good success in the sight of God and man. Trust in the LORD with all your heart, and do not lean on your own understanding. In all your ways acknowledge him, and he will make straight your paths. Be not wise in your own eyes; fear the LORD, and turn away from evil. It will be healing to your flesh and refreshment to your bones. Honor the LORD with your wealth and with the first fruits of all your produce; then your barns will be filled with plenty, and your vats will be bursting with wine. My son, do not despise the LORD's discipline or be weary of his reproof, for the LORD reproves him whom he loves, as a father the son in whom he delights. Proverbs 3:1–10, ESV

Person or situation you are praying for:
Praises and promises:
Prayer:

## 18 October
### He heals the wounds of every shattered heart.

Hallelujah! Praise the Lord! How beautiful it is when we sing our praises to the beautiful God, for praise makes you lovely before him and brings him great delight! The Lord builds up Jerusalem; he gathers up the outcasts and brings them home. He heals the wounds of every shattered heart. He sets his stars in place, calling them all by their names. How great is our God! There's absolutely nothing his power cannot accomplish, and he has infinite understanding of everything. Psalm 147:1–5, TPT

Person or situation you are praying for:
Praises and promises:
Prayer:

## 19 October
### Serve the Lord your God and He will give you bread and water.

Serve the Lord your God and He will give you bread and water. And I will take sickness from among you. Women in your land will not lose their babies before they are born, and will be able to give birth. I will give you a full life. Exodus 23:25, 26, NLV

Person or situation you are praying for:
Praises and promises:
Prayer:

## 20 October
### "Lord, help us! Rescue us! And he did!"

So lift your hands and give thanks to God for his marvelous kindness and for his miracles of mercy for those he loves! For he smashed through heavy prison doors and shattered the steel bars that held us back, just to set us free! Some of us were such fools, bringing on ourselves sorrow and suffering all because of our sins. Sick and feeble, unable to stand the sight of food, we drew near to the gates of death. Then we cried out, "Lord, help us! Rescue us!" And he did! God spoke the words "Be healed," and we were healed, delivered from death's door! So lift your hands and give thanks to God for his marvelous kindness and for his miracles of mercy for those he loves! Bring your praise as an offering and your thanks as a sacrifice as you sing your story of miracles with a joyful song. Psalm 107:15–22, TPT

Person or situation you are praying for:
Praises and promises:
Prayer:

# 21 October
## Asaph's psalm

No one can deny it—God is really good to Israel and to all those with pure hearts. But I nearly missed seeing it for myself. Here's my story: I narrowly missed losing it all. I was stumbling over what I saw with the wicked. For when I saw the boasters with such wealth and prosperity, I became jealous over their smug security. Indulging in whatever they wanted, going where they wanted, doing what they wanted, and with no care in the world. No pain, no problems, they seemed to have it made. They lived as though life would never end. They didn't even try to hide their pride and opulence. Cruelty and violence is part of their lifestyle. Pampered and pompous, vice oozes from their souls; they overflow with vanity. They're such snobs—looking down their noses. They even scoff at God! They are nothing but bullies threatening God's people. Loudmouths with no fear of God, pretending to know it all. Windbags full of hot air, impressing only themselves. Yet the people keep coming back to listen to more of their nonsense. They tell their cohorts, "God will never know. See, he has no clue of what we're doing." These are the wicked ones I'm talking about! They never have to lift a finger, living a life of ease while their riches multiply. Have I been foolish to play by the rules and keep my life pure? Here I am suffering under your discipline day after day. I feel like I'm being punished all day long. If I had given in to my pain and spoken of what I was really feeling, it would have sounded like unfaithfulness to the next generation.

When I tried to understand it all, I just couldn't. It was too puzzling—too much of a riddle to me. But then one day I was brought into the sanctuaries of God, and in the light of glory, my distorted perspective vanished. Then I understood that the destiny of the wicked was near! They're the ones who are on the slippery path, and God will suddenly let them slide off into destruction to be consumed with terrors forever! It will be an instant end to all their life of ease; a blink of the eye and they're swept away by sudden calamity! They're all nothing more than momentary monarchs—soon to disappear like a dream when one awakes. When the rooster crows, Lord God, you'll despise their life of fantasies.

When I saw all of this, what turmoil filled my heart, piercing my opinions with your truth. I was so stupid. I was senseless and ignorant, acting like a brute beast before you, Lord. Yet, in spite of all this, you comfort me by your counsel; you draw me closer to you. You lead me with your secret wisdom. And following you brings me into your brightness and glory! Whom have I in heaven but you? You're all I want! No one on earth means as much to me as you. Lord, so many times I fail; I fall into disgrace. But when I trust in you, I have a strong and glorious presence protecting and anointing me. Forever you're all I need! Those who abandon the worship of God will perish. The false and unfaithful will be silenced, never heard from again. But I'll keep coming closer and closer to you, Lord Yahweh, for your name is good to me. I'll keep telling the world of your awesome works, my faithful and glorious God! Psalm 73, TPT

Person or situation you are praying for:
Praises and promises:

Prayer:

## 22 October

*No matter what, I will sing His praise,*
*for living before His face is my saving grace!*

O God, drinking deeply from the streams of pleasure flowing from your presence. My longings overwhelm me for more of you! My soul thirsts, pants, and longs for the living God. I want to come and see the face of God. Day and night my tears keep falling and my heart keeps crying for your help while my enemies mock me over and over, saying, "Where is this God of yours? Why doesn't he help you?" So I speak over my heartbroken soul, "Take courage. Remember when you used to be right out front leading the procession of praise when the great crowd of worshipers gathered to go into the presence of the Lord? You shouted with joy as the sound of passionate celebration filled the air and the joyous multitude of lovers honored the festival of the Lord!"

So then, my soul, why would you be depressed? Why would you sink into despair? Just keep hoping and waiting on God, your Savior. For no matter what, I will still sing with praise, for living before his face is my saving grace! Here I am depressed and downcast. Yet I will still remember you as I ponder the place where your glory streams down from the mighty mountaintops, lofty and majestic—the mountains of your awesome presence. My deep need calls out to the deep kindness of your love. Your waterfall of weeping sent waves of sorrow over my soul, carrying me away, cascading over me like a thundering cataract. Yet all day long God's promises of love pour over me. Through the night I sing his songs, for my prayer to God has become my life. I will say to God, "You are my mountain of strength; how could you forget me? Why must I suffer this vile oppression of my enemies—these heartless tormentors who are out to kill me?" Their wounding words pierce my heart over and over while they say, "Where is this God of yours?" So I say to my soul, "Don't be discouraged. Don't be disturbed. For I know my God will break through for me." Then I'll have plenty of reasons to praise him all over again. Yes, living before his face is my saving grace! Psalm 42, TPT

Person or situation you are praying for:
Praises and promises:
Prayer:

## 23 October

### Even demons obey Jesus.

The people were awestruck and overwhelmed by his teaching, because he taught in a way that demonstrated God's authority, which was quite unlike the religious scholars. Suddenly, during the meeting, a demon-possessed man screamed out, "Hey! Leave us alone! Jesus the victorious, I know who you are. You're God's Holy One and you have come to destroy us!" Jesus rebuked him, saying, "Silence! You are bound! Come out of him!" The man's body shook violently in spasms, and the demon hurled him to the floor until it finally came out of him with a deafening shriek! The crowd was awestruck and unable to stop saying among themselves, "What is this new teaching that comes with such authority? With merely a word he commands demons to come out and they obey him!" So the reports about Jesus spread like wildfire throughout every community in the region of Galilee. Mark 1:23–28, TPT

Person or situation you are praying for:
Praises and promises:
Prayer:

## 24 October

### Healing current passed from Jesus to the woman with the continual bleeding and she was healed.

And he went with him. And a great crowd followed him and thronged about him. And there was a woman who had had a flow of blood for twelve years, and who had suffered much under many physicians, and had spent all that she had, and was no better but rather grew worse. She had heard the reports about Jesus, and came up behind him in the crowd and touched his garment. For she said, "If I touch even his garments, I shall be made well." And immediately the hemorrhage ceased; and she felt in her body that she was healed of her disease. And Jesus, perceiving in himself that power had gone forth from him, immediately turned about in the crowd, and said, "Who touched my garments?" And his disciples said to him, "You see the crowd pressing around you, and yet you say, 'Who touched me?'" And he looked around to see who had done it. But the woman, knowing what had been done to her, came in fear and trembling and fell down before him, and told him the whole truth. And he said to her, "Daughter, your faith has made you well; go in peace, and be healed of your disease." Mark 5:24–34, RSV

Person or situation you are praying for:
Praises and promises:
Prayer:

## 25 October

*Jesus spent more time healing than He did preaching.*

Jesus walked throughout the region with the joyful message of God's kingdom realm. He taught in their meeting houses, and wherever he went he demonstrated God's power by healing every kind of disease and illness. Matthew 9:35, TPT

Person or situation you are praying for:
Praises and promises:
Prayer:

## 26 October

*Gratitude flows out of a grateful heart when one is healed from an infirmity.*

As he entered one village, ten men approached him, but they kept their distance, for they were lepers. They shouted to him, "Mighty Lord, our wonderful Master! Won't you have mercy on us and heal us?" When Jesus stopped to look at them, he spoke these words: "Go to be examined by the Jewish priests." They set off, and they were healed while walking along the way. One of them, a foreigner from Samaria, when he discovered that he was completely healed, turned back to find Jesus, shouting out joyous praises and glorifying God. When he found Jesus, he fell down at his feet and thanked him over and over, saying to him, "You are the Messiah." This man was a Samaritan. Luke 17:12–16, TPT

Person or situation you are praying for:
Praises and promises:
Prayer:

## 27 October

*"All I know is I was blind but now I can see for the first time in my life!"*

As he passed by, he saw a man blind from his birth. And his disciples asked him, "Rabbi, who sinned, this man or his parents, that he was born blind?" Jesus answered, "It was not that this man sinned, or his parents, but that the works of God might be made manifest in him. We must work the works of him who sent me, while it is day; night comes, when no one can work. As long as I am in the world, I am the light of the world."

As he said this, he spat on the ground and made clay of the spittle and anointed the man's eyes with the clay, saying to him, "Go, wash in the pool of Silo'am" (which means Sent). So he went and washed and came back seeing. The neighbors and those who had seen him before as a beggar, said, "Is not this the man who used to sit and beg?" Some said, "It is he"; others said, "No, but he is like him." He said, "I am the man." They said to him, "Then how were your eyes opened?" He answered, "The man called Jesus made clay and anointed my eyes and said to me, 'Go to Silo'am and wash'; so I went and washed and received my sight." They said to him, "Where is he?" He said, "I do not know." They brought to the Pharisees the man who had formerly been blind.

Now it was a sabbath day when Jesus made the clay and opened his eyes. The Pharisees again asked him how he had received his sight. And he said to them, "He put clay on my eyes, and I washed, and I see." Some of the Pharisees said, "This man is not from God, for he does not keep the sabbath." But others said, "How can a man who is a sinner do such signs?" There was a division among them. So they again said to the blind man, "What do you say about him, since he has opened your eyes?" He said, "He is a prophet."

The Jews did not believe that he had been blind and had received his sight, until they called the parents of the man who had received his sight, and asked them, "Is this your son, who you say was born blind? How then does he now see?" His parents answered, "We know that this is our son, and that he was born blind; but how he now sees we do not know, nor do we know who opened his eyes. Ask him; he is of age, he will speak for himself." His parents said this because they feared the Jews, for the Jews had already agreed that if anyone should confess him to be Christ, he was to be put out of the synagogue. Therefore his parents said, "He is of age, ask him." So for the second time they called the man who had been blind, and said to him, "Give God the praise; we know that this man is a sinner." He answered, "Whether he is a sinner, I do not know; one thing I know, that though I was blind, now I see." John 9:1–25, RSV

Person or situation you are praying for:
Praises and promises:
Prayer:

# 28 October
## Go to the House of Loving-Kindness for healing.

Then Jesus returned to Jerusalem to observe one of the Jewish holy days. Inside the city near the Sheep Gate there is a pool called in Aramaic, The House of Loving Kindness. And this pool is surrounded by five covered porches. Hundreds of sick people were lying there on the porches—the paralyzed, the blind, and the crippled, all of them waiting for their healing. For an angel of God would periodically descend into the pool to stir the waters, and the first one who stepped into the pool after the waters swirled would instantly be healed. Now there was a man who had been disabled for thirty-eight years lying among the multitude of the sick.

When Jesus saw him lying there, he knew that the man had been crippled for a long time. So Jesus said to him, "Do you truly long to be healed?" The sick man answered him, "Sir, there's no way I can get healed, for I have no one who will lower me into the water when the angel comes. As soon as I try to crawl to the edge of the pool, someone else jumps in ahead of me." Then Jesus said to him, "Stand up! Pick up your sleeping mat and you will walk!" Immediately he stood up—he was healed! So he rolled up his mat and walked again!

Now this miracle took place on the Jewish Sabbath. When the Jewish leaders saw the man walking along carrying his sleeping mat, they objected and said, "What are you doing carrying that? Don't you know it's the Sabbath? It's not lawful for you to carry things on the Sabbath!" He answered them, "The man who healed me told me to pick it up and walk." "What man?" they asked him. "Who was this man who ordered you to carry something on a Sabbath?" But the healed man couldn't give them an answer, for he didn't yet know who it was since Jesus had already slipped away into the crowd. A short time later, Jesus found the man at the temple and said to him, "Look at you now! You're healed! Walk away from your sin so that nothing worse will happen to you." Then the man went to the Jewish leaders to inform them, "It was Jesus who healed me!" John 5:1–15, TPT

Person or situation you are praying for:
Praises and promises:
Prayer:

## 29 October

*He healed the sick, raised the dead, made the blind man to see—*
*He was the man from Galilee.*

After this, Jesus left the coastland of Tyre and came through Sidon on his way to Lake Galilee and over into regions of Syria. Some people brought to him a deaf man with a severe speech impediment. They pleaded with Jesus to place his hands on him and heal him. So, Jesus led him away from the crowd to a private spot. Then he stuck his fingers into the man's ears and placed some of his saliva on the man's tongue. Then he gazed into heaven, sighed deeply, and spoke to the man's ears and tongue, "Ethpathakh," which is Aramaic for "Open up, now!" At once the man's ears opened and he could hear perfectly, and his tongue was untied and he began to speak normally. Jesus ordered everyone to keep this miracle a secret, but the more he told them not to, the more the news spread! The people were absolutely beside themselves and astonished beyond measure. And they began to declare, "Everything he does is wonderful! He even makes the deaf hear and the mute speak!" Mark 7:31–37, TPT

Person or situation you are praying for:
Praises and promises:
Prayer:

## 30 October

*On the Sabbath day, Jesus heals the bent woman who had not asked to be healed.*

One Sabbath day, while Jesus was teaching in the synagogue, he encountered a seriously handicapped woman. She was crippled and had been doubled over for eighteen years. Her condition was caused by a demonic spirit of bondage that had left her unable to stand up straight. When Jesus saw her condition, he called her over and gently laid his hands on her. Then he said, "Dear woman, you are free. I release you forever from this crippling spirit." Instantly she stood straight and tall and overflowed with glorious praise to God!

The Jewish leader who was in charge of the synagogue was infuriated over Jesus healing on the Sabbath day. "Six days you are to work," he shouted angrily to the crowd. "Those are the days you should come here for healing, but not on the seventh day!" The Lord said, "You hopeless frauds! Don't you care for your animals on the Sabbath day, untying your ox or donkey from the stall and leading it away to water? If you do this for your animals, what's wrong with allowing this beloved daughter of Abraham, who has been bound by Satan for eighteen long years, to be untied and set free on a Sabbath day?" When they heard this, his critics were completely humiliated. But the crowds shouted with joy over the glorious things Jesus was doing among them. Luke 13:10–17, TPT

Person or situation you are praying for:
Praises and promises:
Prayer:

## 31 October

*Jesus is Lord of the Sabbath day, which includes acts of healing and restoration!*

One day Jesus was on his way to dine with a prominent Jewish religious leader for a Sabbath meal. Everyone was watching him to see if he would heal anyone on the Sabbath. Just then, standing right in front of him was a man suffering with his limbs swollen with fluid. Jesus asked the experts of the law and the Pharisees who were present, "Is it permitted within the law to heal a man on the Sabbath day? Is it right or wrong?" No one dared to answer. So, Jesus turned to the sick man, took hold of him, and released healing to him, then sent him on his way. Jesus said to them all, "If one of your children or one of your animals fell into a well, wouldn't you do all you could to rescue them even if it was a Sabbath day?" There was nothing they could say—all were silenced. Luke 14:1–6, TPT

Person or situation you are praying for:
Praises and promises:
Prayer:

# October Epilogue

A written epilogue, is a way of rounding out a literary work, bringing closure, or summarizing the final scene of a dramatic play. In this case, it is a summary of your prayer life and walk with God during the month of October. This page is for you to record your comments and write one or two summary statements as you have prayed for those who are sick and need healing.

Most of us do not need a designated month to pray for those who are sick and need healing. In fact, it seems like those needing this type of prayer is growing by leaps and bounds. It used to be primarily the elderly who needed our prayers for healing but today, we pray for the entire lifespan continuum from babies in the womb to those who are pushing 100 years of age.

Even with remarkable leaps in medical sciences, for some, it seems like we are in the dark ages of medicine. People are sicker than ever at younger ages. The sick are romanticized with Tik Tok videos and for some with compelling storylines, prayer chains circle the earth requesting a healing miracle. This is uncharted territory. Never in the history of mankind have we paid so much attention to the sick and those suffering with terrible symptoms. We see bodies covered in inflammation and scars, we see the body contorted and contracted in pain. We see unspeakable suffering. It is impossible to 'unsee' some things. We are truly living in Satan's grip. Without getting too deep into a discussion of medical philosophy, suffice to say, disease and infirmity are the result of Satan's hold on mankind. For reasons possibly beyond our understanding, we are sicker than ever before. Matthew records a conversation he and the disciples had with Jesus about their failure to heal a demon possessed man. Jesus then said to them, 'This kind of spirit will not leave a person unless you pray and you do not eat for a time.' Another version goes, '... this kind does not go out except by prayer and fasting.' So now we know. Prayer combined with fasting has great power over infirmity and disease. As you reflect over the past month of praying for those with infirmity and disease, I hope you are convicted more than ever of the power of prayer and fasting.

_____
_____
_____
_____

# November

## Pray for elected political leaders

Noah was an epic preacher and builder, but he only convinced seven people to follow him into the ark. Abraham, the patriarch of the Jews, Christianity and Islam, took Hagar as a second wife and fathered Ishmael before his wife Sarai conceived and Isaac was born. Joseph ultimately and successfully endured many great trials. Moses struck the rock. Eli's sons were out of control. Esther risked everything on her appearance. Gideon kept firing people. Elijah ran from a woman named Jezebel. David messed up a lot! Solomon liked the women. Daniel never faltered. Jonah was grumpy and rebellious. John the Baptist died for his cause. Peter had a temper. Pontius Pilate crucified Jesus. Paul, who murdered many Christians, had an epiphany. The only perfect leader is Jesus, who died to save and redeem us! Now, it would be easy to make the argument that Moses and Elijah came very close to being perfect, as they, along with Enoch, are in heaven with the Lord. But at the end of the day, even their record was imperfect.

There are no perfect children, parents, spouses, friends, bosses, leaders, pastors, prime ministers, presidents, governmental representatives, etc. Because none of us is perfect—even highly accomplished leaders—we should strive to be as congenial as possible when discussing political leaders. Avoid gaslighting leaders. This just makes their job more difficult and may ultimately jeopardize their ability to get useful things done. Avoid making personal jabs and sharp criticisms. Most elected officials are not in office forever. They will move on and be replaced. Allow for them to grow and learn from their mistakes. It remains important we do our best to place honest, hard-working, diligent, moral, and intelligent people in office.

Instead of criticizing every single move politicians make, pray for them. Keep in mind that God sets up and takes down leaders. They serve at His discretion and in a way that furthers His agenda. Read this month's devotionals to see how leaders are described in the Scriptures.

# November Ideas

Pray for leaders who lead by example.
Pray for wise counselors to surround our leaders.
Pray for our leaders to grow and mature in Christ.
Pray for our leaders to walk in the light of the Lord.
Pray for leaders to make decisions that give us safety and security.
Pray we might be conscientious and Christ-like in our civic responsibilities.
Pray we learn to respect all life and be prepared to preserve the life of every person.

1. _____
2. _____
3. _____
4. _____
5. _____
6. _____
7. _____
8. _____
9. _____
10. _____

19.
20.
21.
22.
23.
24.

Pray for elected political leaders.

# 1 November

## Pray with gratitude to God.

Most of all, I'm writing to encourage you to pray with gratitude to God. Pray for all men with all forms of prayers and requests as you intercede with intense passion. And pray for every political leader and representative, so that we would be able to live tranquil, undisturbed lives, as we worship the awe-inspiring God with pure hearts. It is pleasing to our Savior-God to pray for them. He longs for everyone to embrace his life and return to the full knowledge of the truth. 1 Timothy 2:1–4, TPT

Person or situation you are praying for:
Praises and promises:
Prayer:

# 2 November

## Be dependent on no one except Christ.

Finally, brethren, we beseech and exhort you in the Lord Jesus, that as you learned from us how you ought to live and to please God, just as you are doing, you do so more and more. For you know what instructions we gave you through the Lord Jesus. For this is the will of God, your sanctification: that you abstain from unchastity; that each one of you know how to take a wife for himself in holiness and honor, not in the passion of lust like heathen who do not know God; that no man transgress, and wrong his brother in this matter, because the Lord is an avenger in all these things, as we solemnly forewarned you. For God has not called us for uncleanness, but in holiness.

Therefore, whoever disregards this, disregards not man but God, who gives his Holy Spirit to you. But concerning love of the brethren you have no need to have anyone write to you, for you yourselves have been taught by God to love one another; and indeed you do love all the brethren throughout Macedo'nia. But we exhort you, brethren, to do so more and more, to aspire to live quietly, to mind your own affairs, and to work with your hands, as we charged you; so that you may command the respect of outsiders, and be dependent on nobody. 1 Thessalonians 4:1–12, RSV

Person or situation you are praying for:
Praises and promises:
Prayer:

# 3 November
## The desires of the righteous end only in good.

The LORD detests dishonest scales, but accurate weights find favor with him. When pride comes, then comes disgrace, but with humility comes wisdom. The integrity of the upright guides them, but the unfaithful are destroyed by their duplicity. Wealth is worthless in the day of wrath, but righteousness delivers from death. The righteousness of the blameless makes their paths straight, but the wicked are brought down by their own wickedness. The righteousness of the upright delivers them, but the unfaithful are trapped by evil desires. Hopes placed in mortals die with them; all the promise of their power comes to nothing. The righteous person is rescued from trouble, and it falls on the wicked instead. With their mouths the godless destroy their neighbors, but through knowledge the righteous escape. When the righteous prosper, the city rejoices; when the wicked perish, there are shouts of joy. Through the blessing of the upright a city is exalted, but by the mouth of the wicked it is destroyed. Whoever derides their neighbor has no sense, but the one who has understanding holds their tongue. A gossip betrays a confidence, but a trustworthy person keeps a secret. For lack of guidance a nation falls, but victory is won through many advisers. Whoever puts up security for a stranger will surely suffer, but whoever refuses to shake hands in pledge is safe.

A kindhearted woman gains honor, but ruthless men gain only wealth. Those who are kind benefit themselves, but the cruel bring ruin on themselves. A wicked person earns deceptive wages, but the one who sows righteousness reaps a sure reward. Truly the righteous attain life, but whoever pursues evil finds death. The LORD detests those whose hearts are perverse, but he delights in those whose ways are blameless.

Be sure of this: The wicked will not go unpunished, but those who are righteous will go free. Like a gold ring in a pig's snout is a beautiful woman who shows no discretion. The desire of the righteous ends only in good, but the hope of the wicked only in wrath. One person gives freely, yet gains even more; another withholds unduly, but comes to poverty. A generous person will prosper; whoever refreshes others will be refreshed. People curse the one who hoards grain, but they pray God's blessing on the one who is willing to sell. Whoever seeks good finds favor, but evil comes to one who searches for it. Those who trust in their riches will fall, but the righteous will thrive like a green leaf. Whoever brings ruin on their family will inherit only wind, and the fool will be servant to the wise. The fruit of the righteous is a tree of life, and the one who is wise saves lives. If the righteous receive their due on earth, how much more the ungodly and the sinner! Proverbs 11, NIV

Person or situation you are praying for:
Praises and promises:
Prayer:

# 4 November
## I will not let You go, except You bless me.

And Jacob said, O God of my father Abraham, and God of my father Isaac, the LORD which saidst unto me, Return unto thy country, and to thy kindred, and I will deal well with thee: I am not worthy of the least of all the mercies, and of all the truth, which thou hast shewed unto thy servant; for with my staff I passed over this Jordan; and now I am become two bands. Deliver me, I pray thee, from the hand of my brother, from the hand of Esau: for I fear him, lest he will come and smite me, and the mother with the children. And thou saidst, I will surely do thee good, and make thy seed as the sand of the sea, which cannot be numbered for multitude. And he lodged there that same night; and took of that which came to his hand a present for Esau his brother; two hundred she goats, and twenty he goats, two hundred ewes, and twenty rams, thirty milch camels with their colts, forty kine, and ten bulls, twenty she asses, and ten foals. And he delivered them into the hand of his servants, every drove by themselves; and said unto his servants, pass over before me, and put a space betwixt drove and drove. And he commanded the foremost, saying, When Esau my brother meeteth thee, and asketh thee, saying, whose art thou? and whither goest thou? and whose are these before thee? Then thou shalt say, they be thy servant Jacob's; it is a present sent unto my lord Esau: and, behold, also he is behind us. And so commanded he the second, and the third, and all that followed the droves, saying, On this manner shall ye speak unto Esau, when ye find him. And say ye more-over, Behold, thy servant Jacob is behind us. For he said, I will appease him with the present that goeth before me, and afterward I will see his face; peradventure he will accept of me. So went the present over before him: and himself lodged that night in the company. And he rose up that night, and took his two wives, and his two women servants, and his eleven sons, and passed over the ford Jabbok. And he took them, and sent them over the brook, and sent over that he had. And Jacob was left alone; and there wrestled a man with him until the breaking of the day. And when he saw that he prevailed not against him, he touched the hollow of his thigh; and the hollow of Jacob's thigh was out of joint, as he wrestled with him. And he said, let me go, for the day breaketh. And he said, I will not let thee go, except thou bless me. And he said unto him, what is thy name? And he said, Jacob. And he said, thy name shall be called no more Jacob, but Israel: for as a prince hast thou power with God and with men, and hast prevailed. And Jacob asked him, and said, tell me, I pray thee, thy name. And he said, where-fore is it that thou dost ask after my name? And he blessed him there. And Jacob called the name of the place Peniel: for I have seen God face to face, and my life is preserved. And as he passed over Penuel the sun rose upon him, and he halted upon his thigh. Therefore the children of Israel eat not of the sinew which shrank, which is upon the hollow of the thigh, unto this day: because he touched the hollow of Jacob's thigh in the sinew that shrank. Genesis 32:9–32

Person or situation you are praying for:
Praises and promises:
Prayer:

## 5 November

*Don't waste your time doing evil and being hateful.*

Remind people to respect their governmental leaders on every level as law-abiding citizens and to be ready to fulfill their civic duty. And remind them to never tear down anyone with their words or quarrel, but instead be considerate, humble, and courteous to everyone. For it wasn't that long ago that we behaved foolishly in our stubborn disobedience. We were easily led astray as slaves to worldly passions and pleasures. We wasted our lives in doing evil, and with hateful jealousy we hated others. Titus 3:1–3, TPT

Person or situation you are praying for:
Praises and promises:
Prayer:

## 6 November

*Never use your freedom in Christ as a cover-up for doing evil.*

In order to honor the Lord, you must respect and defer to the authority of every human institution whether it be the highest ruler or the governors he puts in place to punish lawbreakers and to praise those who do what's right. For it is God's will for you to silence the ignorance of foolish people by doing what is right. As God's loving servants, you should live in complete freedom, but never use your freedom as a cover-up for evil. Recognize the value of every person and continually show love to every believer. Live your lives with great reverence and in holy awe of God. Honor your rulers. 1 Peter 2:13–17, TPT

Person or situation you are praying for:
Praises and promises:
Prayer:

## 7 November

*It is God who grants authority to leaders.*

The verdict comes down as the watchers decreed; the sentence is passed by order of the holy ones so that all who live on the earth may know that the Most High God is the true sovereign over all kingdoms of the earth; He grants authority to anyone He wishes and installs the lowliest of people into positions of power. Daniel 4:17, VOICE

Person or situation you are praying for:
Praises and promises:
Prayer:

## 8 November
### The king repents.

Manasseh was 12 years old when he became king. He ruled for 55 years in Jerusalem. In GOD's opinion he was a bad king—an evil king. He reintroduced all the moral rot and spiritual corruption that had been scoured from the country when GOD dispossessed the pagan nations in favor of the children of Israel. Much evil—in GOD's view a career in evil. And GOD was angry. As a last straw he placed a carved image of the sex goddess Asherah that he had commissioned in The Temple of God, a flagrant and provocative violation of God's well-known command to both David and Solomon, "In this Temple and in this city Jerusalem, my choice out of all the tribes of Israel, I place my Name—exclusively and forever." He had promised, "Never again will I let my people Israel wander off from this land I've given to their ancestors. But on this condition, that they keep everything I've commanded in the instructions my servant Moses passed on to them." But Manasseh led Judah and the citizens of Jerusalem off the beaten path into practices of evil exceeding even the evil of the pagan nations that GOD had earlier destroyed.

When GOD spoke to Manasseh and his people about this, they ignored him. Then GOD directed the leaders of the troops of the king of Assyria to come after Manasseh. They put a hook in his nose, shackles on his feet, and took him off to Babylon. Now that he was in trouble, he went to his knees in prayer asking for help—total repentance before the God of his ancestors. As he prayed, GOD was touched; GOD listened and brought him back to Jerusalem as king. That convinced Manasseh that GOD was in control. After that Manasseh rebuilt the outside defensive wall of the City of David to the west of the Gihon spring in the valley. It went from the Fish Gate and around the hill of Ophel. He also increased its height. He tightened up the defense system by posting army captains in all the fortress cities of Judah. He also did a good spring cleaning on The Temple, carting out the pagan idols and the goddess statue. He took all the altars he had set up on The Temple hill and throughout Jerusalem and dumped them outside the city. He put the Altar of GOD back in working order and restored worship, sacrificing Peace-Offerings and Thank-Offerings. He issued orders to the people: "You shall serve and worship GOD, the God of Israel."

But the people didn't take him seriously—they used the name "GOD" but kept on going to the old pagan neighborhood shrines and doing the same old things. The rest of the history of Manasseh—his prayer to his God, and the sermons the prophets personally delivered by authority of GOD, the God of Israel—this is all written in The Chronicles of the Kings of Israel. His prayer and how God was touched by his prayer, a list of all his sins and the things he did wrong, the actual places where he built the pagan shrines, the installation of the sex-goddess Asherah sites, and the idolatrous images that he worshiped previous to his conversion—this is all described in the records of the prophets. When Manasseh died, they buried him in the palace garden. His son Amon was the next king. 2 Chronicles 33:1–20, MSG

Person or situation you are praying for:
Praises and promises:

Prayer:

## 9 November

*Learn to cooperate with other governments.*

Now therefore, Tattenai, governor beyond the River, Shetharbozenai, and your companions the Apharsachites, who are beyond the River, you must stay far from there. Leave the work of this house of God alone; let the governor of the Jews and the elders of the Jews build this house of God in its place. Moreover, I make a decree what you shall do for these elders of the Jews for the building of this house of God: that of the king's goods, even of the tribute beyond the River, expenses must be given with all diligence to these men, that they not be hindered. That which they have need of, including young bulls, rams, and lambs, for burnt offerings to the God of heaven; also wheat, salt, wine, and oil, according to the word of the priests who are at Jerusalem, let it be given them day by day without fail; that they may offer sacrifices of pleasant aroma to the God of heaven, and pray for the life of the king, and of his sons.
Ezra 6:6–10, WEB

Person or situation you are praying for:
Praises and promises:
Prayer:


## 10 November

*He bringeth princes to nothing; he maketh the judges of the earth as vanity.*

Fear not. Don't you realize that God is the Creator? Don't you hear the truth? Haven't you been told this from the beginning? Haven't you understood this since he laid a firm foundation for the earth? He sits enthroned high above the circle of the earth; to him the people of earth are like grasshoppers! He stretches out the heavens like a curtain, spreading it open like a tent to live in. He reduces rulers to nothing and makes the elite of the earth as nothing at all. They barely get planted and barely take root in their position of power when the Lord blows on them and they wither away, carried off like straw in the stormy wind.
Isaiah 40:21–24, TPT

Person or situation you are praying for:
Praises and promises:
Prayer:

## 11 November

*I have plans of peace and not evil, to give you a future and hope.*

The prophet Jeremiah wrote a letter from Jerusalem to the elders, priests, prophets, and all the rest who had been taken to Babylon by Nebuchadnezzar. (This was after King Jeconiah of Judah and his mother had been taken into exile, along with servants of the court, officials of Judah and Jerusalem, and many of the craftsmen and artisans.) The letter was hand-carried by Elasah (son of Shaphan) and Gemariah (son of Hilkiah), whom Zedekiah king of Judah dispatched to Babylon on a diplomatic mission to Nebuchadnezzar king of Babylon.

Jeremiah's Letter: this is what the Eternal, Commander of heavenly armies and God of Israel, says to those He exiled from Jerusalem to Babylon: "Build houses—make homes for your families because you are not coming back to Judah anytime soon. Plant gardens, and eat the food you grow there. Marry and have children; find wives for your sons, and give your daughters in marriage, so that they can have children.

During these years of captivity, let your families grow and not die out. Pursue the peace and welfare of the city where I sent you into exile. Pray to Me, the Eternal, for Babylon because if it has peace, you will live in peace." This is what the Eternal, Commander of heavenly armies and God of Israel, says to you: "Do not be fooled by the false prophets and fortune-tellers among you. Do not listen to dreamers or their interpretations of dreams, for I did not send them to you. They are prophesying lies in My name!" So says the Eternal. If you want the truth, this is what the Eternal has to say: "You will remain in Babylon for 70 years. When that time is over, I will come to you, and I will keep My promise of bringing you back home. For I know the plans I have for you," says the Eternal, "plans for peace, not evil, to give you a future and hope—never forget that. At that time, you will call out for Me, and I will hear. You will pray, and I will listen. Jeremiah 29:1–12, VOICE

Person or situation you are praying for:
Praises and promises:
Prayer:

## 12 November

*Love the light and not the darkness.*

And here is the basis for their judgment: The Light of God has now come into the world, but the hearts of people love their darkness more than the Light, because they want the darkness to conceal their evil. So, the wicked [those who do hateful things] hate the Light and try to hide from it, for their lives are fully exposed in the Light. John 3:19, 20, TPT

Person or situation you are praying for:
Praises and promises:
Prayer:

## 13 November
### The coronation of the King

Act I – The nations speak. How dare the nations plan a rebellion. Their foolish plots are futile! Look at how the power brokers of the world rise up to hold their summit as the rulers scheme and confer together against Yahweh and his Anointed King, saying: "Let's come together and break away from the Creator. Once and for all let's cast off these controlling chains of God and his Christ!"

Act II – God speaks. God-Enthroned merely laughs at them; the Sovereign One mocks their madness! Then with the fierceness of his fiery anger he settles the issue and terrifies them to death with these words: "I myself have poured out my King on Zion, my holy mountain.

Act III – The Son speaks. "I will reveal the eternal purpose of God. For he has decreed over me, 'You are my favored Son. And as your Father I have crowned you as my King Eternal. Today I became your Father. Ask me to give you the nations and I will do it, and they shall become your legacy. Your domain will stretch to the ends of the earth. And you will shepherd them with unlimited authority, crushing their rebellion as an iron rod smashes jars of clay!'

Act IV – The Holy Spirit speaks. Listen to me, all you rebel-kings and all you upstart judges of the earth. Learn your lesson while there's still time. Serve and worship the awe-inspiring God. Recognize his greatness and bow before him, trembling with reverence in his presence. Fall facedown before him and kiss the Son before his anger is roused against you. Remember that his wrath can be quickly kindled! But many blessings are waiting for all who turn aside to hide themselves in him! Psalm 2:1–12, TPT

Person or situation you are praying for:
Praises and promises:
Prayer:

## 14 November
### Wash and make yourselves clean.

Wash and make yourselves clean. Take your evil deeds out of my sight; stop doing wrong. Learn to do right; seek justice. Defend the oppressed. Take up the cause of the fatherless; plead the case of the widow. "Come now, let us settle the matter," says the LORD. "Though your sins are like scarlet, they shall be as white as snow; though they are red as crimson, they shall be like wool. If you are willing and obedient, you will eat the good things of the land; but if you resist and rebel, you will be devoured by the sword." For the mouth of the LORD has spoken. Isaiah 1:16–20, NIV

Person or situation you are praying for:
Praises and promises:
Prayer:

# 15 November
## Some days are dark and foreboding, be a good citizen anyway.

Be a good citizen. All governments are under God. Insofar as there is peace and order, it is God's order. So, live responsibly as a citizen. If you are irresponsible to the state, then you're irresponsible with God, and God will hold you responsible. Duly constituted authorities are only a threat if you're trying to get by with something. Decent citizens should have nothing to fear. Do you want to be on good terms with the government? Be a responsible citizen and you'll get on just fine, the government working to your advantage. But if you are breaking the rules right and left, watch out. The police are not there just to be admired in their uniforms. God also has an interest in keeping order, and he uses them to do it. That's why you must live responsibly—not just to avoid punishment but also because it's the right way to live. Romans 13:1–5, MSG

Person or situation you are praying for:
Praises and promises:
Prayer:

# 16 November
## He must increase, I must decrease.

An argument then developed between John's disciples and a particular Jewish man about baptism. So they went to John and asked him, "Teacher, are you aware that the One you told us about at the crossing place—he's now baptizing everyone with larger crowds than yours. People are flocking to him! What do you think about that?" John answered them, "A person cannot receive even one thing unless God bestows it. You heard me tell you before that I am not the Messiah, but certainly I am the messenger sent ahead of him. He is the Bridegroom, and the bride belongs to him. I am the friend of the Bridegroom who stands nearby and listens with great joy to the Bridegroom's voice. And because of his words my joy is complete and overflows! So, it's necessary for him to increase and for me to be diminished. John 3:25–30, TPT

Person or situation you are praying for:
Praises and promises:
Prayer:

## 17 November
### "We must obey God rather than men."

And someone came and told them, "The men whom you put in prison are standing in the temple and teaching the people." Then the captain with the officers went and brought them, but without violence, for they were afraid of being stoned by the people. And when they had brought them, they set them before the council. And the high priest questioned them, saying, "We strictly charged you not to teach in this name, yet here you have filled Jerusalem with your teaching and you intend to bring this man's blood upon us." But Peter and the apostles answered, "We must obey God rather than men. The God of our fathers raised Jesus whom you killed by hanging him on a tree. God exalted him at his right hand as Leader and Savior, to give repentance to Israel and forgiveness of sins. And we are witnesses to these things, and so is the Holy Spirit whom God has given to those who obey him." When they heard this, they were enraged and wanted to kill them. But a Pharisee in the council named Gama'li-el, a teacher of the law, held in honor by all the people, stood up and ordered the men to be put outside for a while. And he said to them, "Men of Israel, take care what you do with these men." Acts 5:25–35, RSV

Person or situation you are praying for:
Praises and promises:
Prayer:


## 18 November
### I want justice! I want fairness! And rivers of it!

I can't stand your religious meetings. I'm fed up with your conferences and conventions. I want nothing to do with your religion projects, your pretentious slogans and goals. I'm sick of your fund-raising schemes, your public relations and image making. I've had all I can take of your noisy ego-music. When was the last time you sang to me? Do you know what I want? I want justice—oceans of it. I want fairness—rivers of it. That's what I want. That's all I want. Amos 5:21–24, MSG

Person or situation you are praying for:
Praises and promises:
Prayer:

# 19 November
## Leaders, commit yourself to the Lord.

... One day in the 18th year of his kingship, with the cleanup of country and Temple complete, King Josiah sent Shaphan son of Azaliah, Maaseiah the mayor of the city, and Joah son of Joahaz the historian to renovate The Temple of GOD. First, they turned over to Hilkiah the high priest all the money collected by the Levitical security guards from Manasseh and Ephraim and the rest of Israel, and from Judah and Benjamin and the citizens of Jerusalem. It was then put into the hands of the foremen managing the work on The Temple of GOD who then passed it on to the workers repairing GOD's Temple—the carpenters, construction workers, and masons so they could buy the lumber and dressed stone for rebuilding the foundations the kings of Judah had allowed to fall to pieces. While the money that had been given for The Temple of GOD was being received and dispersed, Hilkiah the high priest found a copy of The Revelation of Moses. He reported to Shaphan the royal secretary, "I've just found the Book of GOD's Revelation, instructing us in GOD's way—found it in The Temple!" He gave it to Shaphan, who then gave it to the king. And along with the book, he gave this report: "The job is complete—everything you ordered done is done. They took all the money that was collected in The Temple of GOD and handed it over to the managers and workers." And then Shaphan told the king, "Hilkiah the priest gave me a book." Shaphan proceeded to read it out to the king. When the king heard what was written in the book, GOD's Revelation, he ripped his robes in dismay. And then he called for Hilkiah, Ahikam son of Shaphan, Abdon son of Micah, Shaphan the royal secretary, and Asaiah the king's personal aide. He ordered them all: "Go and pray to GOD for me and what's left of Israel and Judah. Find out what we must do in response to what is written in this book that has just been found! GOD's anger must be burning furiously against us — our ancestors haven't obeyed a thing written in this book of GOD, followed none of the instructions directed to us." Hilkiah and those picked by the king went straight to Huldah the prophetess... She lived in Jerusalem... The men consulted with her. In response to them she said, "GOD's word, the God of Israel: Tell the man who sent you here, 'GOD has spoken, I'm on my way to bring the doom of judgment on this place and this people. Every word written in the book read by the king of Judah will happen. And why? Because they've deserted me and taken up with other gods; they've made me thoroughly angry by setting up their god-making businesses. My anger is raging white-hot against this place and nobody is going to put it out.' And also tell the king of Judah, since he sent you to ask GOD for direction, GOD's comment on what he read in the book: 'Because you took seriously the doom of judgment I spoke against this place and people, and because you responded in humble repentance, tearing your robe in dismay and weeping before me, I'm taking you seriously. GOD's word. I'll take care of you; you'll have a quiet death and be buried in peace. You won't be around to see the doom that I'm going to bring upon this place and people...'" 2 Chronicles 34, MSG

Person or situation you are praying for:
Praises and promises:
Prayer:

## 20 November
### Pray for a "road to Damascus" experience for those politicians who persecute believers.

But Saul, still breathing threats and murder against the disciples of the Lord, went to the high priest and asked him for letters to the synagogues at Damascus, so that if he found any belonging to the Way, men or women, he might bring them bound to Jerusalem. Now as he journeyed he approached Damascus, and suddenly a light from heaven flashed about him. And he fell to the ground and heard a voice saying to him, "Saul, Saul, why do you persecute me?" And he said, "Who are you, Lord?" And he said, "I am Jesus, whom you are persecuting; but rise and enter the city, and you will be told what you are to do." The men who were traveling with him stood speechless, hearing the voice but seeing no one. Saul arose from the ground; and when his eyes were opened, he could see nothing; so, they led him by the hand and brought him into Damascus. And for three days he was without sight, and neither ate nor drank.

Now there was a disciple at Damascus named Anani'as. The Lord said to him in a vision, "Anani'as." And he said, "Here I am, Lord." And the Lord said to him, "Rise and go to the street called Straight, and inquire in the house of Judas for a man of Tarsus named Saul; for behold, he is praying, and he has seen a man named Anani'as come in and lay his hands on him so that he might regain his sight." But Anani'as answered, "Lord, I have heard from many about this man, how much evil he has done to thy saints at Jerusalem; and here he has authority from the chief priests to bind all who call upon thy name." But the Lord said to him, "Go, for he is a chosen instrument of mine to carry my name before the Gentiles and kings and the sons of Israel; for I will show him how much he must suffer for the sake of my name."

So Anani'as departed and entered the house. And laying his hands on him he said, "Brother Saul, the Lord Jesus who appeared to you on the road by which you came, has sent me that you may regain your sight and be filled with the Holy Spirit." And immediately something like scales fell from his eyes and he regained his sight. Then he rose and was baptized, and took food and was strengthened. For several days he was with the disciples at Damascus. And in the synagogues immediately he proclaimed Jesus, saying, "He is the Son of God." And all who heard him were amazed, and said, "Is not this the man who made havoc in Jerusalem of those who called on this name? And he has come here for this purpose, to bring them bound before the chief priests." But Saul increased all the more in strength, and confounded the Jews who lived in Damascus by proving that Jesus was the Christ. Acts 9:1–22, RSV

Person or situation you are praying for:
Praises and promises:
Prayer:

## 21 November
### Isaiah's Song of Six Woes: #1 – Grasping Materialism

Woe to those who in their greed buy up house after house to make one grand estate until there is no place for anyone else and only the landowner is left! This is what Yahweh, the Commander of Angel Armies, said in my ears: "Truly, many of your houses will become devastated and your large, impressive mansions will have no one living in them! Indeed, even a vast vineyard will produce only a few gallons of wine, and several bushels of seed will produce only a bushel of harvest!" Isaiah 5:8–10, TPT

Person or situation you are praying for:
Praises and promises:
Prayer:

## 22 November
### Isaiah's Song of Six Woes: #2 – Drunken Pleasure-Seeking

Woe to those who start drinking early in the morning, lingering late into the night to get drunk with wine. Their lavish parties are complete with the music of harps and flutes—and the wine flows! Yet they have no respect for what Yahweh has done, nor do they contemplate the work of his hands! Therefore, my people go into exile for lack of understanding. Their leaders are starving, their multitudes parched with thirst. The shadowy realm of death grows thirsty for souls and opens its mouth even wider to drink in the people! It gulps down the leaders of Jerusalem, along with their noisy, boasting crowds! The people will be humiliated, all of humanity humbled, and the arrogant will be brought low. With justice the Lord Yahweh, Commander of Angel Armies, displays his greatness, and righteousness sets him apart as the holy God. Then lambs will graze, as if in their own pastures, and the refugee will eat in the ruins of the rich. Isaiah 5:11–17, TPT

Person or situation you are praying for:
Praises and promises:
Prayer:

## 23 November
### Isaiah's Song of Six Woes: #3 – Defiant Sinfulness

Woe to those who drag behind them their guilt with ropes made of lies—straining and tugging, harnessed to their bondage! They say, "May God hurry up and bring his judgment so that we can see it once and for all! Let the prophetic plan of the Holy One of Israel quickly come to pass so that we can see what it is!" Isaiah 5:18, 19, TPT

Person or situation you are praying for:
Praises and promises:
Prayer:

## 24 November

### Isaiah's Song of Six Woes: #4 - Perversion of Values

Woe to those who call evil good and good evil, who replace darkness with light and light with darkness, who replace bitter with sweet and sweet with bitter. Isaiah 5:20, TPT

Person or situation you are praying for:
Praises and promises:
Prayer:

## 25 November

### Isaiah's Song of Six Woes: #5 - Arrogant Conceit

Woe to those who are wise in their own eyes and see themselves as clever and shrewd. Isaiah 5:21, TPT

Person or situation you are praying for:
Praises and promises:
Prayer:

## 26 November

### Isaiah's Song of Six Woes: #6 - Injustice

Woe to the champion wine drinkers who are heroes in mixing strong drinks — judges and politicians who acquit the guilty for a bribe and take away the rights of the innocent. Isaiah 5:22, 23, TPT

Person or situation you are praying for:
Praises and promises:
Prayer:

# 27 November

*The wise have wealth and luxury, but fools spend whatever they get.*

The king's heart is like a stream of water directed by the LORD; he guides it wherever he pleases. People may be right in their own eyes, but the LORD examines their heart. The LORD is more pleased when we do what is right and just than when we offer him sacrifices. Haughty eyes, a proud heart, and evil actions are all sin. Good planning and hard work lead to prosperity, but hasty shortcuts lead to poverty. Wealth created by a lying tongue is a vanishing mist and a deadly trap. The violence of the wicked sweeps them away, because they refuse to do what is just. The guilty walk a crooked path; the innocent travel a straight road.

It's better to live alone in the corner of an attic than with a quarrelsome wife in a lovely home. Evil people desire evil; their neighbors get no mercy from them. If you punish a mocker, the simpleminded become wise; if you instruct the wise, they will be all the wiser. The Righteous One knows what is going on in the homes of the wicked; he will bring disaster on them. Those who shut their ears to the cries of the poor will be ignored in their own time of need. A secret gift calms anger; a bribe under the table pacifies fury. Justice is a joy to the godly, but it terrifies evildoers. The person who strays from common sense will end up in the company of the dead. Those who love pleasure become poor; those who love wine and luxury will never be rich. The wicked are punished in place of the godly, and traitors in place of the honest. It's better to live alone in the desert than with a quarrelsome, complaining wife.

The wise have wealth and luxury, but fools spend whatever they get. Whoever pursues righteousness and unfailing love will find life, righteousness, and honor. The wise conquer the city of the strong and level the fortress in which they trust. Watch your tongue and keep your mouth shut, and you will stay out of trouble. Mockers are proud and haughty; they act with boundless arrogance. Despite their desires, the lazy will come to ruin, for their hands refuse to work. Some people are always greedy for more, but the godly love to give! The sacrifice of an evil person is detestable, especially when it is offered with wrong motives. A false witness will be cut off, but a credible witness will be allowed to speak. The wicked bluff their way through, but the virtuous think before they act. No human wisdom or understanding or plan can stand against the LORD. The horse is prepared for the day of battle, but the victory belongs to the LORD. Proverbs 21, NLT

Person or situation you are praying for:
Praises and promises:
Prayer:

## 28 November
*Avoid controversies, genealogies, dissensions, and quarrels over politics.*

Remind them to be submissive to rulers and authorities, to be obedient, to be ready for any honest work, to speak evil of no one, to avoid quarreling, to be gentle, and to show perfect courtesy toward all men. For we ourselves were once foolish, disobedient, led astray, slaves to various passions and pleasures, passing our days in malice and envy, hated by men and hating one another; but when the goodness and loving kindness of God our Savior appeared, he saved us, not because of deeds done by us in righteousness, but in virtue of his own mercy, by the washing of regeneration and renewal in the Holy Spirit, which he poured out upon us richly through Jesus Christ our Savior, so that we might be justified by his grace and become heirs in hope of eternal life. The saying is sure. I desire you to insist on these things, so that those who have believed in God may be careful to apply themselves to good deeds; these are excellent and profitable to men. But avoid stupid controversies, genealogies, dissensions, and quarrels over the law, for they are unprofitable and futile. As for a man who is factious, after admonishing him once or twice, have nothing more to do with him, knowing that such a person is perverted and sinful; he is self-condemned.  Titus 3:1–11, RSV

Person or situation you are praying for:
Praises and promises:
Prayer:

## 29 November
*One day soon, every political argument will be silenced.*

"Time is coming"—GOD's Decree—"when I'll establish a truly righteous David-Branch, A ruler who knows how to rule justly. He'll make sure of justice and keep people united. In his time Judah will be secure again and Israel will live in safety. This is the name they'll give him: 'GOD-Who-Puts-Everything- Right.' " Jeremiah 23:5, TPT

Person or situation you are praying for:
Praises and promises:
Prayer:

## 30 November
### God above everything else.

The Holy One asks: "Can you find anyone or anything to compare to me? Where is the one equal to me?" Lift up your eyes to the sky and see for yourself. Who do you think created the cosmos? He lit every shining star and formed every glowing galaxy, and stationed them all where they belong. He has numbered, counted, and given everyone a name. They shine because of God's incredible power and awesome might; not one fails to appear! Why, then, O Jacob's tribes, would you ever complain? And my chosen Israel, why would you say, "Yahweh isn't paying attention to my situation. He has lost all interest in what happens to me." Don't you know? Haven't you been listening? Yahweh is the one and only everlasting God, the Creator of all you can see and imagine! He never gets weary or worn out. His intelligence is unlimited; he is never puzzled over what to do! He empowers the feeble and infuses the powerless with increasing strength. Even young people faint and get exhausted; athletic ones may stumble and fall. But those who wait for Yahweh's grace will experience divine strength. They will rise up on soaring wings and fly like eagles, run their race without growing weary, and walk through life without giving up.  Isaiah 40:25–31, TPT

Person or situation you are praying for:
Praises and promises:
Prayer:

# November Epilogue

A written epilogue, is a way of rounding out a literary work, bringing closure, or summarizing the final scene of a dramatic play. In this case, it is a summary of your prayer life and walk with God during the month of November. This page is for you to record your comments and write one or two summary statements as you have prayed for elected political leaders.

Most would be hard-pressed to identify an elected political leader they truly like and respect. Most voting people hold their nose and vote for the political candidate that is closest to their dearly held ideals and beliefs. I listen to a radio station that once a day, a person comes on the radio and prays for one federally elected official. It is almost always just a one-line prayer. This seems superficial to me whether or not you agree with the candidate. If you are going to pray for someone you don't know, wouldn't you like to pray they align with Biblical ideologies? This could be for individual liberties, the freedom to worship God, freedom from oppression, life vs. death, for family values vs. the elevation and even protection of immoral behaviours targeting minors, for policies that support families, etc.

As you have prayed for elected political leaders this past month, reflect on your prayers, the specifics of your prayers, the overall themes of your prayers and watch and see how answers to your prayers manifest. Assuming you are a Christian, you realize prophecies in the Bible are unfolding and our time on earth is wrapping up. We won't be slaves to sin forever. A time is coming when everything will seem upside down, but don't despair, Jesus is coming soon! Pray for our elected officials because God has placed them in their positions of great power and influence. Pray their influence is for good and not for evil. Never cease praying these prayers.

_____
_____
_____
_____
_____
_____
_____
_____

# December

## Pray for orphans, prisoners, singles, child and other types of slaves, widowers, and widows.

For many, December is not merry and bright but lonely and sometimes even more gloomy than usual. While many people anticipate reuniting with family and loved ones, some face the prospect of Christmas day being just like any other. Whether or not you celebrate Christmas, the prospect of a lonely Christmas day is difficult for just about anyone. This is why I believe it is important to pray for the lonely people during the month of December, especially if you have been blessed with spending this time with loving family and friends.

Recent data show about 55 percent of the adult population is married and 45 percent are single. Out of the singles, more than 60 percent have never been married, about 23 percent are divorced, and approximately 13 percent are widowed. The widowed acutely feel the isolation of being newly single. Older widows and widowers may go for days and even weeks without any meaningful human-to-human interactions. For many, their humanity slowly slips away into loneliness and depression and for some, death is the only release.

The elderly are not the only ones oftentimes living in solitude and desperation. In the 1950s and 1960s, the USA shifted to a foster home system instead of institutionalized orphanages. Many countries have adopted similar policies. There are approximately 400,000 foster children in the U.S. and an estimated 153 million orphans worldwide. These foster children oftentimes live in sub-par living conditions and live without any meaningful and kind physical touch, hugs, and emotional comfort. Many children living in a home with one or both parents experience extreme disconnection and loneliness which results in a wide range of unacceptable behaviours. Children represent roughly one third of the world's population but account for almost half of the people living in extreme poverty. Many children are sold into sexual slavery. They exist in unthinkable conditions.

The prison population in the U.S. is around 0.7 percent of the population, or roughly 2.3 million and less than 90,000 of this number are incarcerated women. Worldwide, roughly 11 million people are incarcerated. Many prisoners live in harsh environments with few personal effects to remind them of their families and friends. I have regularly been involved in prison ministry over a period of almost 25 years and within two states, California and Georgia. I am currently a volunteer chaplain for the local police department. Two disparate volunteer positions that would seem to contradict the other. I respect and appreciate the law enforcement side and I have seen goodness and even the highest forms of humanity in some prisoners. I have come to realize incarceration, while for some, it may be an answer to the prayers of their friends and family because it provides them with a place to rest, regular food (albeit, not healthy or good quality food) and bare bones necessities, but for most, it quickly becomes a nightmare. I am in no way defending the indefensible. I am a huge proponent of understanding of how certain causes and actions lead to certain outcomes and effects, and acting accordingly. I am just pointing out that the justice system in the USA, from the top to the bottom, is broken.

Many of the characters described in the Old Testament would qualify for life-long imprisonment and even the death penalty. It would be impossible to have a meaningful discussion of all the issues within one or two paragraphs here. Some prisoners are falsely imprisoned. This is a travesty. Most people in prison are legitimately there but once incarcerated they are treated in sub-human ways instead of in redemptive / Biblical ways. They are uncoupled from almost everything that constitutes life, liberty and the pursuit of happiness. They are quickly defined by the worst mistake of their life. Fortunately for some, prison is where they can turn their attention and questions to God. For others, prison time robs them of their humanity and instead of going through a process of personal reflection and reformation, they become less and less human and upon release, they quickly revert to the inhumane and evil behaviours, often modeled to them in prison. Many countries do prison better than the USA and there are certainly many countries which allow much harsher environments to prevail.

I believe prison reform should be a top priority of this country, the USA. All great arguments aside, prisoners are still humans and made in the image of God. God still would have died for the worst of the worst of all prisoners. Most prisoners are Satan's captives. It is for this reason alone, they deserve our most sincere and fervent prayers. When we as Christians pray for prisoners who maybe even personally hurt our family, we join heaven in one of their greatest efforts – to save the most degraded humans in all of the world. To show that Satan cannot claim all of God's children. All of heaven is fighting for even the most degraded and vile prisoners. They are still part of humanity no matter what they have done. Only until the day they die and refuse the promptings of the Holy Spirit are they lost to the Lord. This is why I work in prisons and why we should pray for prisoners.

It is December. Many Christians around the world choose to celebrate the birth of Christ during the month of December, although biblical indicators place Christ's birth sometime at the end of September through the first part of October. For some, this is a joyous time and a time for family and friends to come together and corporately rejoice. However, for those who are single, lonely, orphaned, sex slaves, or in prison, this season tends to magnify their condition. As Christians, we need to be inclusive of those who may not always feel the strong ties of close families and tightly knit Christian communities. And while it may not always be feasible to include singles, orphans, and prisoners in your celebrations, you can take this month to demonstrate compassion and pray for them.

# December Ideas

Pray for the fatherless. Pray to always put God first.
Pray to always guard your heart against worldly influences.
Pray for those who need to repent and turn away from evil.
Pray to have spiritual discernment for God's will in your life.
Pray for communities to embrace those who are disenfranchised.
Pray for those who are incarcerated and want to know You better.
Pray for those who have lost a spouse to accept You as their source of strength.

1. _____
2. _____
3. _____
4. _____
5. _____
6. _____
7. _____
8. _____
9. _____
10. _____

19.
20.
21.
22.
23.
24.
25.

Pray for orphans, prisoners, singles, widowers, and widows.

## 1 December
### God wants an intimate relationship with us.

"Therefore, behold, I will allure her, will bring her into the wilderness, and speak comfort to her. I will give her vineyards from there, and the Valley of Achor as a door of hope; she shall sing there, as in the days of her youth, as in the day when she came up from the land of Egypt. And it shall be, in that day," says the LORD, "That you will call me 'my husband,' and no longer call me 'my master,' for I will take from her mouth the names of the Baals, and they shall be remembered by their name no more. In that day I will make a covenant for them with the beasts of the field, with the birds of the air, and with the creeping things of the ground. Bow and sword of battle I will shatter from the earth, to make them lie down safely. I will betroth you to me forever; yes, I will betroth you to me in righteousness and justice, in loving kindness and mercy; I will betroth you to me in faithfulness, and you shall know the LORD." Hosea 2:14–20, NKJV

Person or situation you are praying for:
Praises and promises:
Prayer:

## 2 December
### We bring Him our little cares and perplexities as well as our greater troubles.

He is doing the judgment of fatherless and widow, and loving the sojourner, to give to him bread and raiment. Deuteronomy 10:18, YLT

Person or situation you are praying for:
Praises and promises:
Prayer:

## 3 December
### Have a tender heart for the orphans, widows, singles, those in prison, etc.

The good-hearted understand what it's like to be poor; the hardhearted haven't the faintest idea. Proverbs 29:7, MSG

Person or situation you are praying for:
Praises and promises:
Prayer:

## 4 December

*Job Addresses Zophar: Spend time in nature and with animals to better know God.*

Job answered: "I'm sure you speak for all the experts, and when you die there'll be no one left to tell us how to live. But don't forget that I also have a brain—I don't intend to play second fiddle to you. It doesn't take an expert to know these things. "I'm ridiculed by my friends: 'So that's the man who had conversations with God!' Ridiculed without mercy: 'Look at the man who never did wrong!' It's easy for the well- to-do to point their fingers in blame, for the well-fixed to pour scorn on the strugglers. Crooks reside safely in high-security houses, insolent blasphemers live in luxury; they've bought and paid for a god who'll protect them. "But ask the animals what they think — let them teach you; let the birds tell you what's going on. Put your ear to the earth—learn the basics. Listen—the fish in the ocean will tell you their stories. Isn't it clear that they all know and agree that GOD is sovereign, that he holds all things in his hand—Every living soul, yes, every breathing creature? Isn't this all just common sense, as common as the sense of taste? Do you think the elderly have a corner on wisdom, that you have to grow old before you understand life? Job 12:1–12, MSG

Person or situation you are praying for:
Praises and promises:
Prayer:

## 5 December

*Don't take advantage of each other.*

There's nothing new to say on the subject. Don't you still have the message of the earlier prophets from the time when Jerusalem was still a thriving, bustling city and the outlying countryside, the Negev and Shephelah, was populated? [This is the message that GOD gave Zechariah.] Well, the message hasn't changed. GOD-of-the-Angel-Armies said then and says now: "Treat one another justly. Love your neighbors. Be compassionate with each other. Don't take advantage of widows, orphans, visitors, and the poor. Don't plot and scheme against one another—that's evil." Zechariah 7:9, 10, MSG

Person or situation you are praying for:
Praises and promises:
Prayer:

## 6 December

*If you are lonely, claim this promise that God will place you in a family.*

To the fatherless he is a father. To the widow he is a champion friend. To the lonely he makes them part of a family. To the prisoners he leads into prosperity until they sing for joy. This is our Holy God in his Holy Place! But for the rebels there is heartache and despair. Psalm 68:6, TPT

Person or situation you are praying for:
Praises and promises:
Prayer:

## 7 December

*God is drawn to humble and tender people.*

My hand made these things so they all belong to me," declares Yahweh. "But there is one my eyes are drawn to: the humble one, the tender one, the trembling one who lives in awe of all I say." Isaiah 66:2, TPT

Person or situation you are praying for:
Praises and promises:
Prayer:

## 8 December

*Be courageous!*

I leave the gift of peace with you—my peace. Not the kind of fragile peace given by the world, but my perfect peace. Don't yield to fear or be troubled in your hearts—instead, be courageous! John 14:27, TPT

Person or situation you are praying for:
Praises and promises:
Prayer:

## 9 December

### My yoke is easy to bear.

Are you weary, carrying a heavy burden? Then come to me. I will refresh your life, for I am your oasis. Simply join your life with mine. Learn my ways and you'll discover that I'm gentle, humble, easy to please. You will find refreshment and rest in me. For all that I require of you will be pleasant and easy to bear.  Matthew 11:28–30, TPT

Person or situation you are praying for:
Praises and promises:
Prayer:

## 10 December

### When Jesus sets you free, you are free indeed!

The Spirit of the Lord is upon me, and he has anointed me to be hope for the poor, freedom for the brokenhearted, and new eyes for the blind, and to preach to prisoners, "You are set free!" I have come to share the message of Jubilee, for the time of God's great acceptance has begun. Luke 4:18, 19, TPT

Person or situation you are praying for:
Praises and promises:
Prayer:

## 11 December

### God constantly guards us.

From Peter, an apostle of Jesus the Anointed One, to the chosen ones who have been scattered abroad like "seed" into the nations living as refugees, to those living in Pontus, Galatia, Cappadocia, and throughout the Roman provinces of Asia and Bithynia. You are not forgotten, for you have been chosen and destined by Father God. The Holy Spirit has set you apart to be God's holy ones, obedient followers of Jesus Christ who have been gloriously sprinkled with his blood. May God's delightful grace and peace cascade over you many times over! Celebrate with praises the God and Father of our Lord Jesus Christ, who has shown us his extravagant mercy. For his fountain of mercy has given us a new life—we are reborn to experience a living, energetic hope through the resurrection of Jesus Christ from the dead. We are reborn into a perfect inheritance that can never perish, never be defiled, and never diminish. It is promised and preserved forever in the heavenly realm for you! Through our faith, the mighty power of God constantly guards us until our full salvation is ready to be revealed in the last time. 1 Peter 1:1–5, TPT

Person or situation you are praying for:
Praises and promises:
Prayer:

## 12 December
### God suffers with us and heals our wounds.

He heals the wounds of every shattered heart. Psalm 143:8, TPT

Person or situation you are praying for:
Praises and promises:
Prayer:

## 13 December
### Our most bitter grief may be followed by the greatest victory.

I tell you the truth. You will cry and be sad, but the world will be happy. You will be sad, but your sadness will become joy. When a woman gives birth to a baby, she has pain, because her time has come. But when her baby is born, she forgets the pain. She forgets because she is so happy that a child has been born into the world. It is the same with you. Now you are sad. But I will see you again and you will be happy. And no one will take away your joy. John 16:20–22, ICB

Person or situation you are praying for:
Praises and promises:
Prayer:

## 14 December
### Pray for those burdened with debt to see the folly in debt accumulation.

The rich rules over the poor, and the borrower is the slave of the lender. Proverbs 22:7, RSV

Person or situation you are praying for:
Praises and promises:
Prayer:

## 15 December
### Pray for those whose hearts have been broken.

The LORD is close to those whose hearts have been broken. He saves those whose spirits have been crushed. The person who does what is right may have many troubles. But the LORD saves him from all of them. Psalm 34:18, 19, NIRV

Person or situation you are praying for:
Praises and promises:
Prayer:

## 16 December
*A series of small victories leads to high places with the Lord.*

Though the fig tree does not blossom, nor fruit be on the vines, the produce of the olive fail and the fields yield no food, the flock be cut off from the fold and there be no herd in the stalls, yet I will rejoice in the LORD, I will joy in the God of my salvation. GOD, the Lord, is my strength; he makes my feet like hinds' feet, he makes me tread upon my high places. To the choirmaster: with stringed instruments.  Habakkuk 3:17–19, RSV

Person or situation you are praying for:
Praises and promises:
Prayer:

## 17 December
*Pray for the poor and destitute.*

Speak up for the people who have no voice, for the rights of all the down-and-outers. Speak out for justice! Stand up for the poor and destitute! Proverbs 31:8, 9, MSG

Person or situation you are praying for:
Praises and promises:
Prayer:

## 18 December
*God weeps along with man.*

The LORD is close to the brokenhearted and saves those who are crushed in spirit. The righteous person may have many troubles, but the LORD delivers him from them all; he protects all his bones, not one of them will be broken. Psalm 34:18–20, NIV

Person or situation you are praying for:
Praises and promises:
Prayer:

## 19 December
*God sees the tears of a brokenhearted soul.*

You keep track of all my sorrows. You have collected all my tears in your bottle. You have recorded each one in your book. Psalm 56:8, TPT

Person or situation you are praying for:
Praises and promises:
Prayer:

## 20 December
*Always speak the truth because we all belong to each other.*

So, with the wisdom given to me from the Lord I say: You should not live like the unbelievers around you who walk in their empty delusions. Their corrupted logic has been clouded because their hearts are so far from God—their blinded understanding and deep-seated moral darkness keeps them from the true knowledge of God. Because of spiritual apathy, they surrender their lives to lewdness, impurity, and sexual obsession. But this is not the way of life that Christ has unfolded within you. If you have really experienced the Anointed One, and heard his truth, it will be seen in your life; for we know that the ultimate reality is embodied in Jesus! And he has taught you to let go of the lifestyle of the ancient man, the old self-life, which was corrupted by sinful and deceitful desires that spring from delusions. Now it's time to be made new by every revelation that's been given to you. And to be transformed as you embrace the glorious Christ-within as your new life and live in union with him! For God has re-created you all over again in his perfect righteousness, and you now belong to him in the realm of true holiness.

So, discard every form of dishonesty and lying so that you will be known as one who always speaks the truth, for we all belong to one another. But don't let the passion of your emotions lead you to sin! Don't let anger control you or be fuel for revenge, not for even a day. Don't give the slanderous accuser, the Devil, an opportunity to manipulate you! If any one of you has stolen from someone else, never do it again. Instead, be industrious, earning an honest living, and then you'll have enough to bless those in need. And never let ugly or hateful words come from your mouth, but instead let your words become beautiful gifts that encourage others; do this by speaking words of grace to help them. The Holy Spirit of God has sealed you in Jesus Christ until you experience your full salvation. So never grieve the Spirit of God or take for granted his holy influence in your life. Lay aside bitter words, temper tantrums, revenge, profanity, and insults. But instead be kind and affectionate toward one another. Has God graciously forgiven you? Then graciously forgive one another in the depths of Christ's love.
Ephesians 4:17–32, TPT

Person or situation you are praying for:
Praises and promises:
Prayer:

## 21 December
### God with us.

All praise to the God and Father of our Master, Jesus the Messiah! Father of all mercy! God of all healing counsel! He comes alongside us when we go through hard times, and before you know it, he brings us alongside someone else who is going through hard times so that we can be there for that person just as God was there for us. We have plenty of hard times that come from following the Messiah, but no more so than the good times of his healing comfort—we get a full measure of that, too. 2 Corinthians 1:3–5, MSG

Person or situation you are praying for:
Praises and promises:
Prayer:

## 22 December
### Instead of worrying, pray!

Don't fret or worry. Instead of worrying, pray. Let petitions and praises shape your worries into prayers, letting God know your concerns. Before you know it, a sense of God's wholeness, everything coming together for good, will come and settle you down. It's wonderful what happens when Christ displaces worry at the center of your life. Ephesians 4:6, 7, MSG

Person or situation you are praying for:
Praises and promises:
Prayer:

## 23 December
### Keep pressing toward the goal.

Not that I have already obtained this or am already perfect; but I press on to make it my own, because Christ Jesus has made me his own. Brethren, I do not consider that I have made it my own; but one thing I do, forgetting what lies behind and straining forward to what lies ahead, I press on toward the goal for the prize of the upward call of God in Christ Jesus. Let those of us who are mature be thus minded; and if in anything you are otherwise minded, God will reveal that also to you. Only let us hold true to what we have attained. Brethren, join in imitating me, and mark those who so live as you have an example in us. For many, of whom I have often told you and now tell you even with tears, live as enemies of the cross of Christ. Their end is destruction, their god is the belly, and they glory in their shame, with minds set on earthly things. But our commonwealth is in heaven, and from it we await a Savior, the Lord Jesus Christ, who will change our lowly body to be like his glorious body, by the power which enables him even to subject all things to himself. Philippians 3:12–21, RSV

Person or situation you are praying for:
Praises and promises:
Prayer:

## 24 December

### Be anxious for nothing.

But if God so clothes the grass of the field, which today is alive and tomorrow is thrown into the oven, will he not much more clothe you, O men of little faith? Therefore, do not be anxious, saying, "What shall we eat?" or "What shall we drink?" or "What shall we wear?" For the Gentiles seek all these things; and your heavenly Father knows that you need them all. But seek first his kingdom and his righteousness, and all these things shall be yours as well. "There-fore, do not be anxious about tomorrow, for tomorrow will be anxious for itself. Let the day's own trouble be sufficient for the day. Matthew 6:30–34, RSV

Person or situation you are praying for:
Praises and promises:
Prayer:


## 25 December

### Accept the gift of perfect peace centered in Christ.

I leave the gift of peace with you—my peace. Not the kind of fragile peace given by the world, but my perfect peace. Don't yield to fear or be troubled in your hearts—instead, be courageous! Remember what I've told you, that I must go away, but I promise to come back to you. So, if you truly love me, you will be glad for me, since I'm returning to my Father, who is greater than I. So, when all of these things happen, you will still trust and cling to me. I won't speak with you much longer, for the ruler of this dark world is coming. But he has no power over me, for he has nothing to use against me. I am doing exactly what the Father destined for me to accomplish, so that the world will discover how much I love my Father. Now come with me. John 14:27–31, TPT

Person or situation you are praying for:
Praises and promises:
Prayer:

## 26 December

*Patient endurance refines our character.*

Our faith in Jesus transfers God's righteousness to us and he now declares us flawless in his eyes. This means we can now enjoy true and lasting peace with God, all because of what our Lord Jesus, the Anointed One, has done for us. Our faith guarantees us permanent access into this marvelous kindness that has given us a perfect relationship with God. What incredible joy bursts forth within us as we keep on celebrating our hope of experiencing God's glory! But that's not all! Even in times of trouble we have a joyful confidence, knowing that our pressures will develop in us patient endurance. And patient endurance will refine our character, and proven character leads us back to hope. And this hope is not a disappointing fantasy, because we can now experience the endless love of God cascading into our hearts through the Holy Spirit who lives in us! Romans 5:1–5, TPT

Person or situation you are praying for:
Praises and promises:
Prayer:


## 27 December

*Someday soon, God will make our crooked paths straight!*

Thus says the LORD to His anointed, to Cyrus, whose right hand I have held—to subdue nations before him and loose the armor of kings, to open before him the double doors, so that the gates will not be shut: "I will go before you and make the crooked places straight; I will break in pieces the gates of bronze and cut the bars of iron. I will give you the treasures of darkness and hidden riches of secret places, that you may know that I, the LORD, who call you by your name, am the God of Israel. For Jacob my servant's sake, and Israel my elect, I have even called you by your name; I have named you, though you have not known me. I am the LORD, and there is no other; there is no God besides me. I will gird you, though you have not known me, that they may know from the rising of the sun to its setting that there is none besides me. I am the LORD, and there is no other; I form the light and create darkness, I make peace and create calamity; I, the LORD, do all these things. Rain down, you heavens, from above, and let the skies pour down righteousness; let the earth open, let them bring forth salvation, and let righteousness spring up together. I, the LORD, have created it." Isaiah 45:1–8, NKJV

Person or situation you are praying for:
Praises and promises:
Prayer:

## 28 December
### He makes everything new!

I heard a voice thunder from the Throne: "Look! Look! God has moved into the neighborhood, making his home with men and women! They're his people, he's their God. He'll wipe every tear from their eyes. Death is gone for good—tears gone, crying gone, pain gone—all the first order of things gone." The Enthroned continued, "Look! I'm making everything new. Write it all down—each word dependable and accurate." Revelation 21:4, 5, MSG

Person or situation you are praying for:
Praises and promises:
Prayer:


## 29 December
### Nothing can separate us from God's love.

What then shall we say to this? If God is for us, who is against us? He who did not spare his own Son but gave him up for us all, will he not also give us all things with him? Who shall bring any charge against God's elect? It is God who justifies; who is to condemn? Is it Christ Jesus, who died, yes, who was raised from the dead, who is at the right hand of God, who indeed intercedes for us? Who shall separate us from the love of Christ? Shall tribulation, or distress, or persecution, or famine, or nakedness, or peril, or sword? As it is written, "For thy sake we are being killed all the day long; we are regarded as sheep to be slaughtered." No, in all these things we are more than conquerors through him who loved us. For I am sure that neither death, nor life, nor angels, nor principalities, nor things present, nor things to come, nor powers, nor height, nor depth, nor anything else in all creation, will be able to separate us from the love of God in Christ Jesus our Lord. Romans 8:31–39, RSV

Person or situation you are praying for:
Praises and promises:
Prayer:

## 30 December
### Show others how much you care about their spiritual journey.

With promises like this to pull us on, dear friends, let's make a clean break with everything that defiles or distracts us, both within and without. Let's make our entire lives fit and holy temples for the worship of God. Trust us. We've never hurt a soul, never exploited or taken advantage of anyone. Don't think I'm finding fault with you. I told you earlier that I'm with you all the way, no matter what. I have, in fact, the greatest confidence in you. If only you knew how proud I am of you! I am overwhelmed with joy despite all our troubles. When we arrived in Macedonia province, we couldn't settle down. The fights in the church and the fears in our hearts kept us on pins and needles. We couldn't relax because we didn't know how it would turn out. Then the God who lifts up the downcast lifted our heads and our hearts with the arrival of Titus. We were glad just to see him, but the true reassurance came in what he told us about you: how much you cared, how much you grieved, how concerned you were for me. I went from worry to tranquility in no time! 2 Corinthians 7:1–7, MSG

Person or situation you are praying for:
Praises and promises:
Prayer:

## 31 December
### God our shepherd. Don't miss out on a journey with Him!

The Eternal is my shepherd, He cares for me always. He provides me rest in rich, green fields beside streams of refreshing water. He soothes my fears; He makes me whole again, steering me off worn, hard paths to roads where truth and righteousness echo His name. Even in the unending shadows of death's darkness, I am not overcome by fear. Because you are with me in those dark moments, near with your protection and guidance, I am comforted. You spread out a table before me, provisions in the midst of attack from my enemies; You care for all my needs, anointing my head with soothing, fragrant oil, filling my cup again and again with Your grace. Certainly, your faithful protection and loving provision will pursue me where I go, always, everywhere. I will always be with the Eternal, in your house forever. Psalm 23, VOICE

Person or situation you are praying for:
Praises and promises:
Prayer:

# December Epilogue

A written epilogue, is a way of rounding out a literary work, bringing closure, or summarizing the final scene of a dramatic play. In this case, it is a summary of your prayer life and walk with God during the month of December. This page is for you to record your comments and write one or two summary statements as you have prayed for foster children, orphans, singles, slaves of all types, widowers, and widows, etc.

Over this past month, you have broadened your worldview. You have prayed for those who are different from you. You have joined with heaven in ways that please God. This means you have cooperated with God in the salvation of the lost, the lowest of the low. In reality, we who live in beautiful homes and have beautiful lives are no better in God's eyes than the vilest of all prisoners. We all fall short of His glory. We all fail Him whether or not we commit blue collar or white-collar crimes such as pride and haughtiness.

When we pray and minister to the homeless, orphans, foster children, singles, and even prisoners, we have done the same to God. We all reflect His image and when we pray for each other, we shore up our humanity and are changed into His likeness. This is the process of sanctification. Praising His name, claiming Bible promises and praying connect us to the Infinite one.

One of the first hints we have about the nature of God is to understand the nature of sin. Someday it will be "no more." The sinner and sin will be gone. The converse is true. One day, very soon, perfection will be restored, the perfect balance and nature of the universe will be restored, however, it will be different than before God made man and the earth. Never again will sin be contemplated or enacted. Never again will jealousy and self-centeredness mar the worship of Christ. All power, honor, glory, and credit will be in its rightful place. We humans will throw down our crowns at the Savior's feet. One of my favorite authors describes this event in the book Spiritual Gifts, vol 1, p 771, "Again the heavenly host cried out, Who is this King of glory? The escorting angels in melodious strains answered, The Lord of hosts! He is the King of glory! And the heavenly train passed into the city. Then all the heavenly host surrounded the Son of God, their majestic commander, and with the deepest adoration, bowed, casting their glittering crowns at his feet. And then they touched their golden harps, and in sweet, melodious strains, filled all heaven with their rich music and songs to the Lamb who was slain, yet lives in majesty and glory."

As Jesus rode a donkey into Jerusalem, the crowd thronged around him. The rulers came out of their homes to see what the commotion was about. Let's pick up the story from Redemption, on page 128, "They inquire who and what is the cause of all this tumultuous rejoicing. As they, with much authority, repeat their question, —Who is this? the disciples, filled with a spirit of inspiration, are heard above all the noise of the crowd, repeating in eloquent strains the prophecies which answered this question. Adam will tell you, **it is the seed of the woman that shall bruise the serpent's head**. Ask Abraham, he will tell you, **it is Melchizedek, King of Salem, King of Peace**. Jacob will tell you, **He is Shiloh of the tribe of Judah**. Isaiah will tell you, **Immanuel, Wonderful, Counsellor, the Mighty God, the everlasting Father, the Prince of Peace**. Jeremiah will tell you, **The Branch of David, the Lord, our righteousness**. Daniel will tell you, **He is the Messiah**. Hosea will tell you, **He is the Lord God of Hosts, the Lord is his memorial**. John the Baptist will tell you, **He is the Lamb of God who taketh away the sin of the world**. The great Jehovah has proclaimed from his throne, **this is my beloved Son**. We, his disciples, declare, **this is Jesus, the Messiah, the Prince of Life, the Redeemer of the world**. And even the Prince of the powers of darkness acknowledges him, saying, "**I know thee who thou art, the Holy One of God**."

There is no other like him. Get to know him through praise, reading the Word and through prayer. Don't miss out on this incredible journey to eternity with Him. We take two things with us to Heaven: our character and converts! Pray like your life and the lives of others depends on your prayers, because they do.

Made in the USA
Middletown, DE
07 September 2025